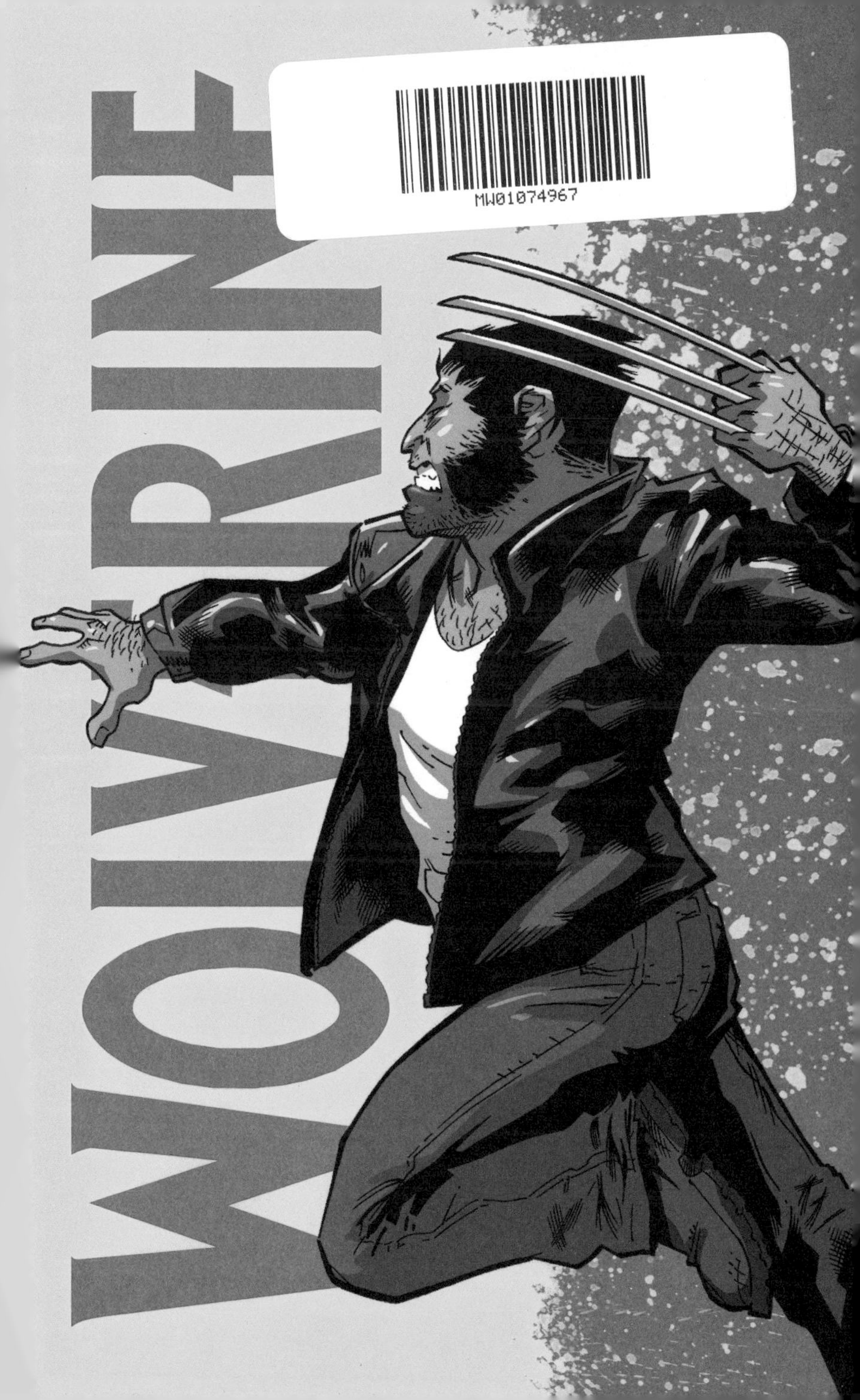
WOLVERINE

"KINGDOM OF NO"
WRITER: **FRED VAN LENTE**
ARTISTS: **GURIHIRU**
LETTERER: **DAVE SHARPE**
COVER ARTISTS: **ED McGUINNESS**, **MARK FARMER**
& **JUSTIN PONSOR**
EDITOR: **NATHAN COSBY**
CONSULTING EDITOR: **RALPH MACCHIO**

"AND NOW...THE WOLVERINE!"
WRITER: **LEN WEIN**
PENCILER: **HERB TRIMPE**
INKER: **JACK ABEL**
COLORIST: **GLYNIS WEIN**
LETTERER: **ARTIE SIMEK**
COVER ARTIST: **HERB TRIMPE**
EDITOR: **ROY THOMAS**

"ROCK GODS"
WRITER: **PETER DAVID**
ARTIST: **SCOTT KOBLISH**
COLOR ARTIST: **ULISES ARREOLA**
LETTERER: **VC'S JOE CARAMAGNA**
COVER ARTISTS: **DENNIS CALERO** & **SOTOCOLOR**
EDITOR: **NATHAN COSBY**
CONSULTING EDITOR: **RALPH MACCHIO**

SPIDER-MAN #3
WRITER: **PAUL TOBIN**
PENCILER: **MATTEO LOLLI**
INKERS: **TERRY PALLOT** & **ANDREW HENNESSY**
COLORIST: **SOTOCOLOR**
LETTERER: **DAVE SHARPE**
COVER ARTISTS: **KARL KERSCHL**, **SERGE LaPOINTE**
& **THOMAS MASON**
ASSISTANT EDITOR: **MICHAEL HORWITZ**
EDITOR: **NATHAN COSBY**

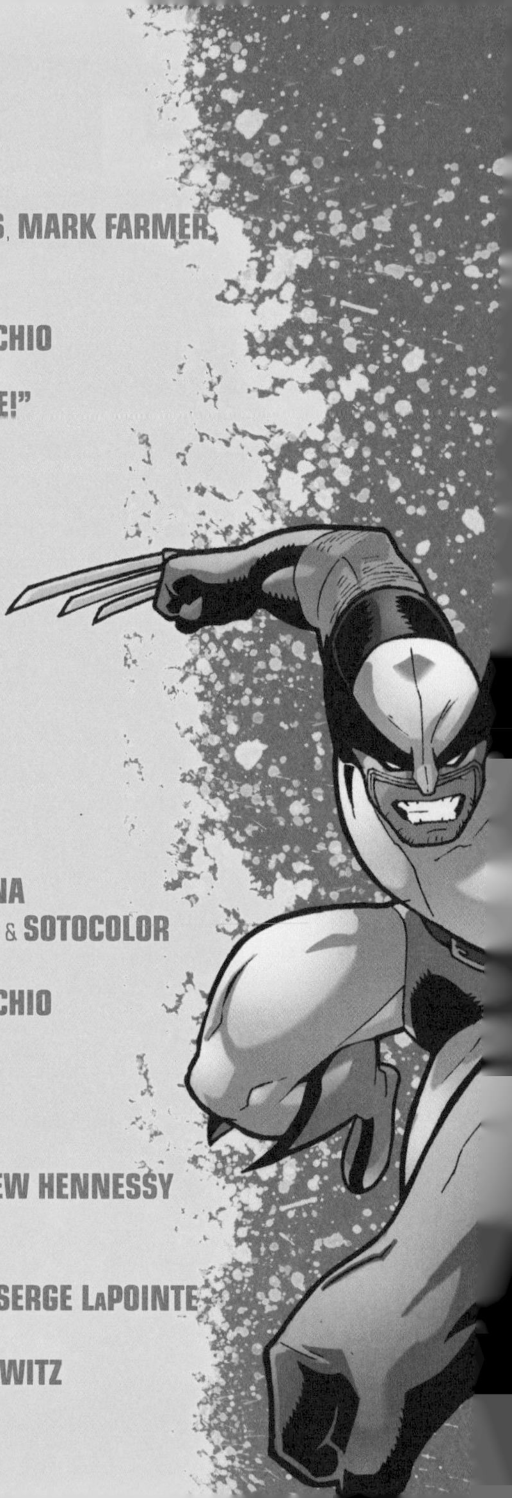

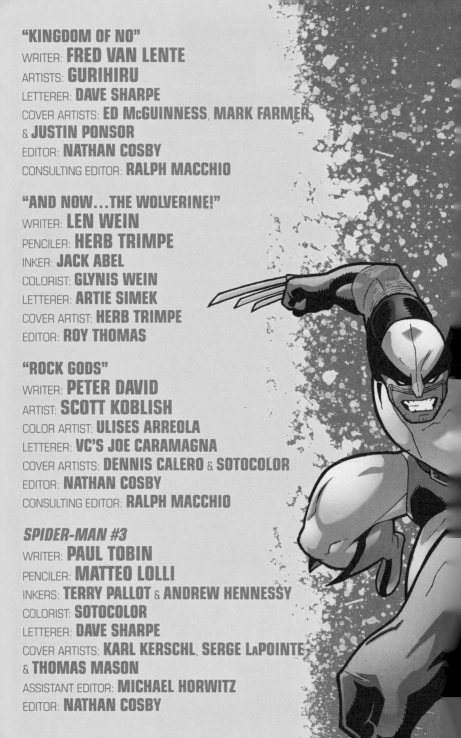

COLLECTION EDITOR & DESIGN: CORY LEVINE
ASSISTANT EDITORS: ALEX STARBUCK & NELSON RIBEIRO
EDITORS, SPECIAL PROJECTS: JENNIFER GRÜNWALD & MARK D. BEAZLEY
SENIOR EDITOR, SPECIAL PROJECTS: JEFF YOUNGQUIST
MARVEL MASTERWORKS EDITOR: CORY SEDLMEIER
SVP OF PRINT & DIGITAL PUBLISHING SALES: DAVID GABRIEL

EDITOR IN CHIEF: AXEL ALONSO • CHIEF CREATIVE OFFICER: JOE QUESADA
PUBLISHER: DAN BUCKLEY • EXECUTIVE PRODUCER: ALAN FINE

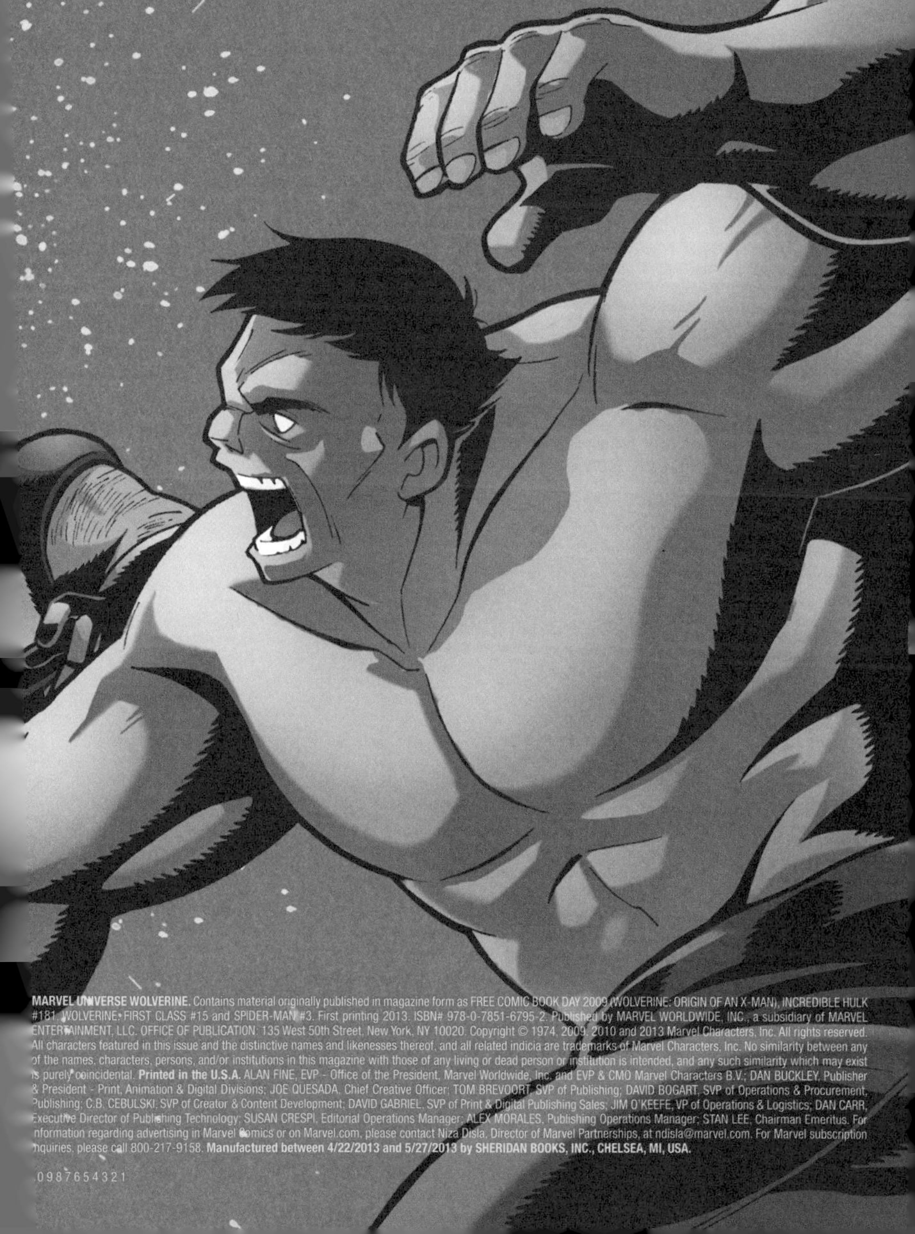

0987654321

WOLVERINE

ORIGIN OF AN
X-MAN

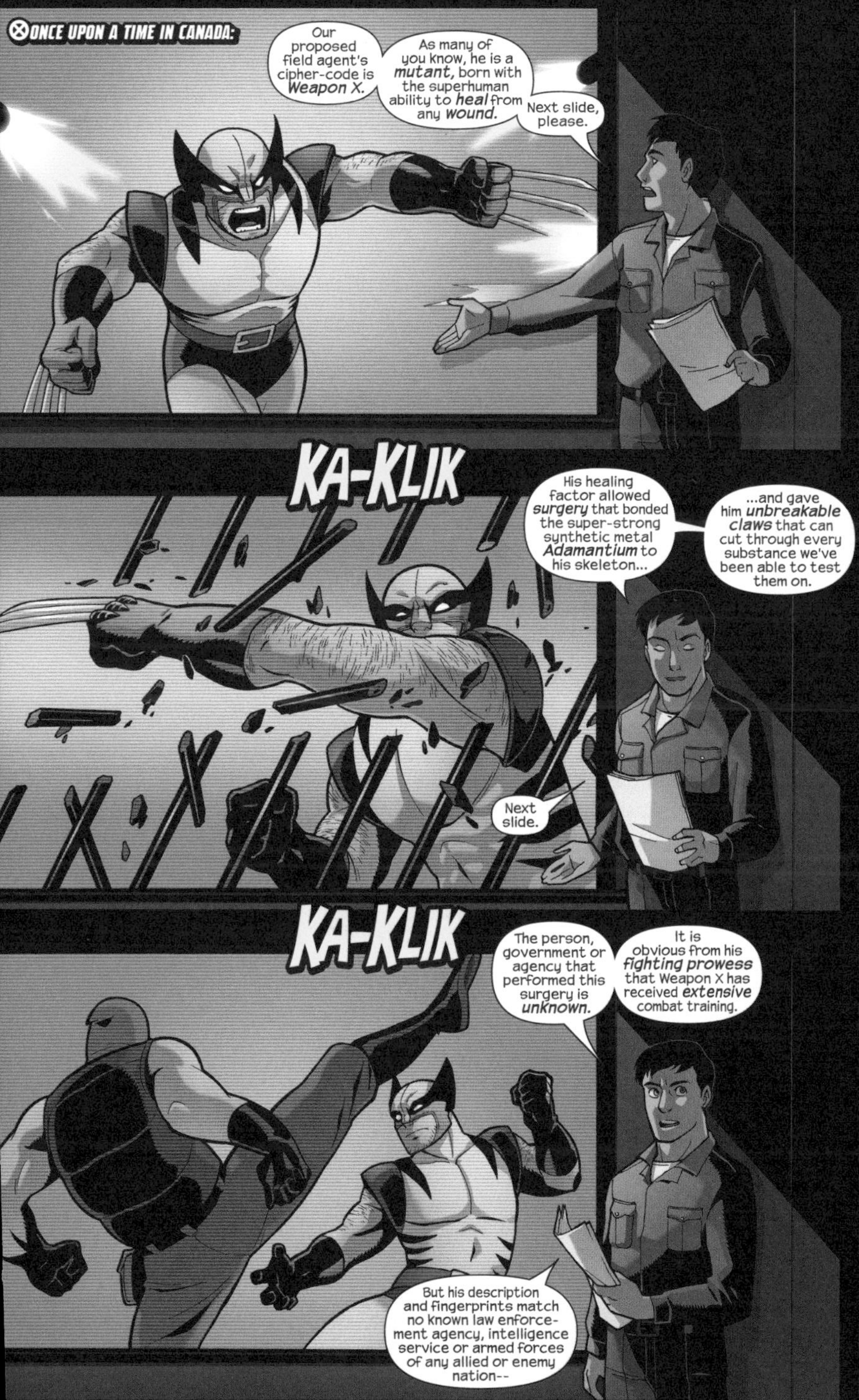
ONCE UPON A TIME IN CANADA:
Our proposed field agent's cipher-code is Weapon X.
As many of you know, he is a mutant, born with the superhuman ability to heal from any wound.
Next slide, please.
KA-KLIK
His healing factor allowed surgery that bonded the super-strong synthetic metal Adamantium to his skeleton...
...and gave him unbreakable claws that can cut through every substance we've been able to test them on.
Next slide.
KA-KLIK
The person, government or agency that performed this surgery is unknown.
It is obvious from his fighting prowess that Weapon X has received extensive combat training.
But his description and fingerprints match no known law enforcement agency, intelligence service or armed forces of any allied or enemy nation--

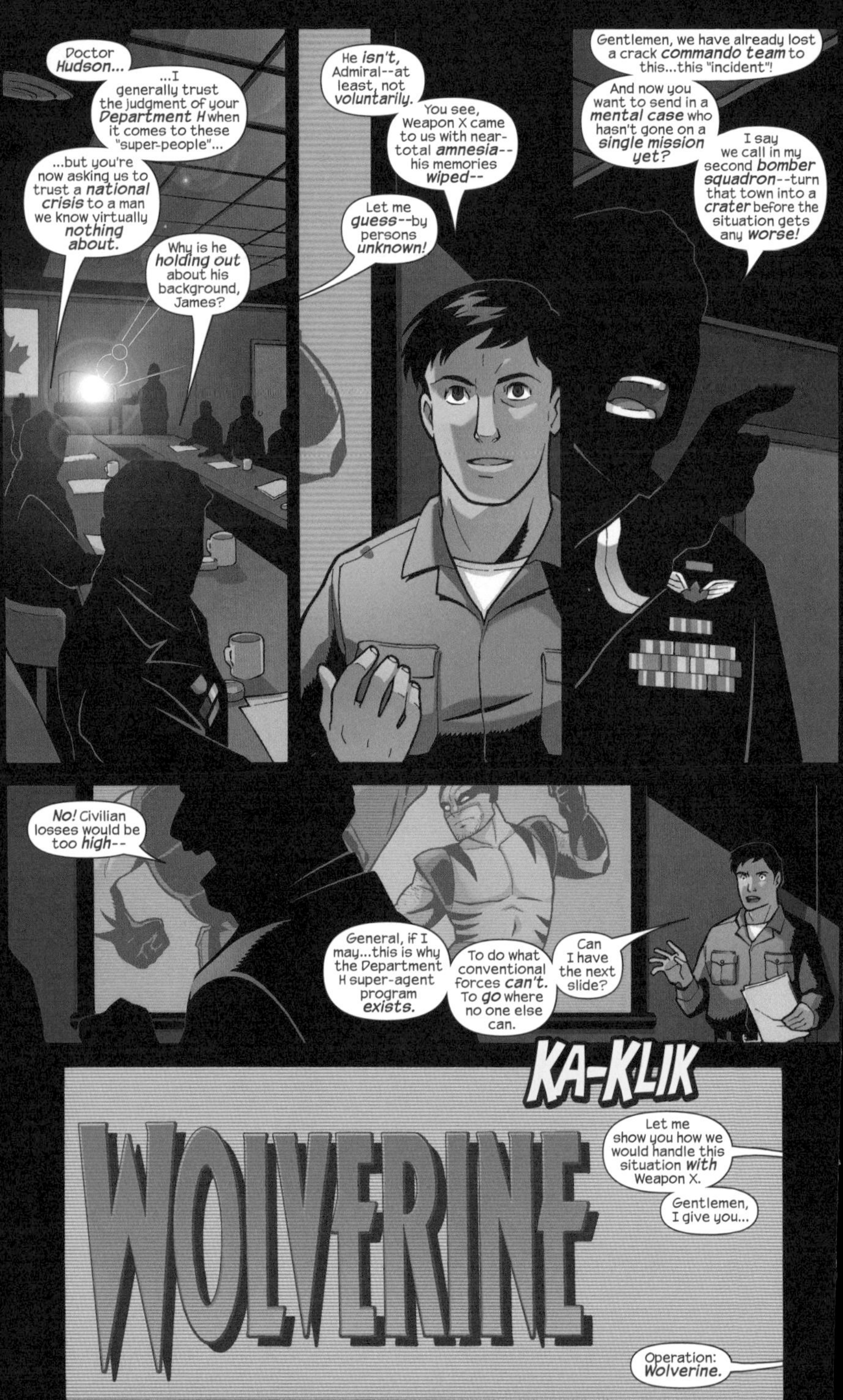

Doctor Hudson...
...I generally trust the judgment of your Department H when it comes to these "super-people"...
...but you're now asking us to trust a national crisis to a man we know virtually nothing about.
Why is he holding out about his background, James?
He isn't, Admiral--at least, not voluntarily.
You see, Weapon X came to us with near-total amnesia--his memories wiped--
Let me guess--by persons unknown!
Gentlemen, we have already lost a crack commando team to this...this "incident"!
And now you want to send in a mental case who hasn't gone on a single mission yet?
I say we call in my second bomber squadron--turn that town into a crater before the situation gets any worse!
No! Civilian losses would be too high--
General, if I may...this is why the Department H super-agent program exists.
To do what conventional forces can't. To go where no one else can.
Can I have the next slide?
KA-KLIK
WOLVERINE
Let me show you how we would handle this situation with Weapon X.
Gentlemen, I give you...
Operation: Wolverine.

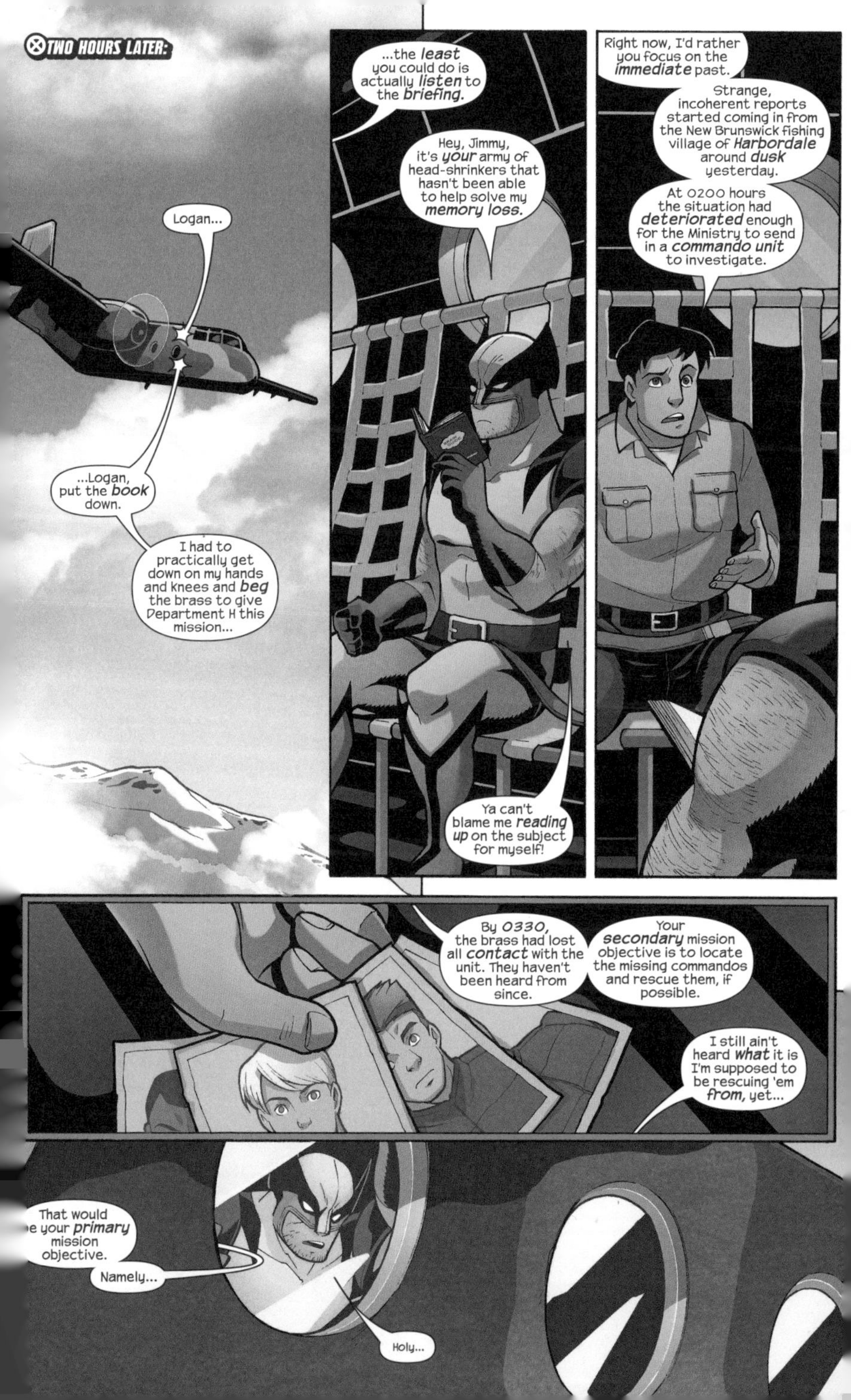
TWO HOURS LATER:
Logan...
...Logan, put the book down.
I had to practically get down on my hands and knees and beg the brass to give Department H this mission...
...the least you could do is actually listen to the briefing.
Hey, Jimmy, it's your army of head-shrinkers that hasn't been able to help solve my memory loss.
Ya can't blame me reading up on the subject for myself!
Right now, I'd rather you focus on the immediate past.
Strange, incoherent reports started coming in from the New Brunswick fishing village of Harbordale around dusk yesterday.
At 0200 hours the situation had deteriorated enough for the Ministry to send in a commando unit to investigate.
By 0330, the brass had lost all contact with the unit. They haven't been heard from since.
Your secondary mission objective is to locate the missing commandos and rescue them, if possible.
I still ain't heard what it is I'm supposed to be rescuing 'em from, yet...
That would be your primary mission objective.
Namely...
Holy...

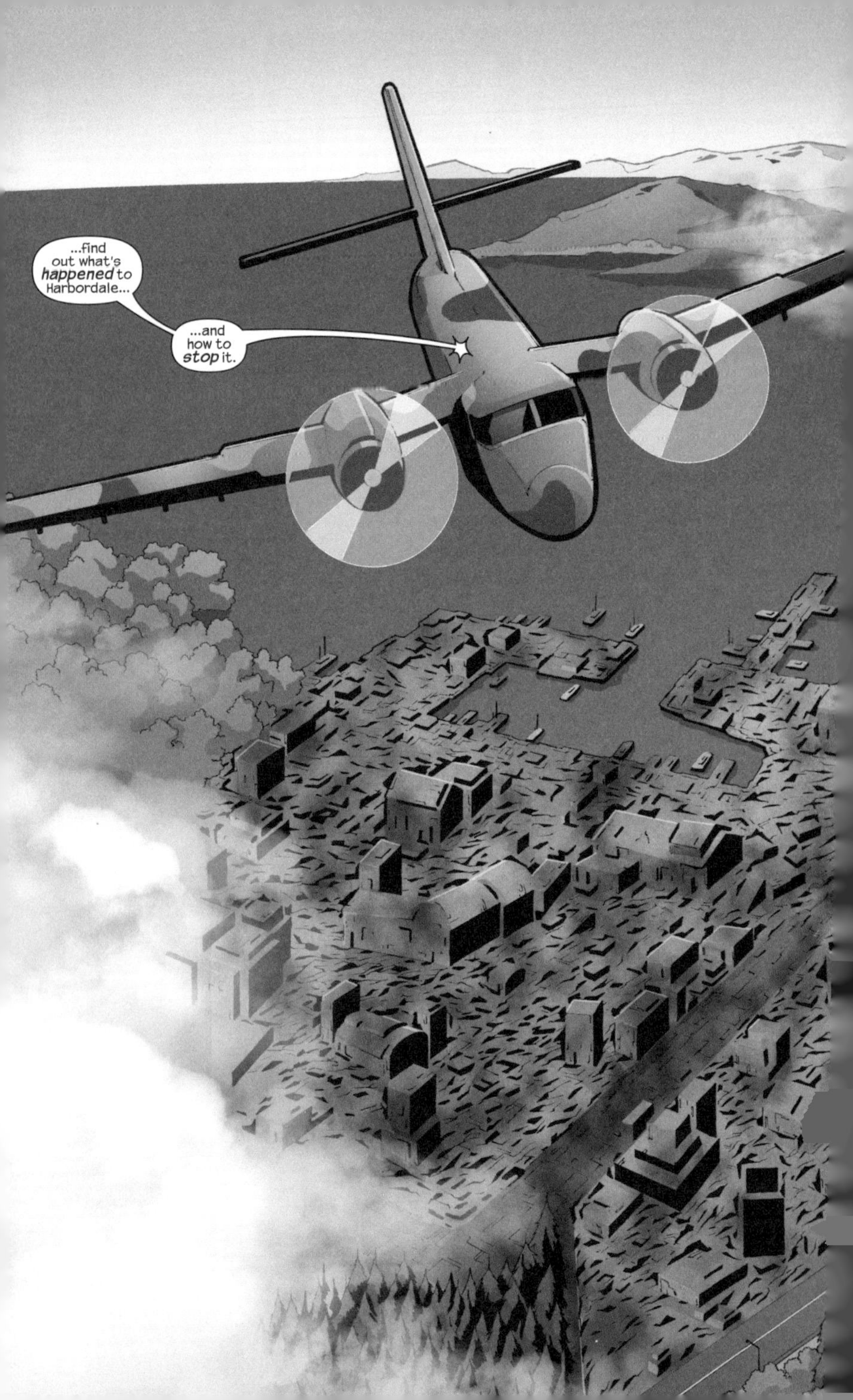
...find out what's happened to Harbordale...
...and how to stop it.

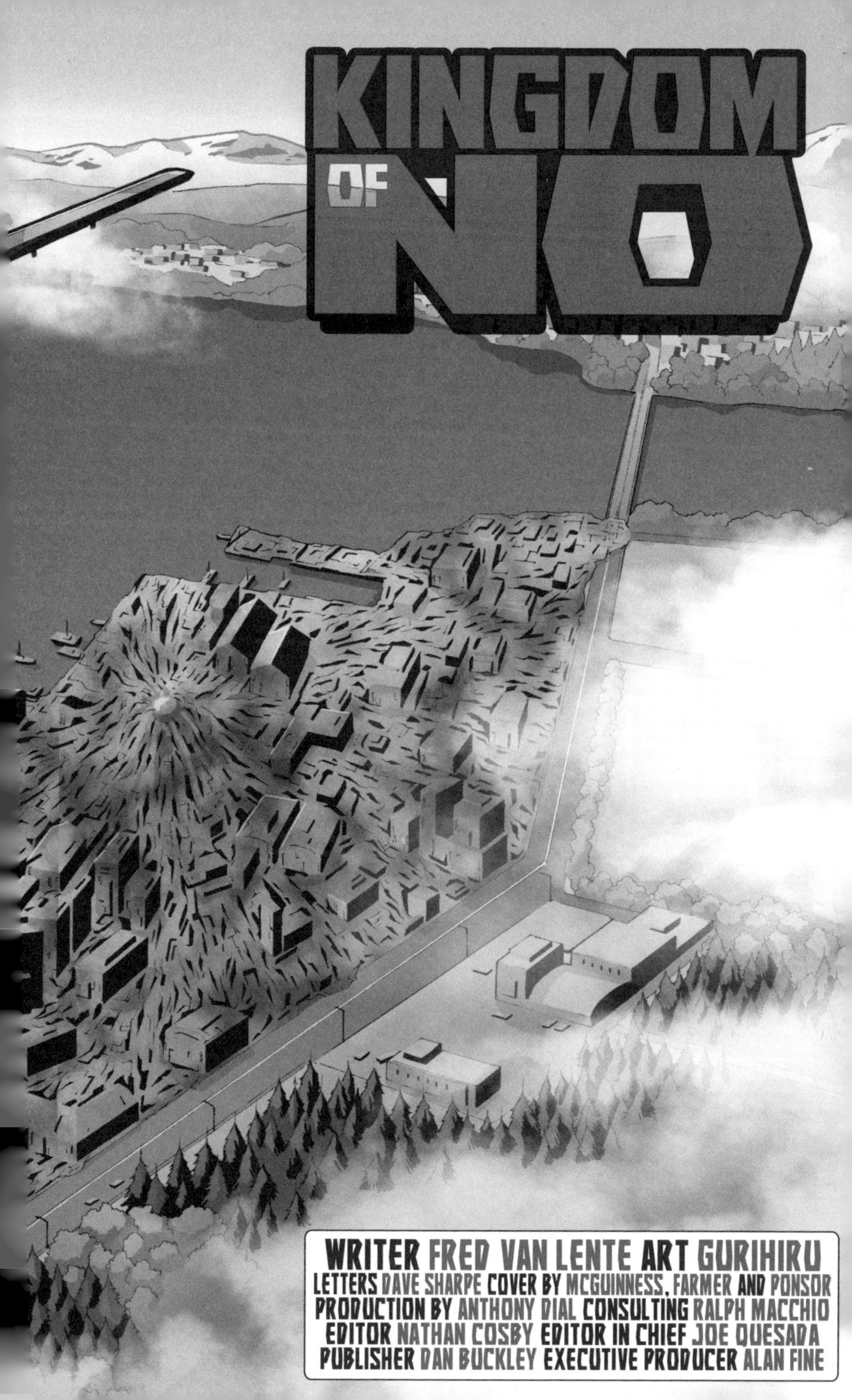
KINGDOM OF NO
WRITER FRED VAN LENTE ART GURIHIRU
LETTERS DAVE SHARPE COVER BY MCGUINNESS, FARMER AND PONSOR
PRODUCTION BY ANTHONY DIAL CONSULTING RALPH MACCHIO
EDITOR NATHAN COSBY EDITOR IN CHIEF JOE QUESADA
PUBLISHER DAN BUCKLEY EXECUTIVE PRODUCER ALAN FINE

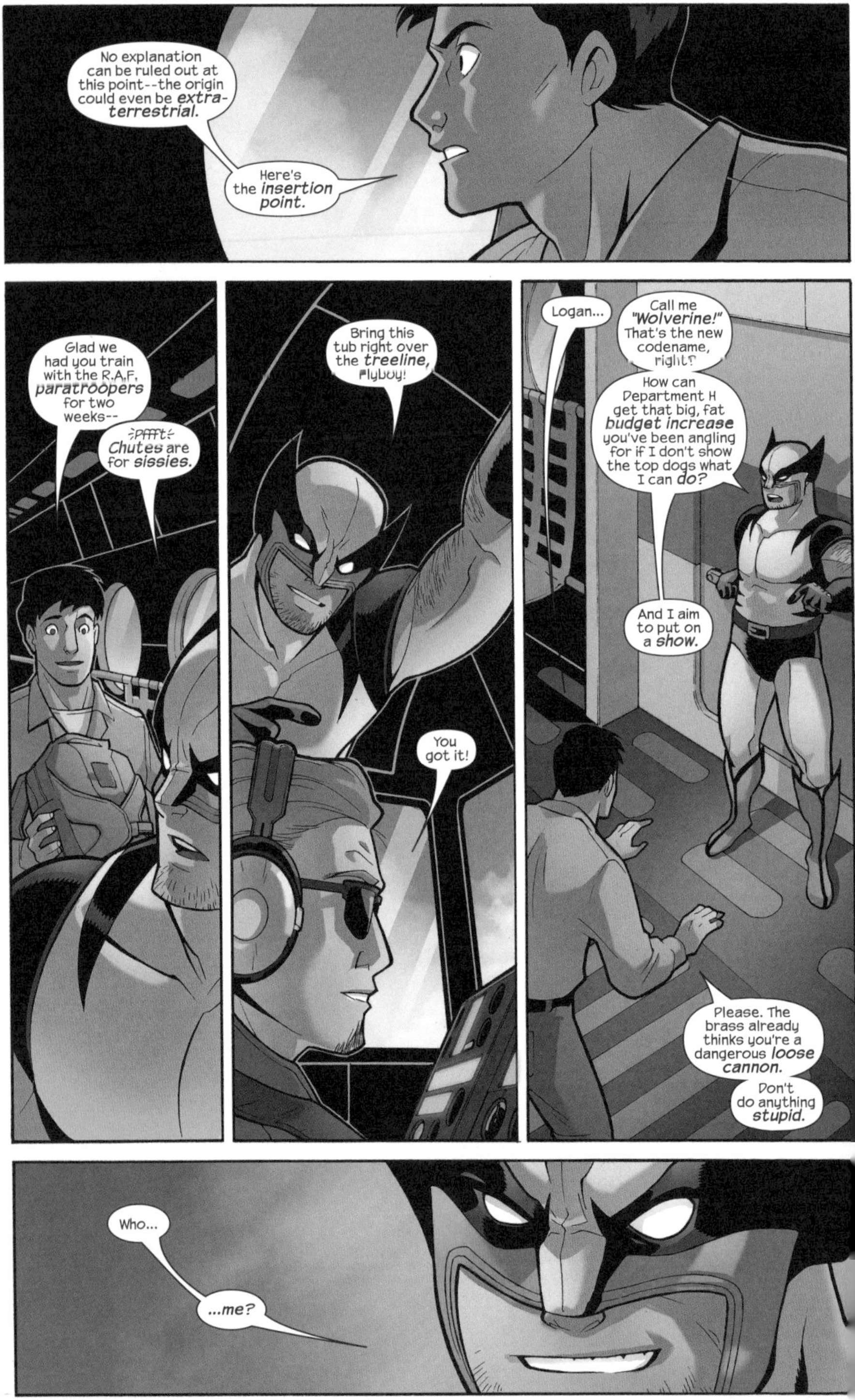
No explanation can be ruled out at this point--the origin could even be *extra-terrestrial.*
Here's the *insertion point.*
Glad we had you train with the R.A.F. *paratroopers* for two weeks--
PFFFT! *Chutes* are for *sissies.*
Bring this tub right over the *treeline,* Flyboy!
You got it!
Logan...
Call me *"Wolverine!"* That's the new codename, right?
How can Department H get that big, fat *budget increase* you've been angling for if I don't show the top dogs what I can *do?*
And I aim to put on a *show.*
Please. The brass already thinks you're a dangerous *loose cannon.*
Don't do anything *stupid.*
Who...
...*me?*

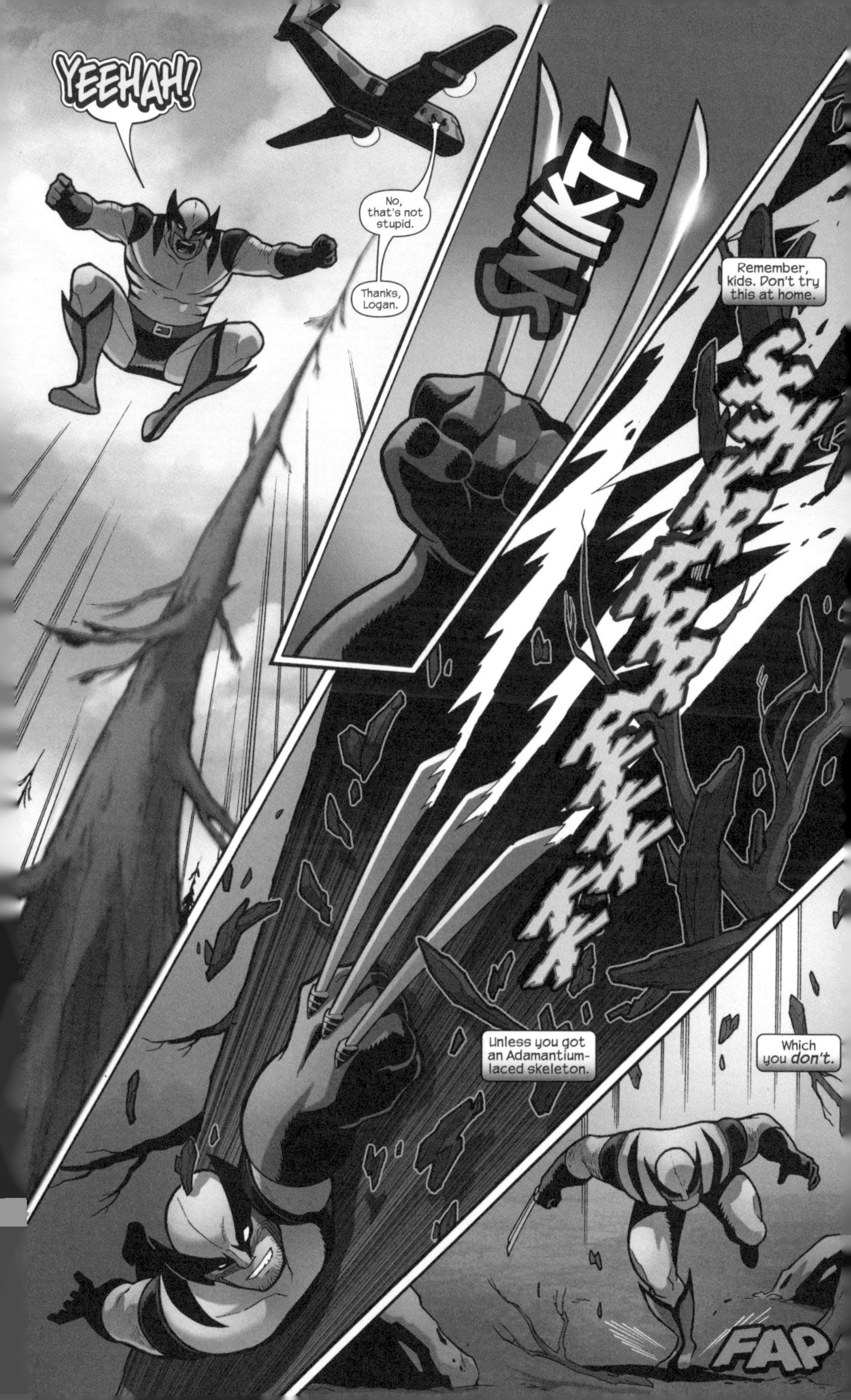
YEEHAH!
No, that's not stupid.
Thanks, Logan.
SNIKT
Remember, kids. Don't try this at home.
Unless you got an Adamantium-laced skeleton.
Which you don't.
FAP

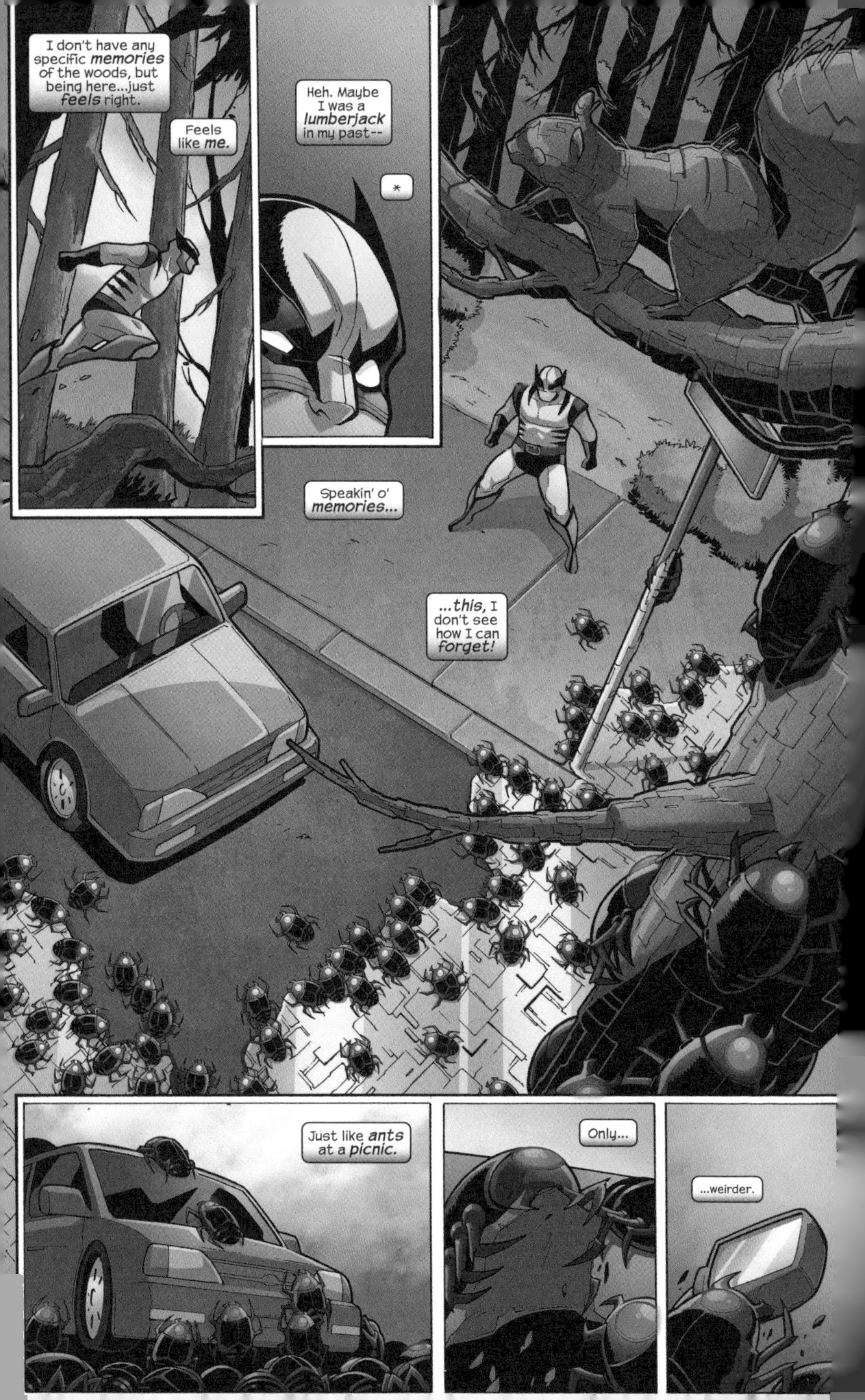

I don't have any specific memories of the woods, but being here...just feels right.
Feels like me.
Heh. Maybe I was a lumberjack in my past--
*
Speakin' o' memories...
...this, I don't see how I can forget!
Just like ants at a picnic.
Only...
...weirder.

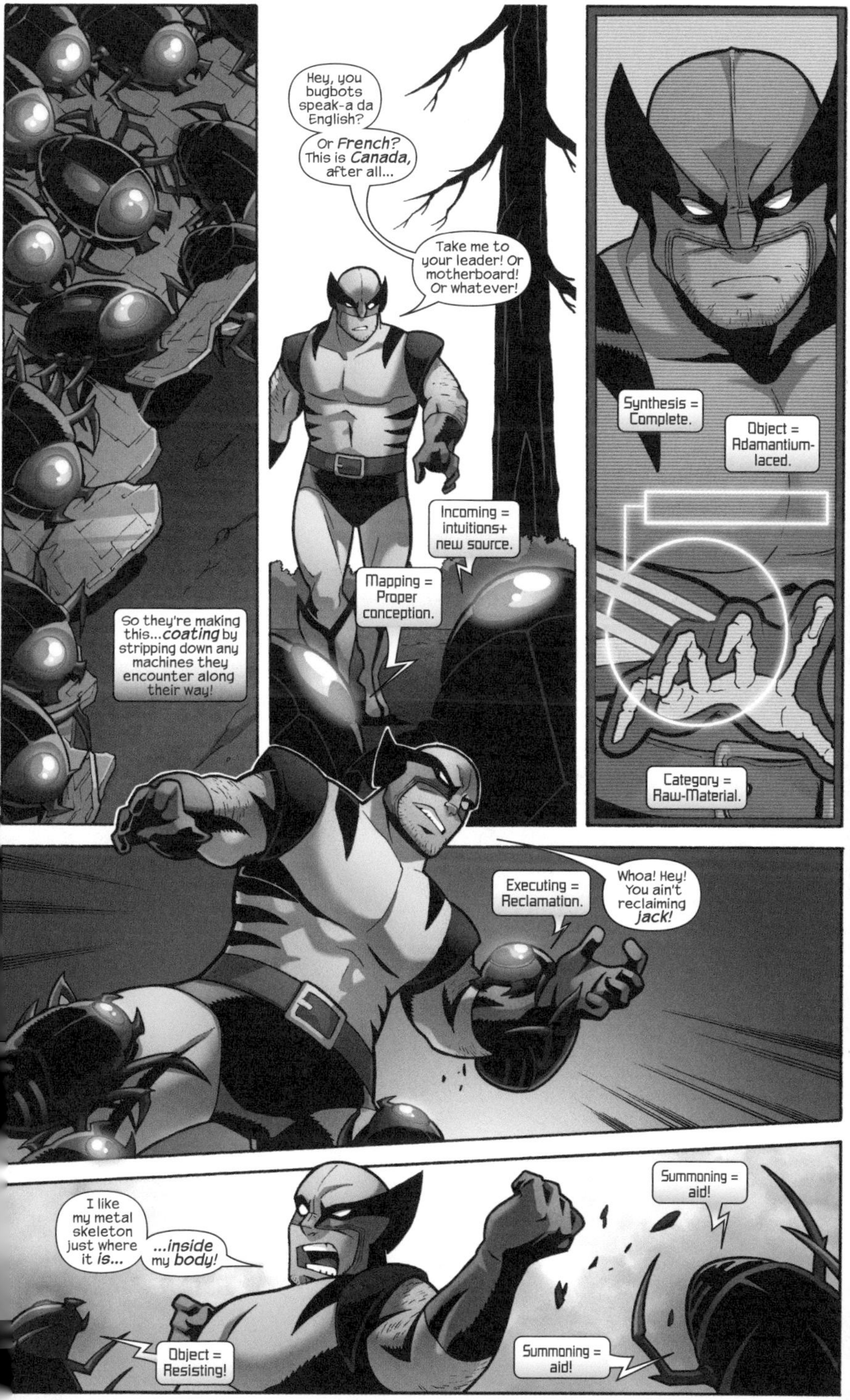
So they're making this...coating by stripping down any machines they encounter along their way!
Hey, you bugbots speak-a da English?
Or French? This is Canada, after all...
Take me to your leader! Or motherboard! Or whatever!
Incoming = intuitions+ new source.
Mapping = Proper conception.
Synthesis = Complete.
Object = Adamantium-laced.
Category = Raw-Material.
Executing = Reclamation.
Whoa! Hey! You ain't reclaiming jack!
I like my metal skeleton just where it is...
...inside my body!
Summoning = aid!
Object = Resisting!
Summoning = aid!

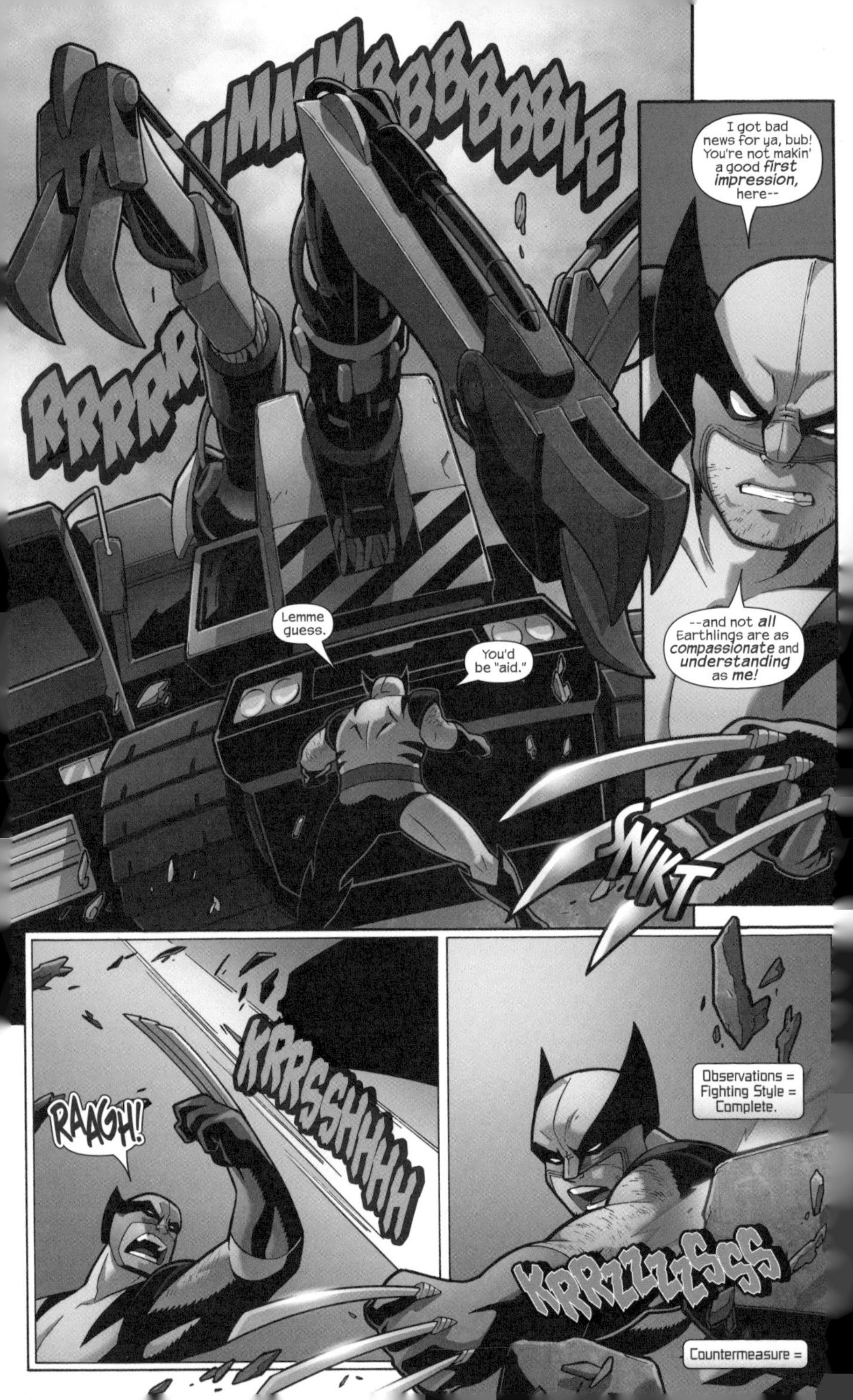
RRRRRUMMMBBBBBBLE
I got bad news for ya, bub! You're not makin' a good first impression, here--
--and not all Earthlings are as compassionate and understanding as me!
Lemme guess.
You'd be "aid."
SNIKT
KRRSHHHH
RAAGH!
Observations = Fighting Style = Complete.
KRRZZZZSSS
Countermeasure =

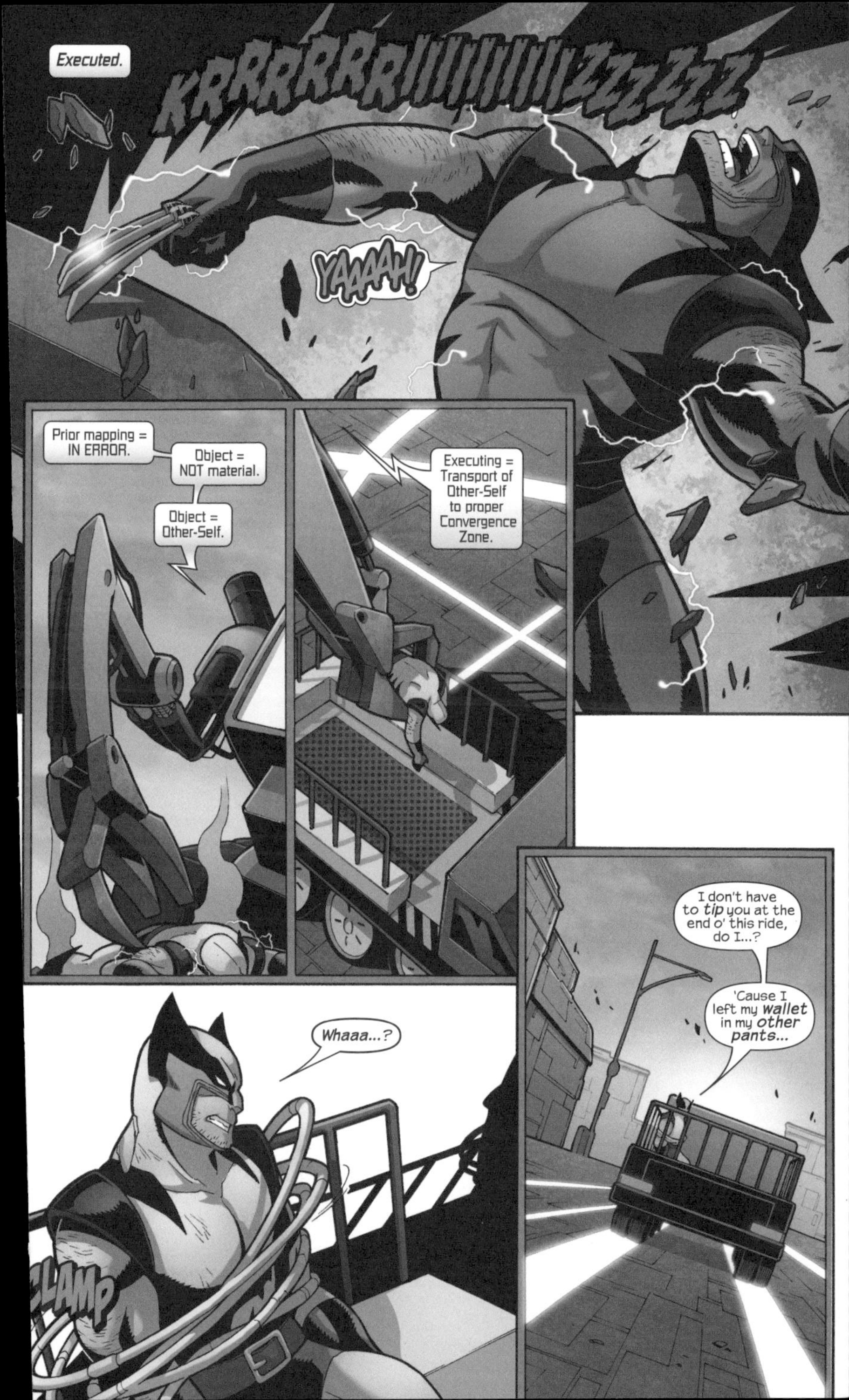
Executed.
KRRRRRRRIIIIIIIIIIIIIZZZZZZ
YAAAAH!!
Prior mapping = IN ERROR.
Object = NOT material.
Object = Other-Self.
Executing = Transport of Other-Self to proper Convergence Zone.
Whaaa...?
CLAMP
I don't have to tip you at the end o' this ride, do I...?
'Cause I left my wallet in my other pants...

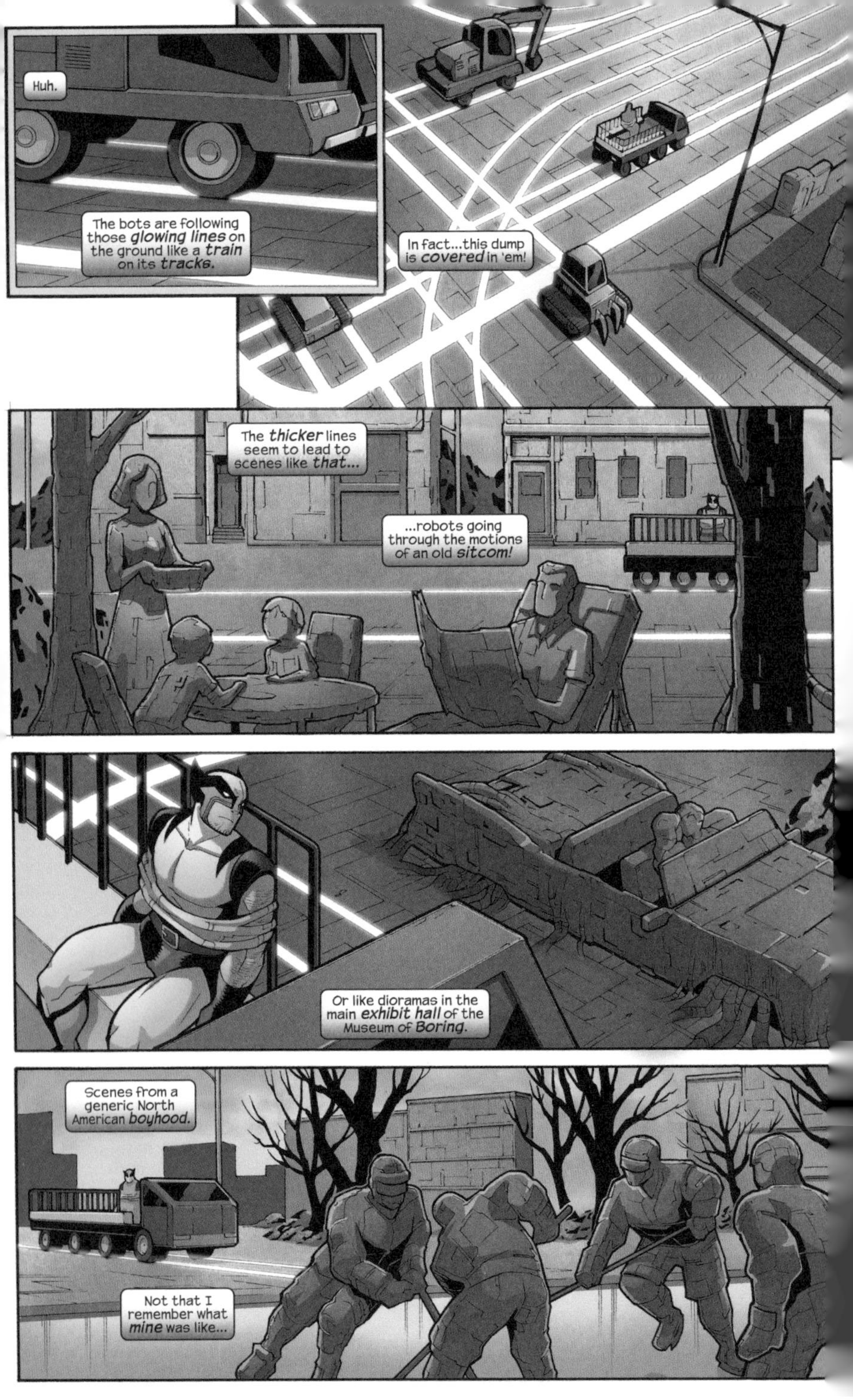
Huh.
The bots are following those *glowing lines* on the ground like a *train* on its *tracks*.
In fact...this dump is *covered* in 'em!
The *thicker* lines seem to lead to scenes like *that*...
...robots going through the motions of an old *sitcom!*
Or like dioramas in the main *exhibit hall* of the Museum of *Boring*.
Scenes from a generic North American *boyhood*.
Not that I remember what *mine* was like...

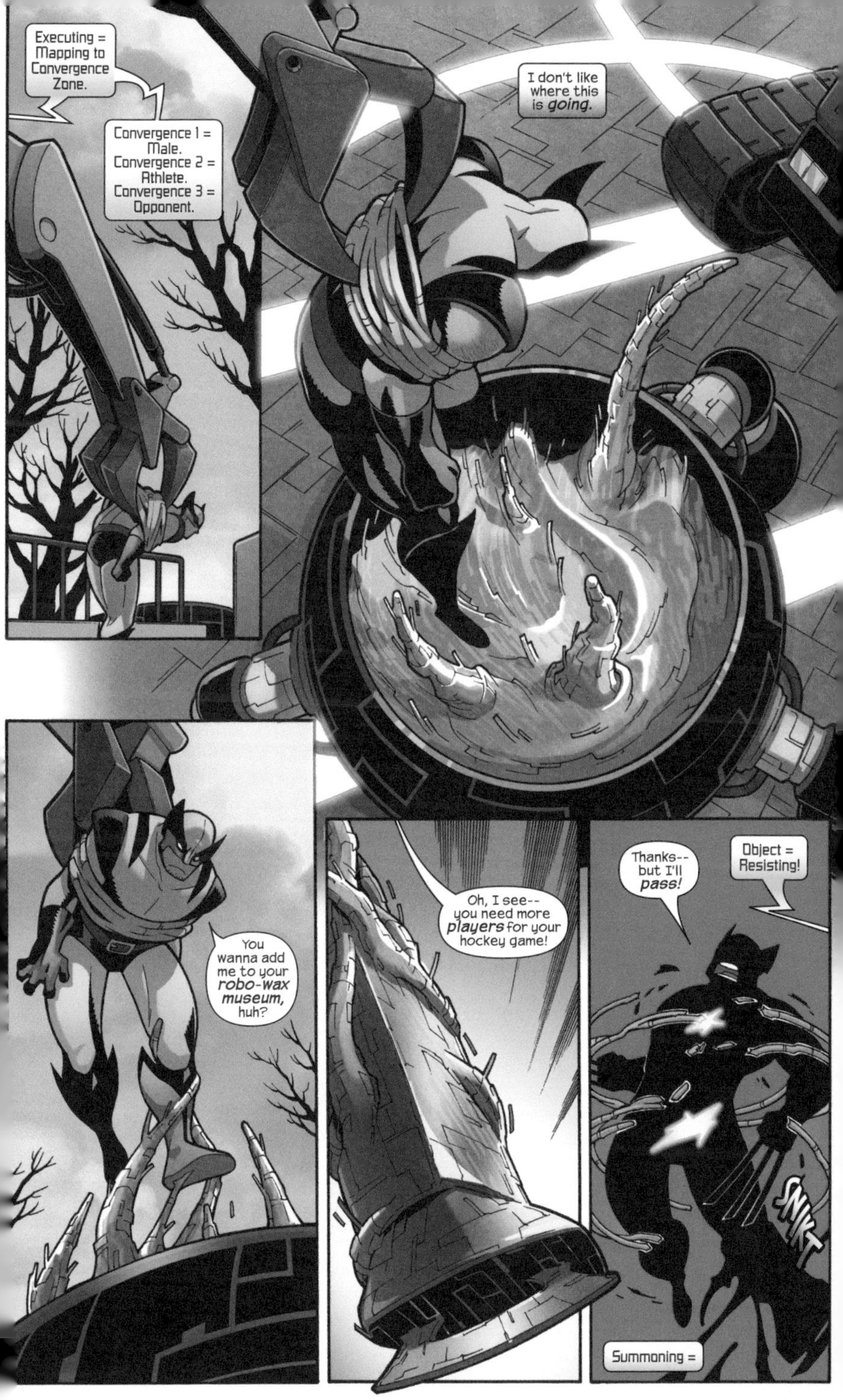
Executing = Mapping to Convergence Zone.
Convergence 1 = Male. Convergence 2 = Athlete. Convergence 3 = Opponent.
I don't like where this is going.
You wanna add me to your robo-wax museum, huh?
Oh, I see-- you need more players for your hockey game!
Thanks-- but I'll pass!
Object = Resisting!
SNIKT
Summoning =

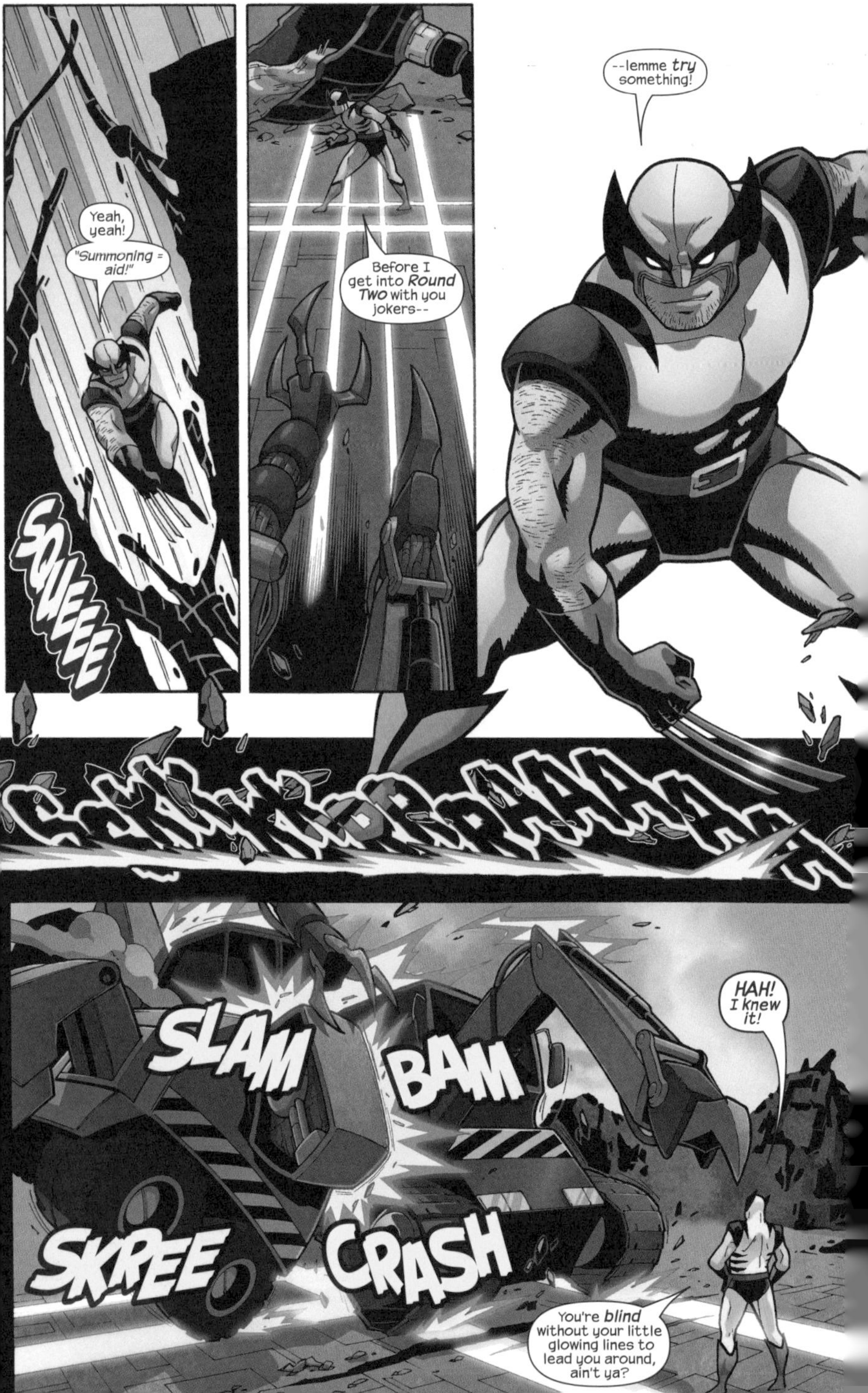
Yeah, yeah!
"Summoning = aid!"
SQUEEE
Before I get into *Round Two* with you jokers--
--lemme *try* something!
SLAM
BAM
HAH! I knew it!
SKREE
CRASH
You're *blind* without your little glowing lines to lead you around, ain't ya?

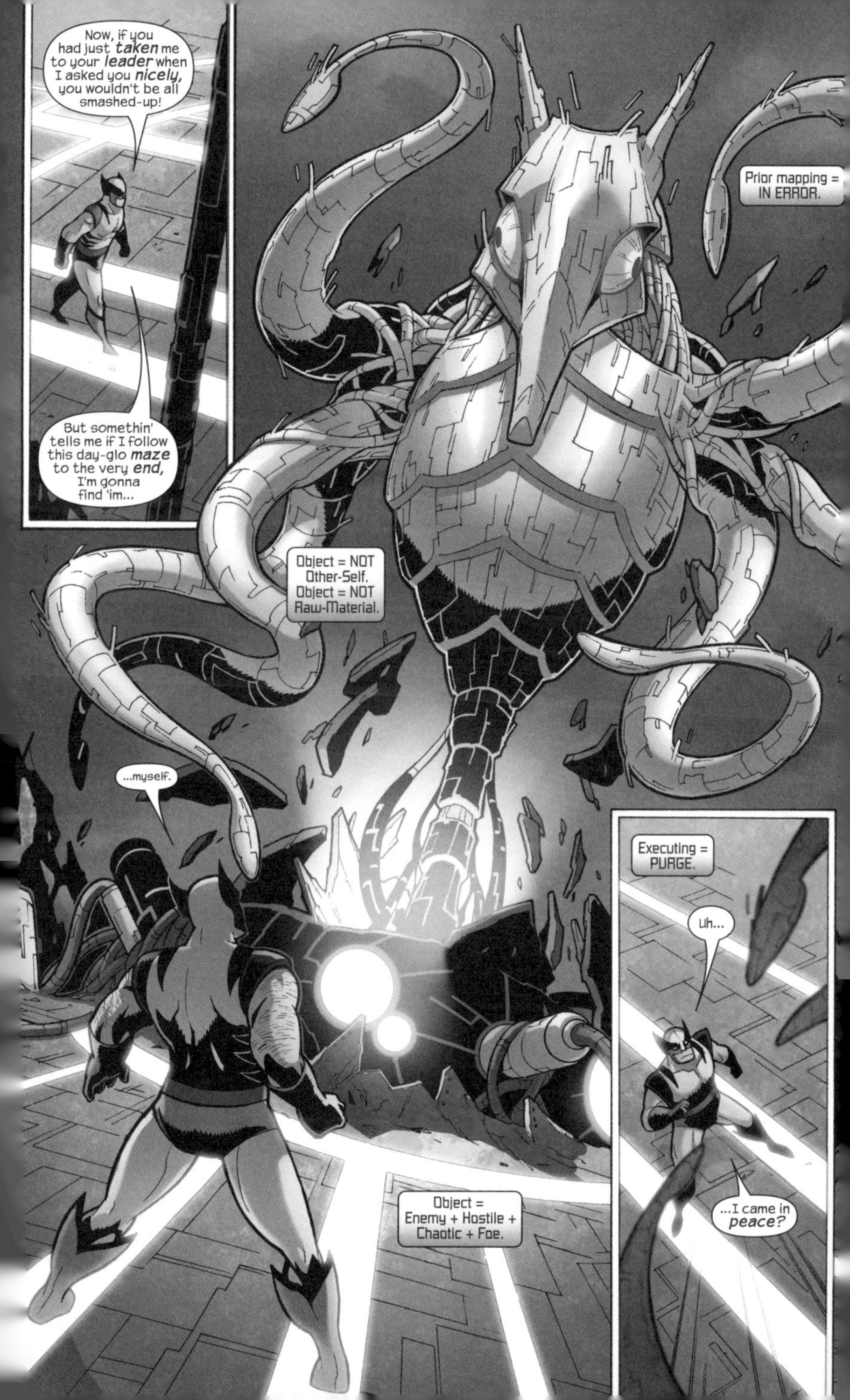
Now, if you had just *taken* me to your *leader* when I asked you *nicely,* you wouldn't be all smashed-up!
But somethin' tells me if I follow this day-glo *maze* to the very *end,* I'm gonna find 'im...
Prior mapping = IN ERROR.
Object = NOT Other-Self. Object = NOT Raw-Material.
...myself.
Object = Enemy + Hostile + Chaotic + Foe.
Executing = PURGE.
Uh...
...I came in *peace?*

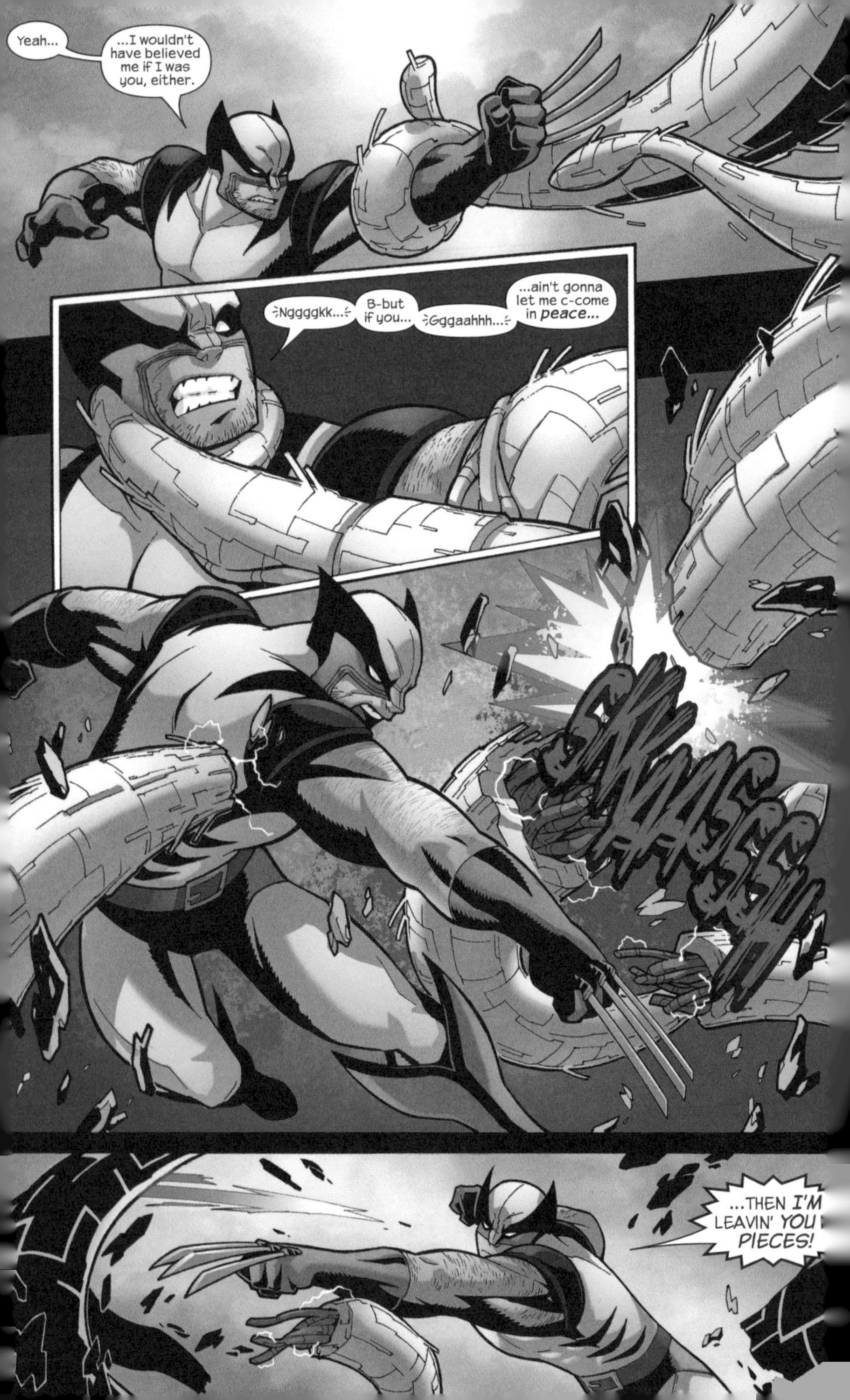
Yeah...
...I wouldn't have believed me if I was you, either.
Nggggkk...
B-but if you...
Gggaahhh...
...ain't gonna let me c-come in *peace*...
SKRASCCH
...THEN *I'M* LEAVIN' *YOU* *PIECES!*

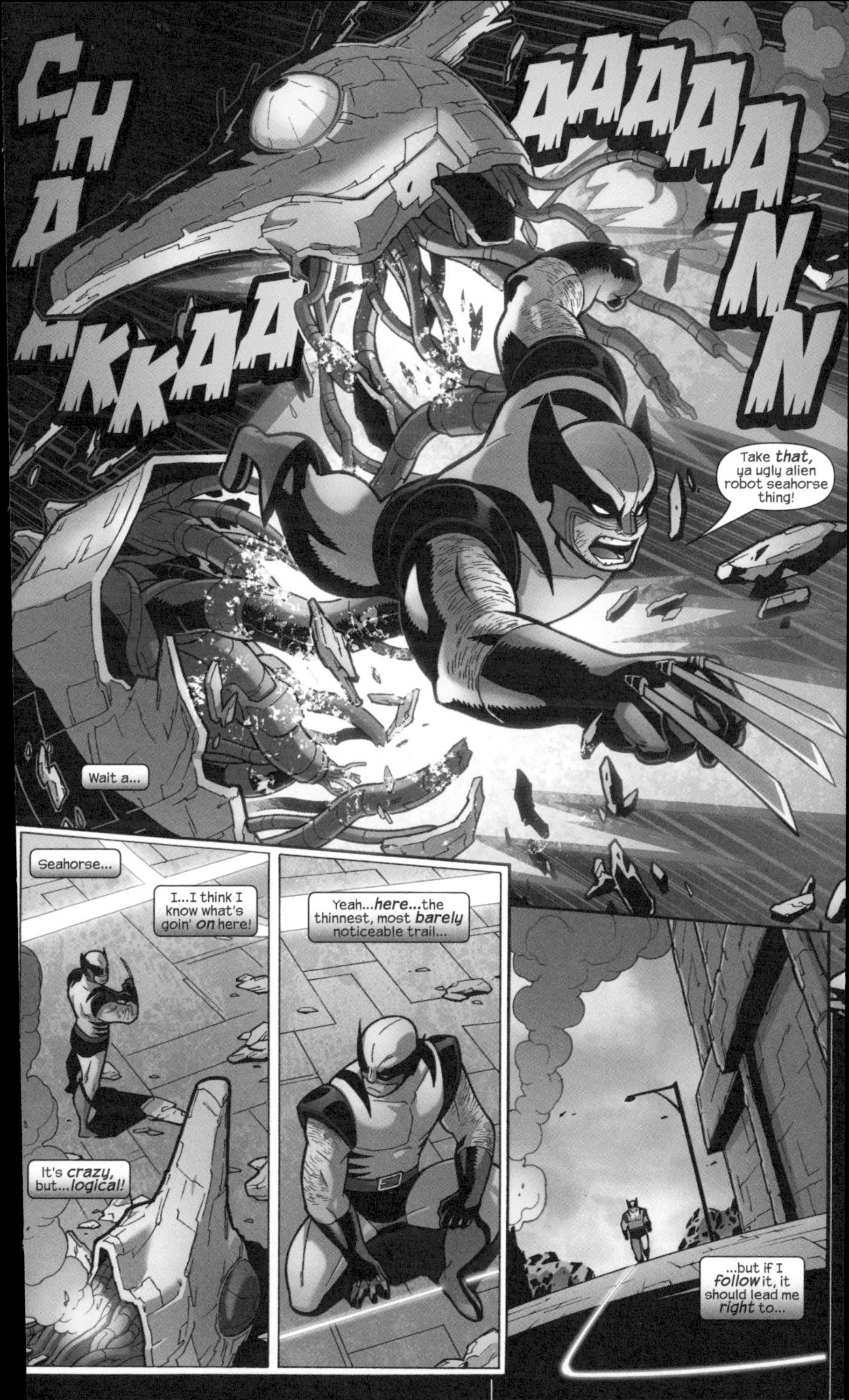

CHAKKAAAAAAAAANN
Take *that*, ya ugly alien robot seahorse thing!
Wait a...
Seahorse...
I...I think I know what's goin' *on* here!
It's *crazy*, but...*logical!*
Yeah...*here...*the thinnest, most *barely* noticeable trail...
...but if I *follow* it, it should lead me *right* to...

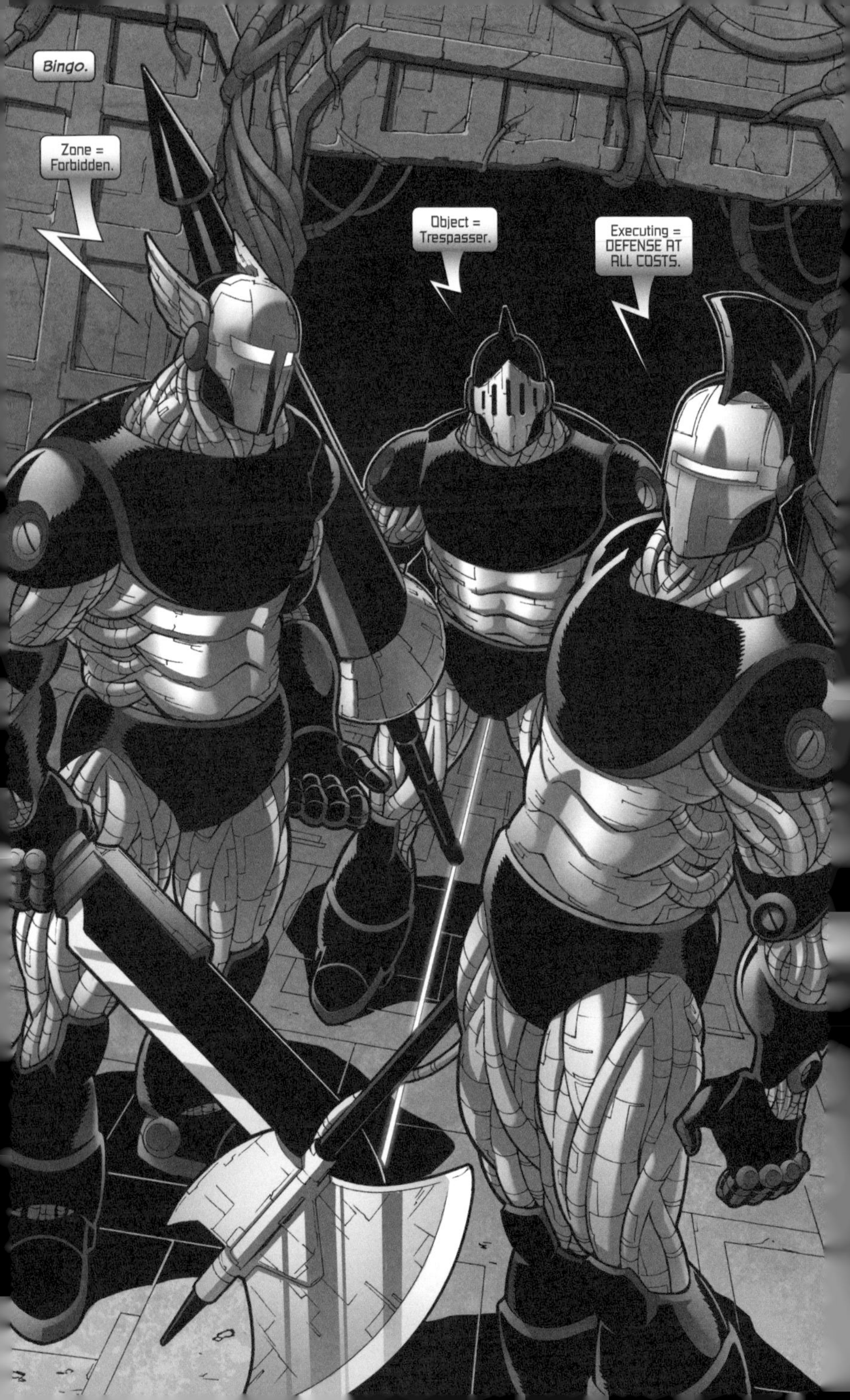
Bingo.
Zone = Forbidden.
Object = Trespasser.
Executing = DEFENSE AT ALL COSTS.

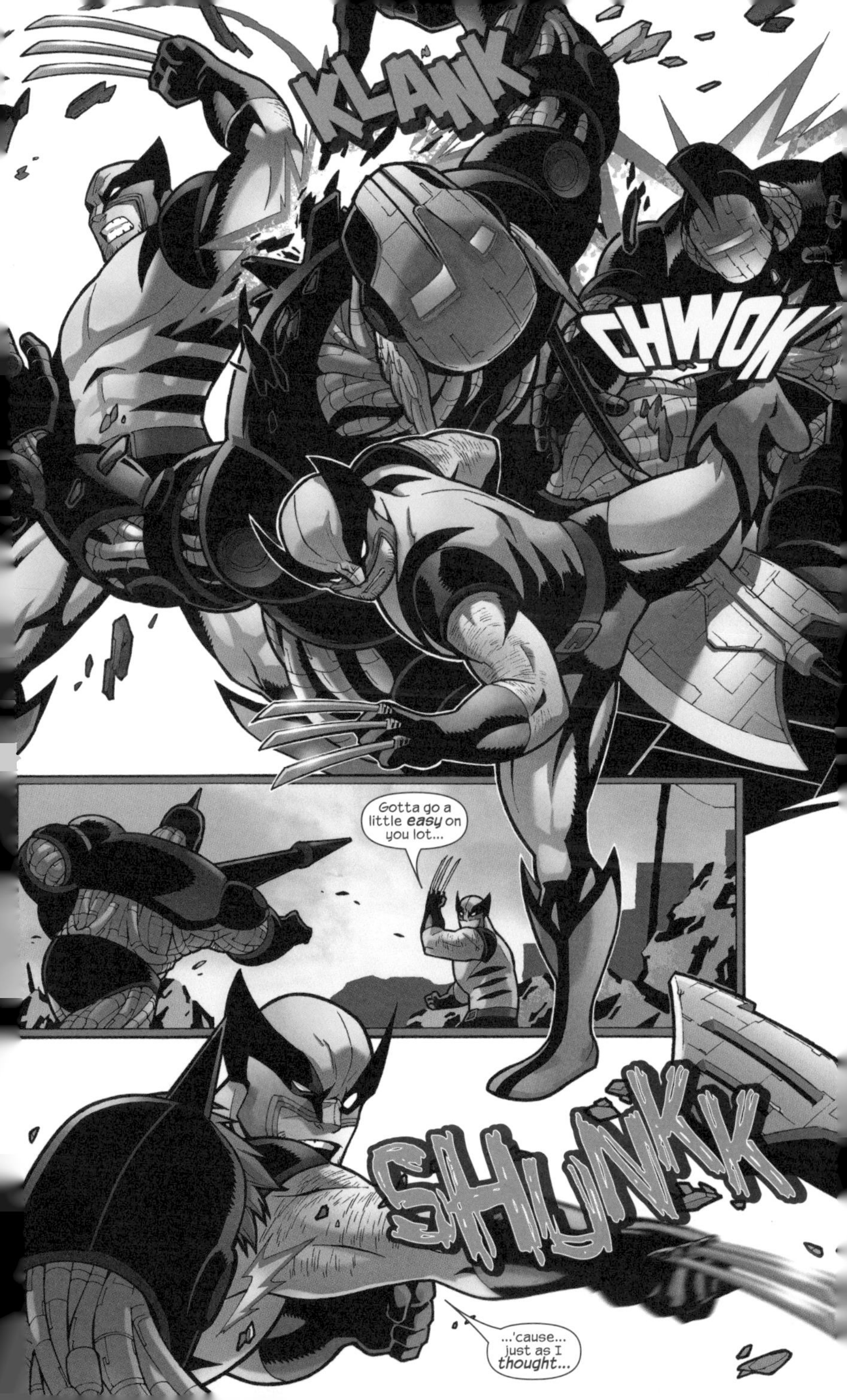
KLANK
CHWOK
Gotta go a little easy on you lot...
SHUNKK
...'cause... just as I thought...

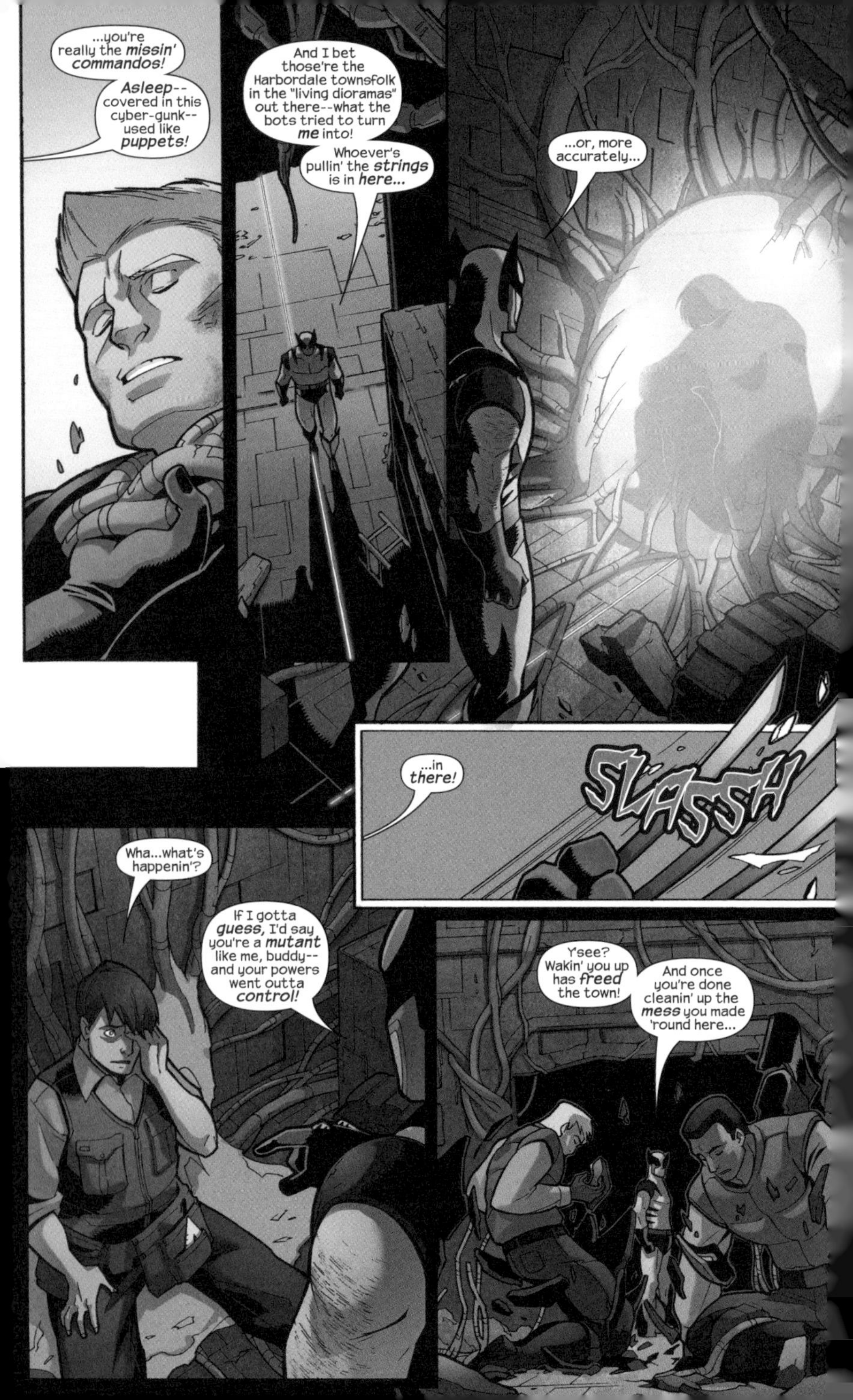
...you're really the missin' commandos!
Asleep--covered in this cyber-gunk--used like puppets!
And I bet those're the Harbordale townsfolk in the "living dioramas" out there--what the bots tried to turn me into!
Whoever's pullin' the strings is in here...
...or, more accurately...
...in there!
SLASSH
Wha...what's happenin'?
If I gotta guess, I'd say you're a mutant like me, buddy--and your powers went outta control!
Y'see? Wakin' you up has freed the town!
And once you're done cleanin' up the mess you made 'round here...

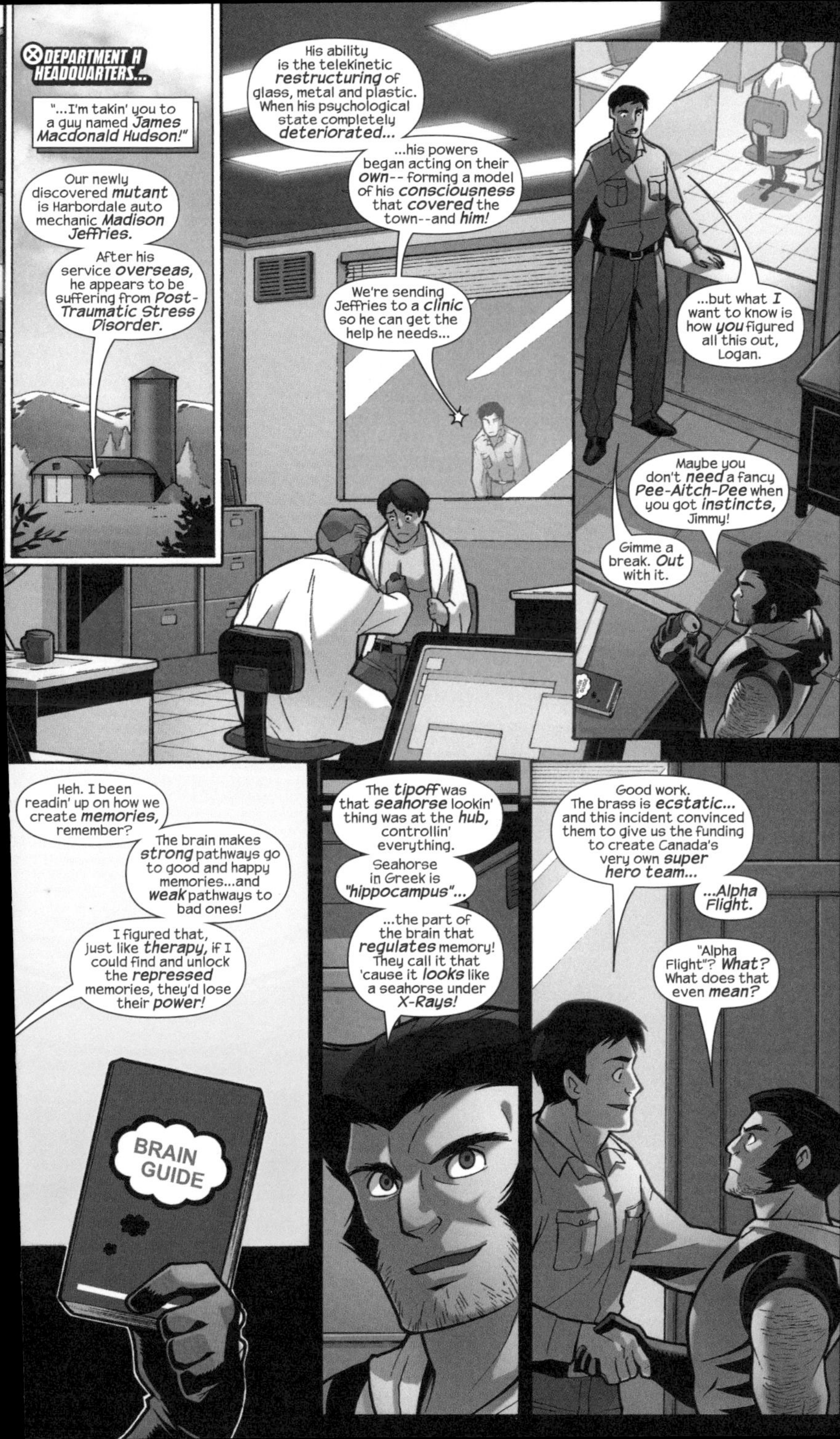

DEPARTMENT H HEADQUARTERS...
"...I'm takin' you to a guy named James Macdonald Hudson!"
Our newly discovered mutant is Harbordale auto mechanic Madison Jeffries.
After his service overseas, he appears to be suffering from Post-Traumatic Stress Disorder.
His ability is the telekinetic restructuring of glass, metal and plastic. When his psychological state completely deteriorated...
...his powers began acting on their own-- forming a model of his consciousness that covered the town--and him!
We're sending Jeffries to a clinic so he can get the help he needs...
...but what I want to know is how you figured all this out, Logan.
Maybe you don't need a fancy Pee-Aitch-Dee when you got instincts, Jimmy!
Gimme a break. Out with it.
Heh. I been readin' up on how we create memories, remember?
The brain makes strong pathways go to good and happy memories...and weak pathways to bad ones!
I figured that, just like therapy, if I could find and unlock the repressed memories, they'd lose their power!
BRAIN GUIDE
The tipoff was that seahorse lookin' thing was at the hub, controllin' everything.
Seahorse in Greek is "hippocampus"...
...the part of the brain that regulates memory! They call it that 'cause it looks like a seahorse under X-Rays!
Good work. The brass is ecstatic... and this incident convinced them to give us the funding to create Canada's very own super hero team...
...Alpha Flight.
"Alpha Flight"? What? What does that even mean?

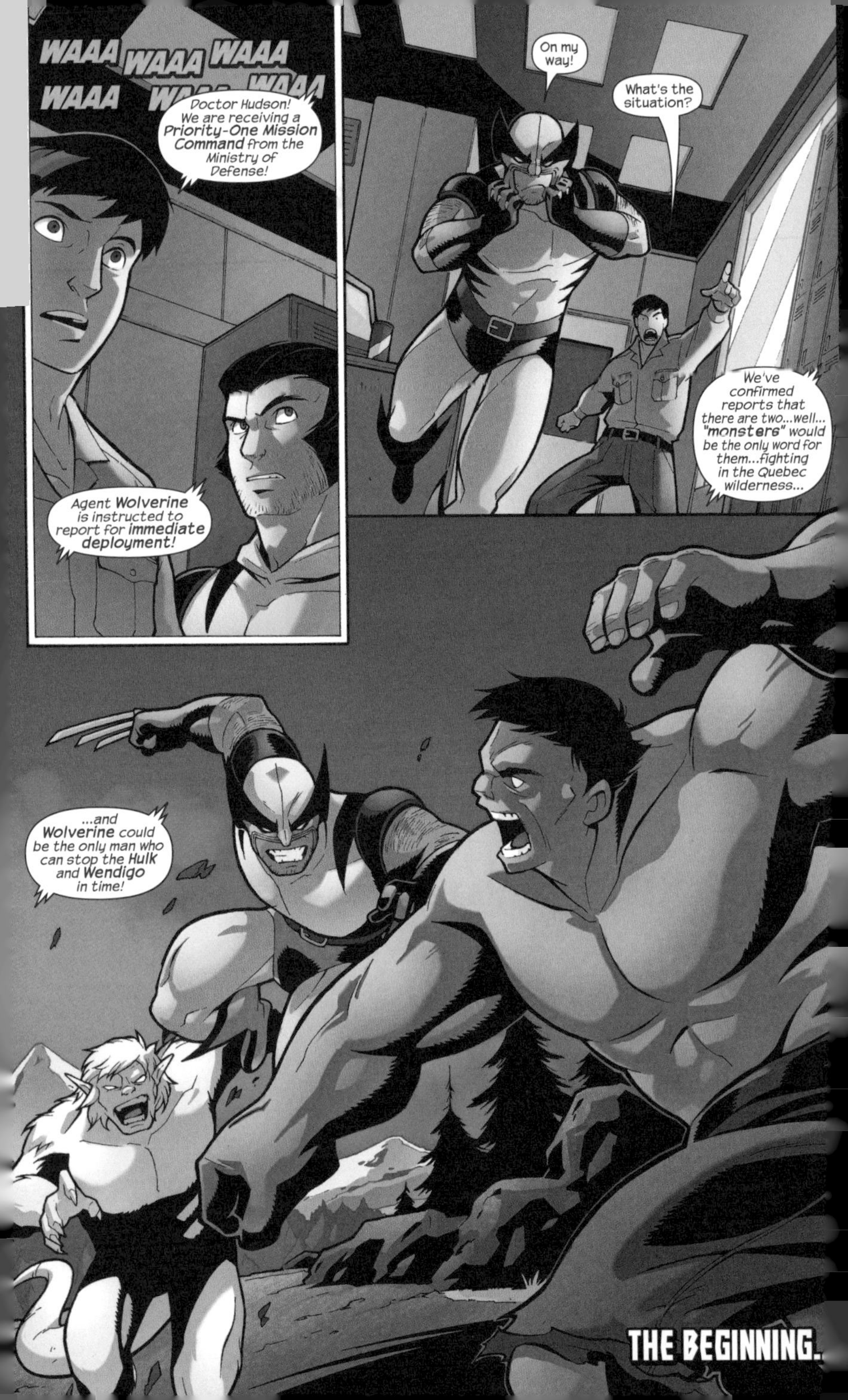
WAAA WAAA WAAA
WAAA
Doctor Hudson! We are receiving a Priority-One Mission Command from the Ministry of Defense!
Agent Wolverine is instructed to report for immediate deployment!
On my way!
What's the situation?
We've confirmed reports that there are two...well... "monsters" would be the only word for them...fighting in the Quebec wilderness...
...and Wolverine could be the only man who can stop the Hulk and Wendigo in time!
THE BEGINNING.

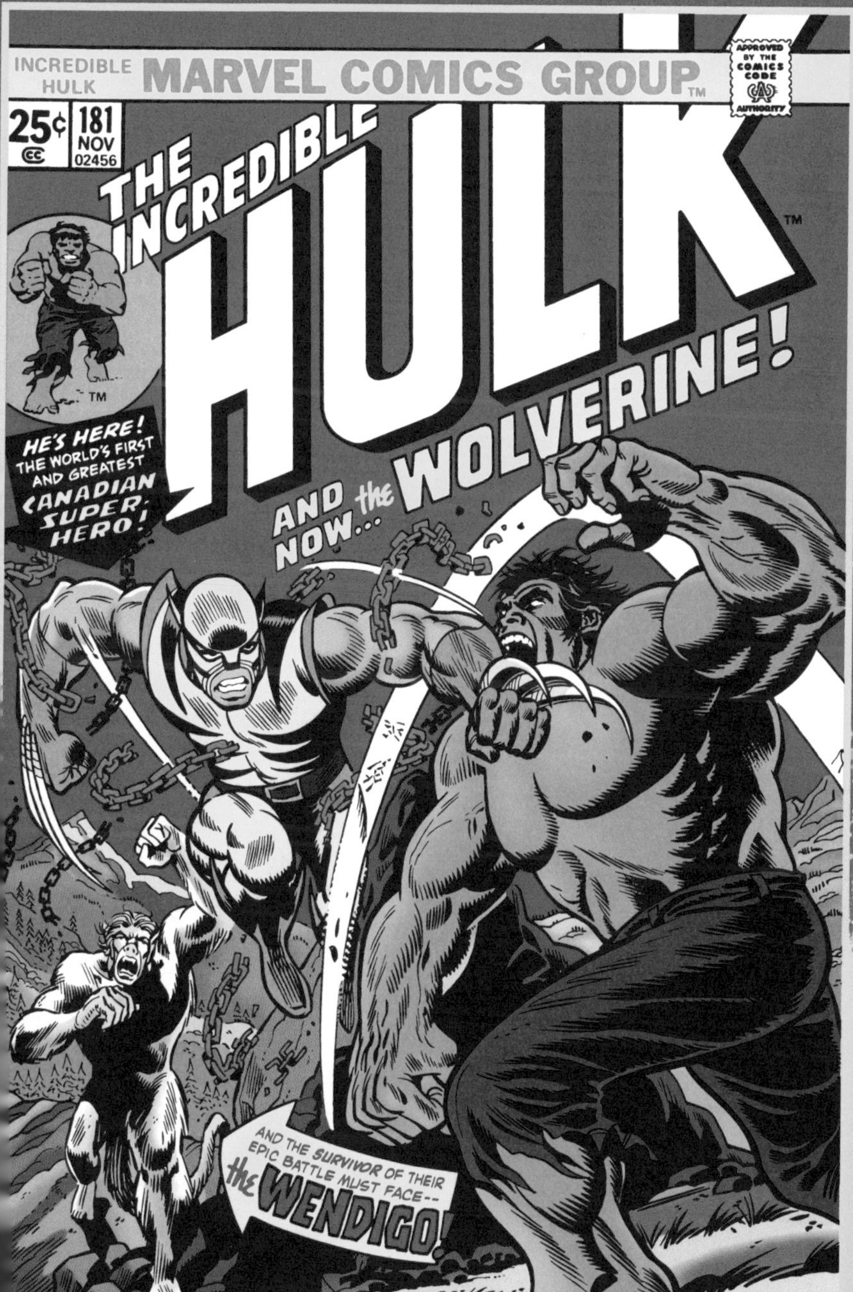
INCREDIBLE HULK
MARVEL COMICS GROUP
APPROVED BY THE COMICS CODE AUTHORITY
25¢
181 NOV 02456
THE INCREDIBLE HULK
HE'S HERE! THE WORLD'S FIRST AND GREATEST CANADIAN SUPER-HERO!
AND NOW... the WOLVERINE!
AND THE SURVIVOR OF THEIR EPIC BATTLE MUST FACE-- the WENDIGO!

Caught in the heart of a ***Nuclear Explosion,*** victim of ***Gamma-Radiation*** gone wild, ***Doctor Robert Bruce Banner*** now finds himself transformed in times of stress into seven feet, one thousand pounds of unfettered ***Fury***—the most powerful creature to ever walk the earth—

Stan Lee PRESENTS: **THE INCREDIBLE HULK!**™

LEN WEIN & HERB TRIMPE ✱ JACK ABEL ✱ GLYNIS WEIN, *COLORIST* ✱ ROY THOMAS
WRITER *ARTIST* *INKER* ARTIE SIMEK, *LETTERER* *EDITOR*

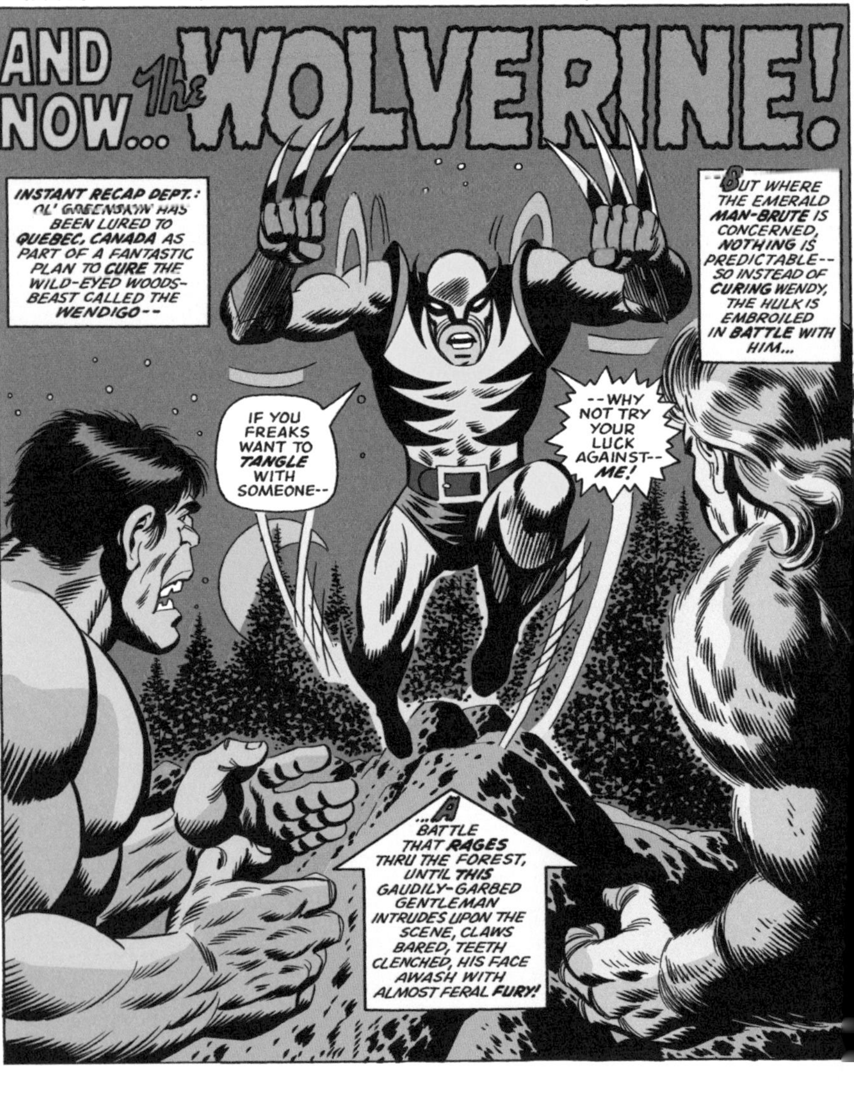
AND NOW... THE WOLVERINE!
INSTANT RECAP DEPT.: OL' GREENSKIN HAS BEEN LURED TO QUEBEC, CANADA AS PART OF A FANTASTIC PLAN TO CURE THE WILD-EYED WOODS-BEAST CALLED THE WENDIGO--
--BUT WHERE THE EMERALD MAN-BRUTE IS CONCERNED, NOTHING IS PREDICTABLE--SO INSTEAD OF CURING WENDY, THE HULK IS EMBROILED IN BATTLE WITH HIM...
IF YOU FREAKS WANT TO TANGLE WITH SOMEONE--
--WHY NOT TRY YOUR LUCK AGAINST--ME!
...A BATTLE THAT RAGES THRU THE FOREST, UNTIL THIS GAUDILY-GARBED GENTLEMAN INTRUDES UPON THE SCENE, CLAWS BARED, TEETH CLENCHED, HIS FACE AWASH WITH ALMOST FERAL FURY!

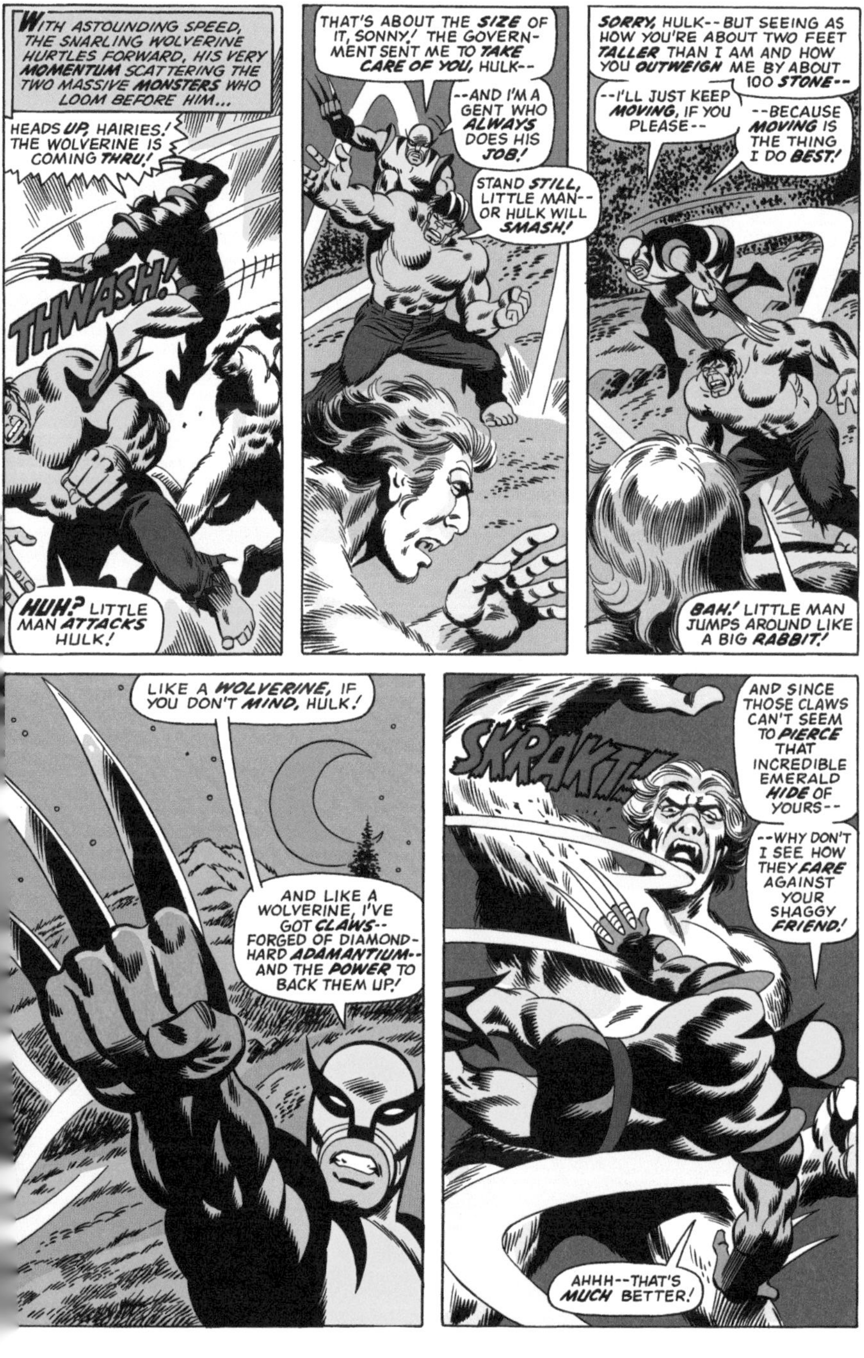
WITH ASTOUNDING SPEED, THE SNARLING WOLVERINE HURTLES FORWARD, HIS VERY MOMENTUM SCATTERING THE TWO MASSIVE MONSTERS WHO LOOM BEFORE HIM...
HEADS UP, HAIRIES! THE WOLVERINE IS COMING THRU!
THWASH!
HUH? LITTLE MAN ATTACKS HULK!
THAT'S ABOUT THE SIZE OF IT, SONNY! THE GOVERNMENT SENT ME TO TAKE CARE OF YOU, HULK--
--AND I'M A GENT WHO ALWAYS DOES HIS JOB!
STAND STILL, LITTLE MAN-- OR HULK WILL SMASH!
SORRY, HULK-- BUT SEEING AS HOW YOU'RE ABOUT TWO FEET TALLER THAN I AM AND HOW YOU OUTWEIGN ME BY ABOUT 100 STONE--
--I'LL JUST KEEP MOVING, IF YOU PLEASE--
--BECAUSE MOVING IS THE THING I DO BEST!
BAH! LITTLE MAN JUMPS AROUND LIKE A BIG RABBIT!
LIKE A WOLVERINE, IF YOU DON'T MIND, HULK!
AND LIKE A WOLVERINE, I'VE GOT CLAWS-- FORGED OF DIAMOND-HARD ADAMANTIUM-- AND THE POWER TO BACK THEM UP!
SKRAKT!
AND SINCE THOSE CLAWS CAN'T SEEM TO PIERCE THAT INCREDIBLE EMERALD HIDE OF YOURS--
--WHY DON'T I SEE HOW THEY FARE AGAINST YOUR SHAGGY FRIEND!
AHHH--THAT'S MUCH BETTER!

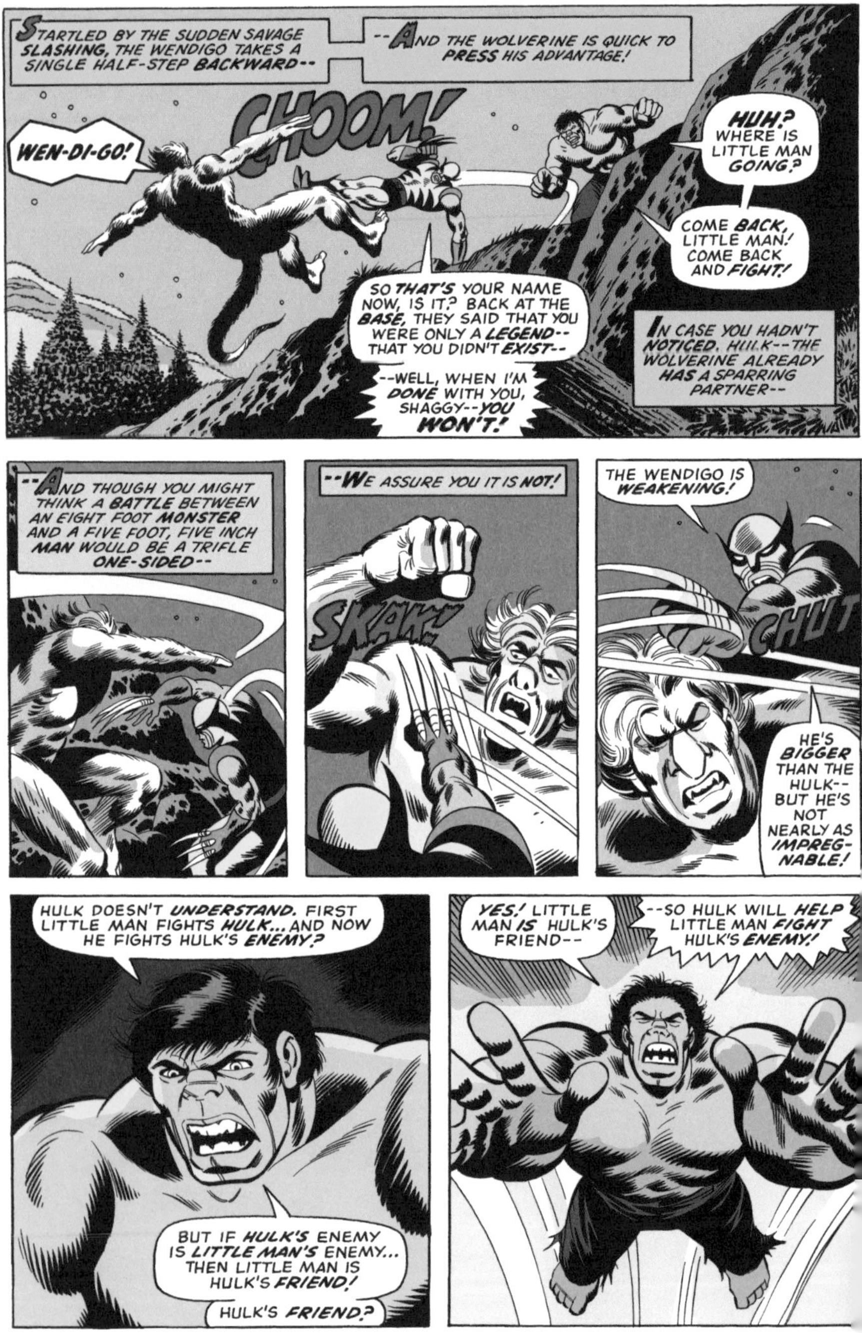

STARTLED BY THE SUDDEN SAVAGE SLASHING, THE WENDIGO TAKES A SINGLE HALF-STEP BACKWARD--
--AND THE WOLVERINE IS QUICK TO PRESS HIS ADVANTAGE!
CHOOM!
WEN-DI-GO!
HUH? WHERE IS LITTLE MAN GOING?
COME BACK, LITTLE MAN! COME BACK AND FIGHT!
SO THAT'S YOUR NAME NOW, IS IT? BACK AT THE BASE, THEY SAID THAT YOU WERE ONLY A LEGEND-- THAT YOU DIDN'T EXIST--
--WELL, WHEN I'M DONE WITH YOU, SHAGGY--YOU WON'T!
IN CASE YOU HADN'T NOTICED, HULK--THE WOLVERINE ALREADY HAS A SPARRING PARTNER--
--AND THOUGH YOU MIGHT THINK A BATTLE BETWEEN AN EIGHT FOOT MONSTER AND A FIVE FOOT, FIVE INCH MAN WOULD BE A TRIFLE ONE-SIDED--
--WE ASSURE YOU IT IS NOT!
SKAK!
THE WENDIGO IS WEAKENING!
CHUT
HE'S BIGGER THAN THE HULK-- BUT HE'S NOT NEARLY AS IMPREGNABLE!
HULK DOESN'T UNDERSTAND. FIRST LITTLE MAN FIGHTS HULK... AND NOW HE FIGHTS HULK'S ENEMY?
BUT IF HULK'S ENEMY IS LITTLE MAN'S ENEMY... THEN LITTLE MAN IS HULK'S FRIEND!
HULK'S FRIEND?
YES! LITTLE MAN IS HULK'S FRIEND--
--SO HULK WILL HELP LITTLE MAN FIGHT HULK'S ENEMY!

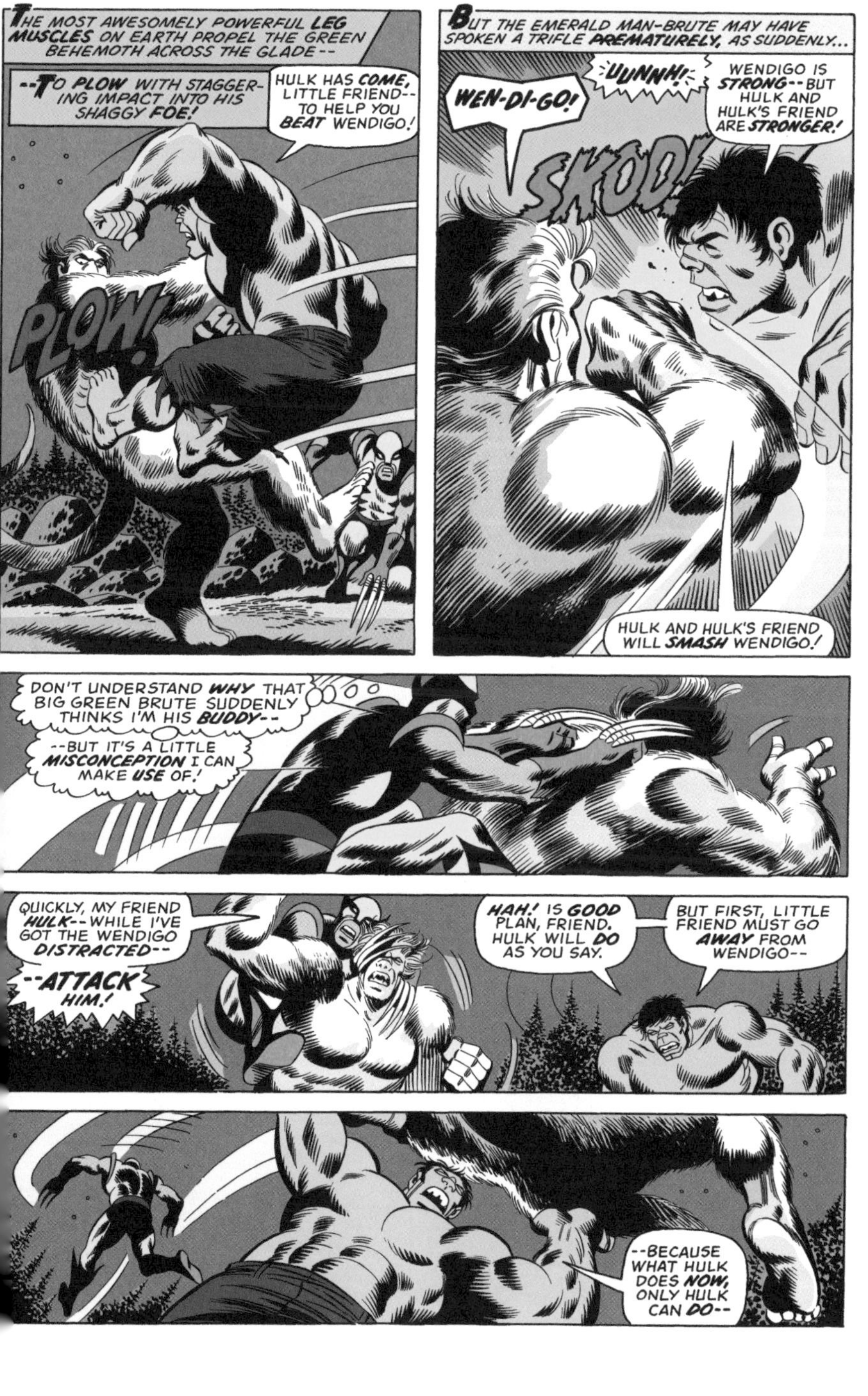
THE MOST AWESOMELY POWERFUL LEG MUSCLES ON EARTH PROPEL THE GREEN BEHEMOTH ACROSS THE GLADE--
--TO PLOW WITH STAGGERING IMPACT INTO HIS SHAGGY FOE!
HULK HAS COME, LITTLE FRIEND-- TO HELP YOU BEAT WENDIGO!
PLOW!
BUT THE EMERALD MAN-BRUTE MAY HAVE SPOKEN A TRIFLE PREMATURELY, AS SUDDENLY...
UUNNH!
WEN-DI-GO!
WENDIGO IS STRONG--BUT HULK AND HULK'S FRIEND ARE STRONGER!
SKOD!
HULK AND HULK'S FRIEND WILL SMASH WENDIGO!
DON'T UNDERSTAND WHY THAT BIG GREEN BRUTE SUDDENLY THINKS I'M HIS BUDDY--
--BUT IT'S A LITTLE MISCONCEPTION I CAN MAKE USE OF!
QUICKLY, MY FRIEND HULK--WHILE I'VE GOT THE WENDIGO DISTRACTED--
--ATTACK HIM!
HAH! IS GOOD PLAN, FRIEND. HULK WILL DO AS YOU SAY.
BUT FIRST, LITTLE FRIEND MUST GO AWAY FROM WENDIGO--
--BECAUSE WHAT HULK DOES NOW, ONLY HULK CAN DO--

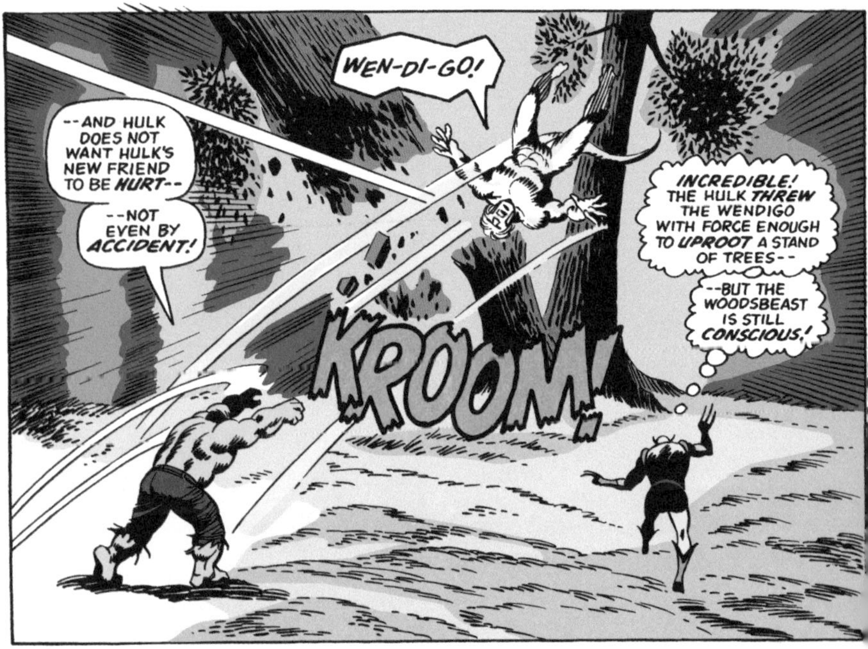
--AND HULK DOES NOT WANT HULK'S NEW FRIEND TO BE HURT--
--NOT EVEN BY ACCIDENT!
WEN-DI-GO!
INCREDIBLE! THE HULK THREW THE WENDIGO WITH FORCE ENOUGH TO UPROOT A STAND OF TREES--
--BUT THE WOODSBEAST IS STILL CONSCIOUS!
KROOM!

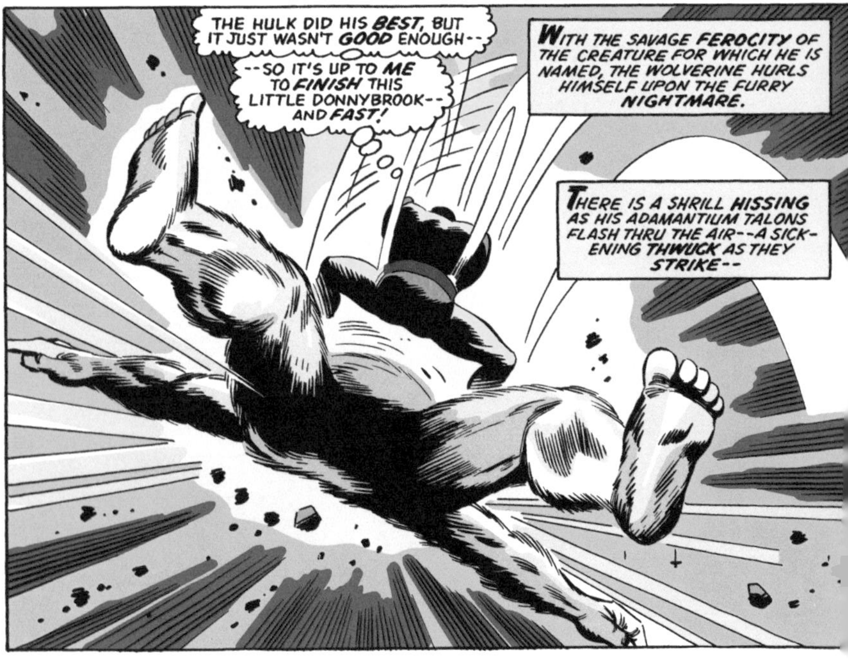
THE HULK DID HIS BEST, BUT IT JUST WASN'T GOOD ENOUGH--
--SO IT'S UP TO ME TO FINISH THIS LITTLE DONNYBROOK--AND FAST!
WITH THE SAVAGE FEROCITY OF THE CREATURE FOR WHICH HE IS NAMED, THE WOLVERINE HURLS HIMSELF UPON THE FURRY NIGHTMARE.
THERE IS A SHRILL HISSING AS HIS ADAMANTIUM TALONS FLASH THRU THE AIR--A SICKENING THWUCK AS THEY STRIKE--

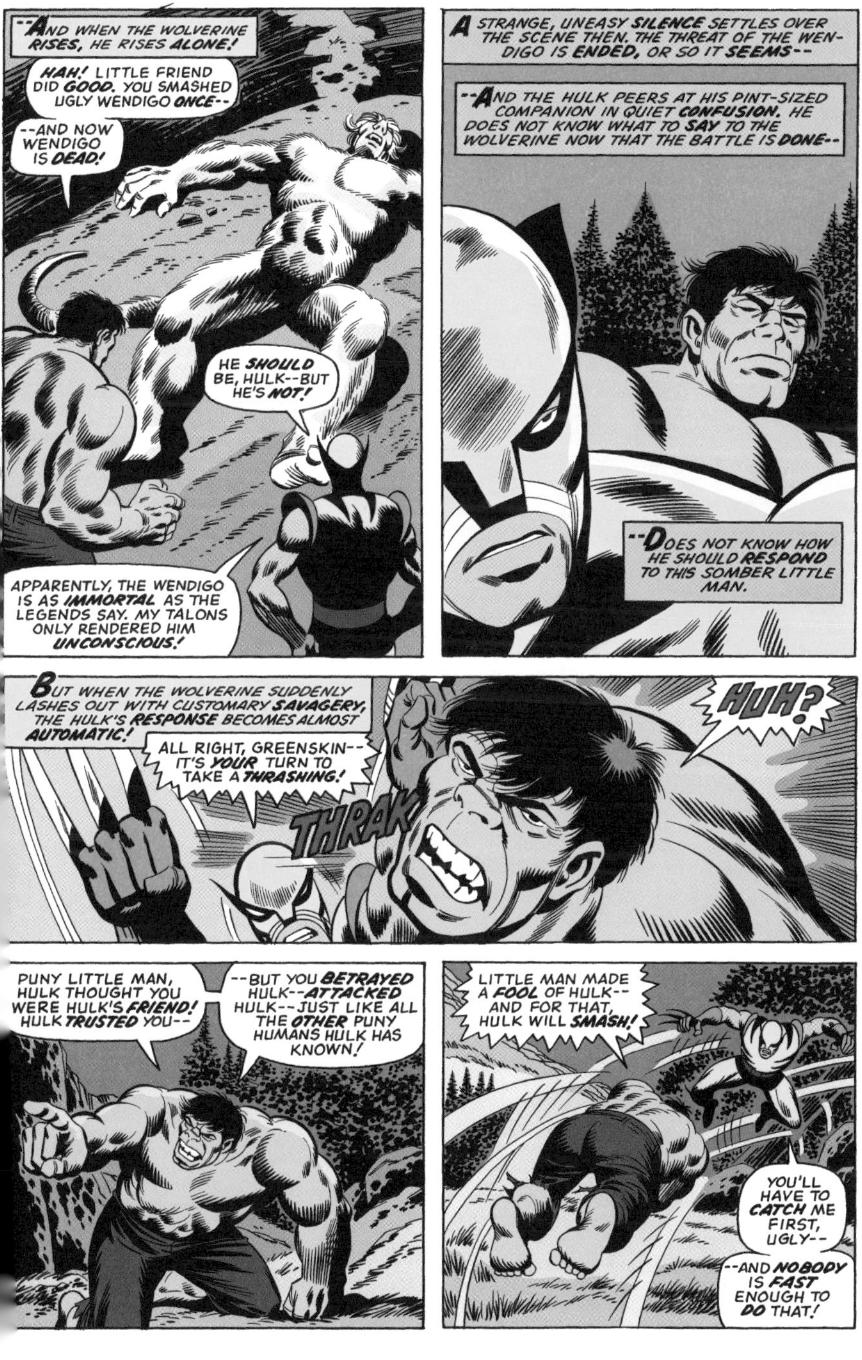
--AND WHEN THE WOLVERINE RISES, HE RISES ALONE!
HAH! LITTLE FRIEND DID GOOD. YOU SMASHED UGLY WENDIGO ONCE--
--AND NOW WENDIGO IS DEAD!
HE SHOULD BE, HULK--BUT HE'S NOT!
APPARENTLY, THE WENDIGO IS AS IMMORTAL AS THE LEGENDS SAY. MY TALONS ONLY RENDERED HIM UNCONSCIOUS!
A STRANGE, UNEASY SILENCE SETTLES OVER THE SCENE THEN. THE THREAT OF THE WENDIGO IS ENDED, OR SO IT SEEMS--
--AND THE HULK PEERS AT HIS PINT-SIZED COMPANION IN QUIET CONFUSION. HE DOES NOT KNOW WHAT TO SAY TO THE WOLVERINE NOW THAT THE BATTLE IS DONE--
--DOES NOT KNOW HOW HE SHOULD RESPOND TO THIS SOMBER LITTLE MAN.
BUT WHEN THE WOLVERINE SUDDENLY LASHES OUT WITH CUSTOMARY SAVAGERY, THE HULK'S RESPONSE BECOMES ALMOST AUTOMATIC!
ALL RIGHT, GREENSKIN--IT'S YOUR TURN TO TAKE A THRASHING!
THRAK
HUH?
PUNY LITTLE MAN, HULK THOUGHT YOU WERE HULK'S FRIEND! HULK TRUSTED YOU--
--BUT YOU BETRAYED HULK--ATTACKED HULK--JUST LIKE ALL THE OTHER PUNY HUMANS HULK HAS KNOWN!
LITTLE MAN MADE A FOOL OF HULK--AND FOR THAT, HULK WILL SMASH!
YOU'LL HAVE TO CATCH ME FIRST, UGLY--
--AND NOBODY IS FAST ENOUGH TO DO THAT!

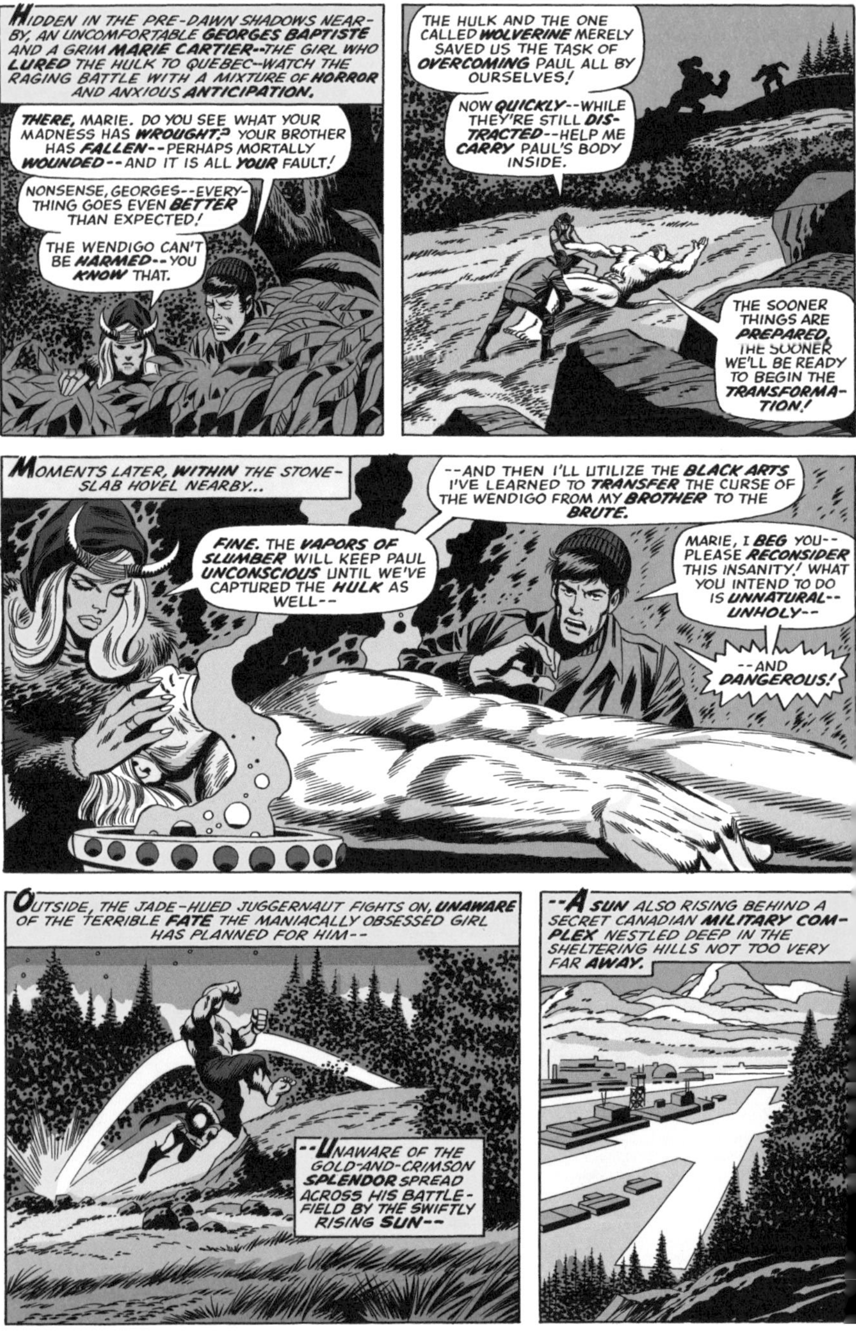
HIDDEN IN THE PRE-DAWN SHADOWS NEARBY, AN UNCOMFORTABLE GEORGES BAPTISTE AND A GRIM MARIE CARTIER--THE GIRL WHO LURED THE HULK TO QUEBEC--WATCH THE RAGING BATTLE WITH A MIXTURE OF HORROR AND ANXIOUS ANTICIPATION.
THERE, MARIE. DO YOU SEE WHAT YOUR MADNESS HAS WROUGHT? YOUR BROTHER HAS FALLEN--PERHAPS MORTALLY WOUNDED--AND IT IS ALL YOUR FAULT!
NONSENSE, GEORGES--EVERYTHING GOES EVEN BETTER THAN EXPECTED!
THE WENDIGO CAN'T BE HARMED--YOU KNOW THAT.
THE HULK AND THE ONE CALLED WOLVERINE MERELY SAVED US THE TASK OF OVERCOMING PAUL ALL BY OURSELVES!
NOW QUICKLY--WHILE THEY'RE STILL DISTRACTED--HELP ME CARRY PAUL'S BODY INSIDE.
THE SOONER THINGS ARE PREPARED, THE SOONER WE'LL BE READY TO BEGIN THE TRANSFORMATION!
MOMENTS LATER, WITHIN THE STONE-SLAB HOVEL NEARBY...
FINE. THE VAPORS OF SLUMBER WILL KEEP PAUL UNCONSCIOUS UNTIL WE'VE CAPTURED THE HULK AS WELL--
--AND THEN I'LL UTILIZE THE BLACK ARTS I'VE LEARNED TO TRANSFER THE CURSE OF THE WENDIGO FROM MY BROTHER TO THE BRUTE.
MARIE, I BEG YOU--PLEASE RECONSIDER THIS INSANITY! WHAT YOU INTEND TO DO IS UNNATURAL--UNHOLY--
--AND DANGEROUS!
OUTSIDE, THE JADE-HUED JUGGERNAUT FIGHTS ON, UNAWARE OF THE TERRIBLE FATE THE MANIACALLY OBSESSED GIRL HAS PLANNED FOR HIM--
--UNAWARE OF THE GOLD-AND-CRIMSON SPLENDOR SPREAD ACROSS HIS BATTLEFIELD BY THE SWIFTLY RISING SUN--
--A SUN ALSO RISING BEHIND A SECRET CANADIAN MILITARY COMPLEX NESTLED DEEP IN THE SHELTERING HILLS NOT TOO VERY FAR AWAY.

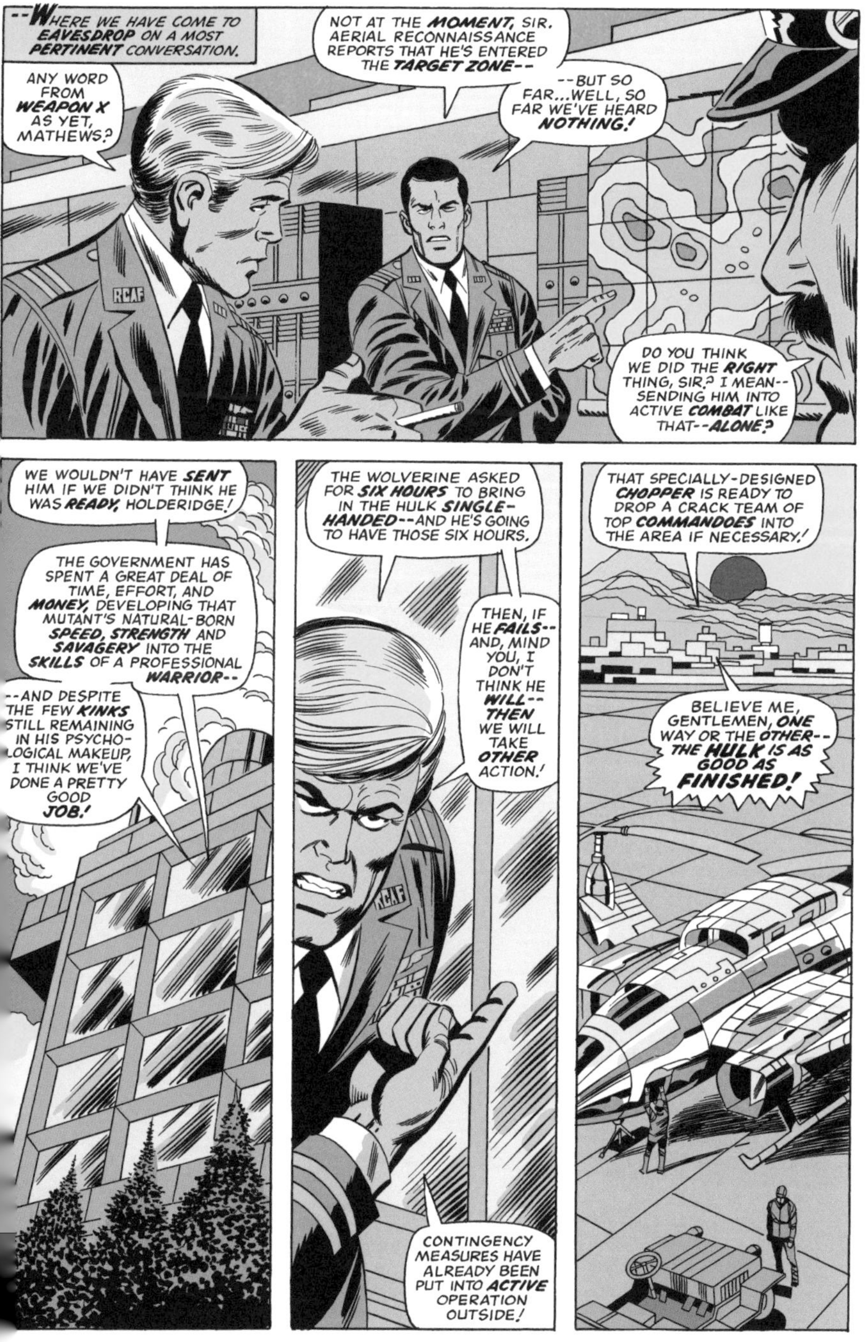
--WHERE WE HAVE COME TO EAVESDROP ON A MOST PERTINENT CONVERSATION.
ANY WORD FROM WEAPON X AS YET, MATHEWS?
NOT AT THE MOMENT, SIR. AERIAL RECONNAISSANCE REPORTS THAT HE'S ENTERED THE TARGET ZONE--
--BUT SO FAR...WELL, SO FAR WE'VE HEARD NOTHING!
RCAF
DO YOU THINK WE DID THE RIGHT THING, SIR? I MEAN--SENDING HIM INTO ACTIVE COMBAT LIKE THAT--ALONE?
WE WOULDN'T HAVE SENT HIM IF WE DIDN'T THINK HE WAS READY, HOLDERIDGE!
THE GOVERNMENT HAS SPENT A GREAT DEAL OF TIME, EFFORT, AND MONEY, DEVELOPING THAT MUTANT'S NATURAL-BORN SPEED, STRENGTH AND SAVAGERY INTO THE SKILLS OF A PROFESSIONAL WARRIOR--
--AND DESPITE THE FEW KINKS STILL REMAINING IN HIS PSYCHOLOGICAL MAKEUP, I THINK WE'VE DONE A PRETTY GOOD JOB!
THE WOLVERINE ASKED FOR SIX HOURS TO BRING IN THE HULK SINGLE-HANDED--AND HE'S GOING TO HAVE THOSE SIX HOURS.
THEN, IF HE FAILS--AND, MIND YOU, I DON'T THINK HE WILL--THEN WE WILL TAKE OTHER ACTION!
RCAF
CONTINGENCY MEASURES HAVE ALREADY BEEN PUT INTO ACTIVE OPERATION OUTSIDE!
THAT SPECIALLY-DESIGNED CHOPPER IS READY TO DROP A CRACK TEAM OF TOP COMMANDOES INTO THE AREA IF NECESSARY!
BELIEVE ME, GENTLEMEN, ONE WAY OR THE OTHER--THE HULK IS AS GOOD AS FINISHED!

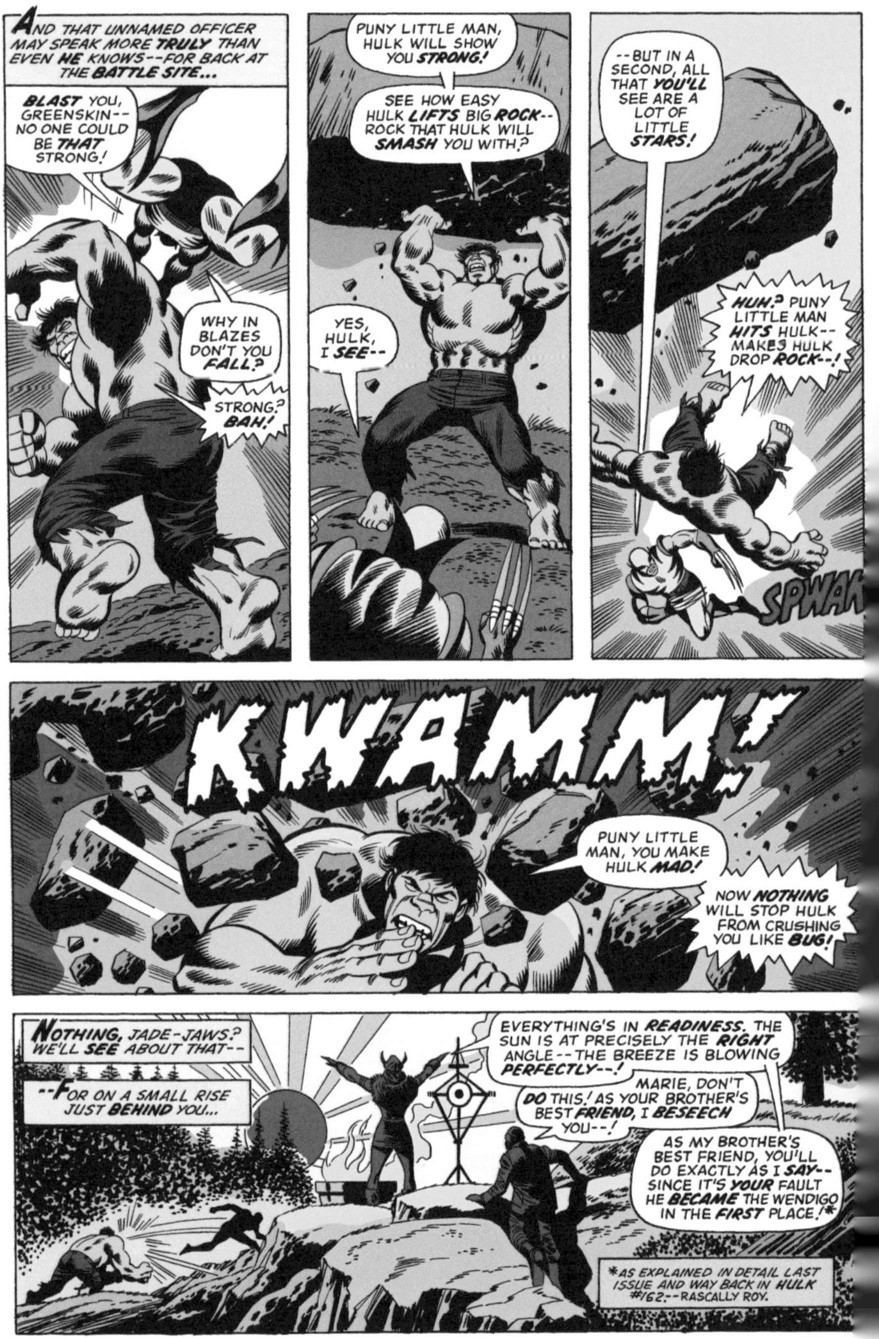
AND THAT UNNAMED OFFICER MAY SPEAK MORE TRULY THAN EVEN HE KNOWS--FOR BACK AT THE BATTLE SITE...
BLAST YOU, GREENSKIN--NO ONE COULD BE THAT STRONG!
WHY IN BLAZES DON'T YOU FALL?
STRONG? BAH!
PUNY LITTLE MAN, HULK WILL SHOW YOU STRONG!
SEE HOW EASY HULK LIFTS BIG ROCK--ROCK THAT HULK WILL SMASH YOU WITH?
YES, HULK, I SEE--
--BUT IN A SECOND, ALL THAT YOU'LL SEE ARE A LOT OF LITTLE STARS!
HUH? PUNY LITTLE MAN HITS HULK--MAKES HULK DROP ROCK--!
SPWAK
KWAMM!
PUNY LITTLE MAN, YOU MAKE HULK MAD!
NOW NOTHING WILL STOP HULK FROM CRUSHING YOU LIKE BUG!
NOTHING, JADE-JAWS? WE'LL SEE ABOUT THAT--
--FOR ON A SMALL RISE JUST BEHIND YOU...
EVERYTHING'S IN READINESS. THE SUN IS AT PRECISELY THE RIGHT ANGLE--THE BREEZE IS BLOWING PERFECTLY--!
MARIE, DON'T DO THIS! AS YOUR BROTHER'S BEST FRIEND, I BESEECH YOU--!
AS MY BROTHER'S BEST FRIEND, YOU'LL DO EXACTLY AS I SAY--SINCE IT'S YOUR FAULT HE BECAME THE WENDIGO IN THE FIRST PLACE!*
*AS EXPLAINED IN DETAIL LAST ISSUE AND WAY BACK IN HULK #162.--RASCALLY ROY.

NOW STAND ASIDE AS I PREPARE THE MYSTIC *SPELL OF SUBJUGATION*--

--OR *YOU* MAY BE CAUGHT IN ITS GRASP AS *WELL!*

*W*ITH THAT, MARIE CARTIER TURNS HER FACE *SKYWARD*-- MUTTERS AN ARCANE *CHANT* BENEATH HER BREATH--

*--T*HEN POURS A DUSTY GRAY *PUMICE* FROM THE VIAL IN HER HAND.

A PUMICE THAT GLOWS *GOLDEN* WITH THE DAWN SUN'S RAYS AS IT PLUNGES INTO AN ORNATELY-CARVED *VESSEL*--

*--T*HUS RELEASING BILLOWING CLOUDS OF AN ALMOST-INVISIBLE *GAS*--

--A GAS CARRIED DOWN THE RISE TO THE BATTLE-FIELD BELOW BY THE BRISK MORNING *BREEZE.*

*F*OR SEVERAL SECONDS, THE CONFLICT *CONTINUES,* UNMINDFUL OF THE ALL-PERVADING *MIST.*

*T*HEN THE TWO COMBATANTS *STAGGER*--GASP DESPERATELY FOR *BREATH*--AND *FALL!*

*A*ND IT IS A *TRIUMPHANT* ENCHANTRESS WHO COMES TO CLAIM HER *PRIZE.*

YOU *SEE*, GEORGES? I *TOLD* YOU EVERY-THING WOULD *WORK OUT* IN THE END, DIDN'T I ?

UNFORTUNATELY, MARIE, EVERY-THING IS NOT *ENDED*-- NOT *YET!*

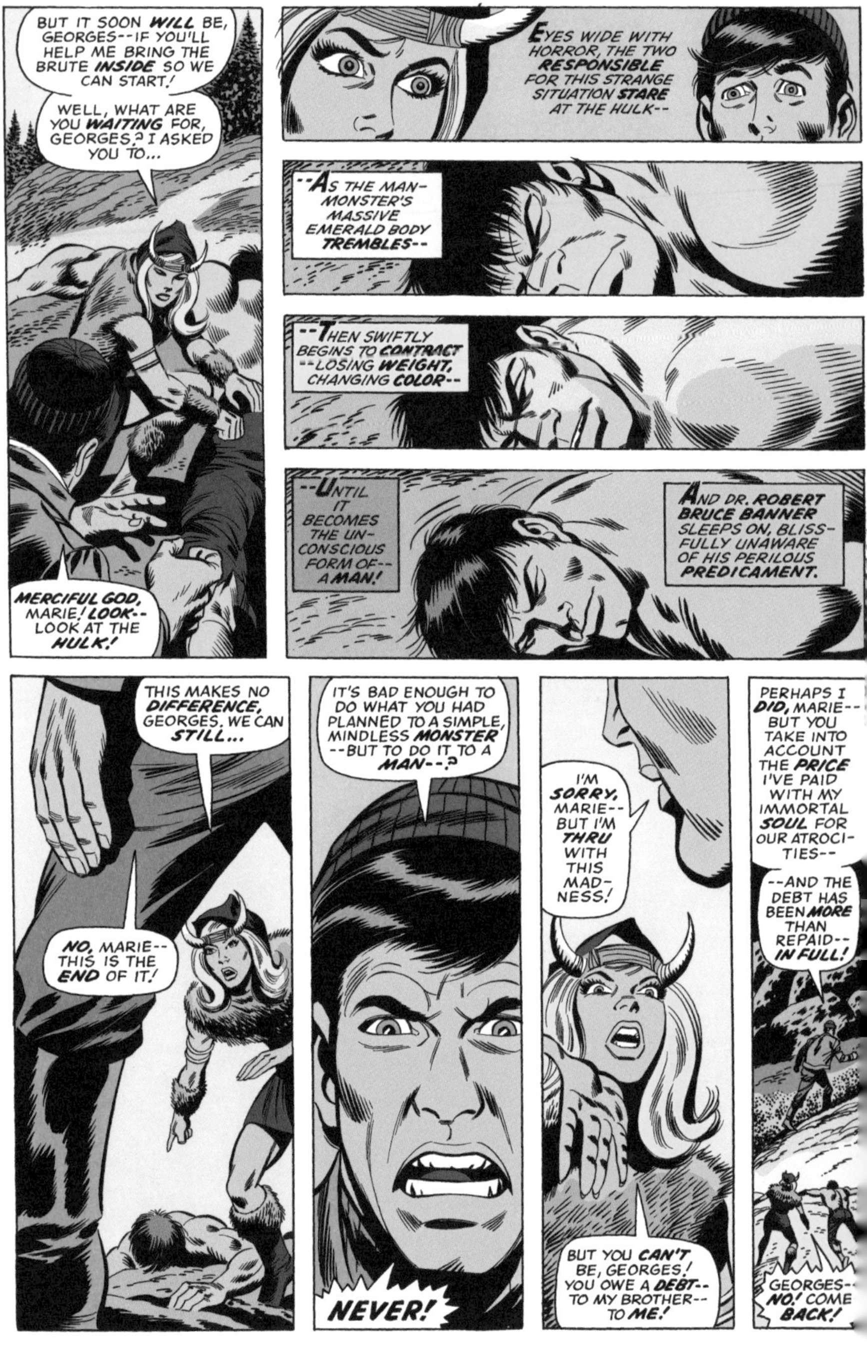

BUT IT SOON WILL BE, GEORGES--IF YOU'LL HELP ME BRING THE BRUTE INSIDE SO WE CAN START!
WELL, WHAT ARE YOU WAITING FOR, GEORGES? I ASKED YOU TO...
MERCIFUL GOD, MARIE! LOOK--LOOK AT THE HULK!
EYES WIDE WITH HORROR, THE TWO RESPONSIBLE FOR THIS STRANGE SITUATION STARE AT THE HULK--
--AS THE MAN-MONSTER'S MASSIVE EMERALD BODY TREMBLES--
--THEN SWIFTLY BEGINS TO CONTRACT--LOSING WEIGHT, CHANGING COLOR--
--UNTIL IT BECOMES THE UN-CONSCIOUS FORM OF--A MAN!
AND DR. ROBERT BRUCE BANNER SLEEPS ON, BLISS-FULLY UNAWARE OF HIS PERILOUS PREDICAMENT.
THIS MAKES NO DIFFERENCE, GEORGES. WE CAN STILL...
NO, MARIE--THIS IS THE END OF IT!
IT'S BAD ENOUGH TO DO WHAT YOU HAD PLANNED TO A SIMPLE, MINDLESS MONSTER--BUT TO DO IT TO A MAN--?
NEVER!
I'M SORRY, MARIE--BUT I'M THRU WITH THIS MAD-NESS!
BUT YOU CAN'T BE, GEORGES! YOU OWE A DEBT--TO MY BROTHER--TO ME!
PERHAPS I DID, MARIE--BUT YOU TAKE INTO ACCOUNT THE PRICE I'VE PAID WITH MY IMMORTAL SOUL FOR OUR ATROCI-TIES--
--AND THE DEBT HAS BEEN MORE THAN REPAID--IN FULL!
GEORGES--NO! COME BACK!

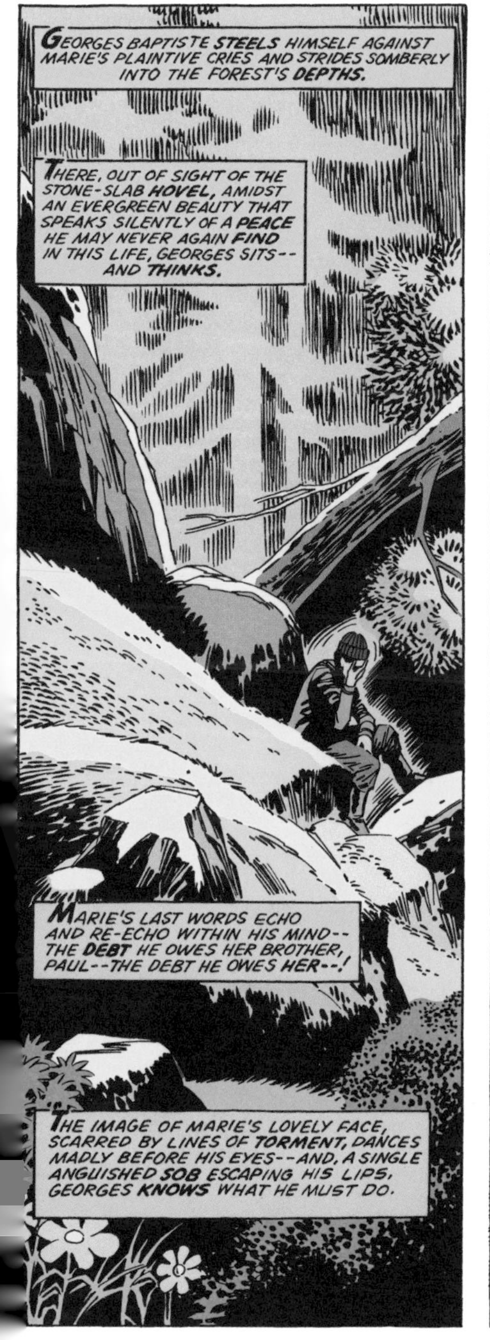
GEORGES BAPTISTE STEELS HIMSELF AGAINST MARIE'S PLAINTIVE CRIES AND STRIDES SOMBERLY INTO THE FOREST'S DEPTHS.
THERE, OUT OF SIGHT OF THE STONE-SLAB HOVEL, AMIDST AN EVERGREEN BEAUTY THAT SPEAKS SILENTLY OF A PEACE HE MAY NEVER AGAIN FIND IN THIS LIFE, GEORGES SITS-- AND THINKS.
MARIE'S LAST WORDS ECHO AND RE-ECHO WITHIN HIS MIND-- THE DEBT HE OWES HER BROTHER, PAUL--THE DEBT HE OWES HER--!
THE IMAGE OF MARIE'S LOVELY FACE, SCARRED BY LINES OF TORMENT, DANCES MADLY BEFORE HIS EYES--AND, A SINGLE ANGUISHED SOB ESCAPING HIS LIPS, GEORGES KNOWS WHAT HE MUST DO.

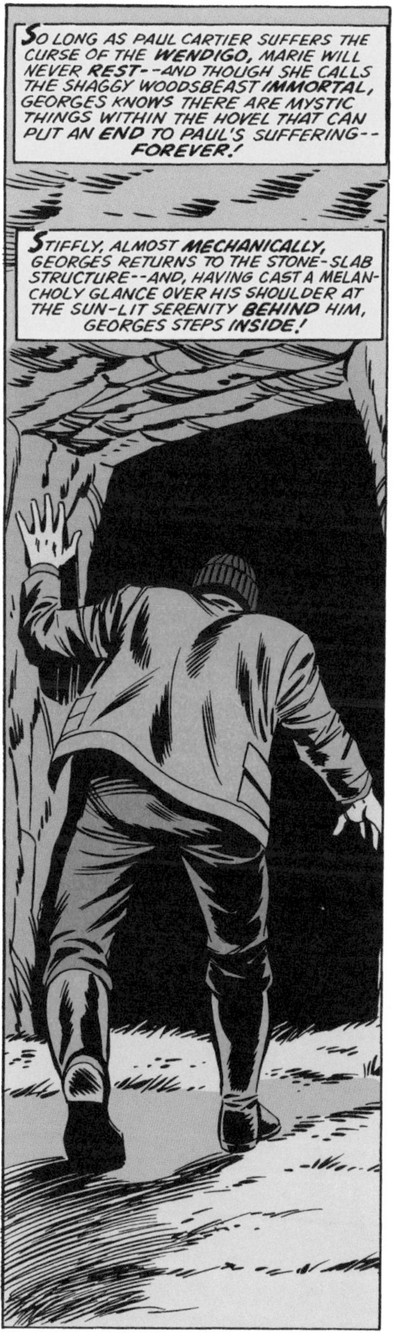
SO LONG AS PAUL CARTIER SUFFERS THE CURSE OF THE WENDIGO, MARIE WILL NEVER REST--AND THOUGH SHE CALLS THE SHAGGY WOODSBEAST IMMORTAL, GEORGES KNOWS THERE ARE MYSTIC THINGS WITHIN THE HOVEL THAT CAN PUT AN END TO PAUL'S SUFFERING-- FOREVER!
STIFFLY, ALMOST MECHANICALLY, GEORGES RETURNS TO THE STONE-SLAB STRUCTURE--AND, HAVING CAST A MELANCHOLY GLANCE OVER HIS SHOULDER AT THE SUN-LIT SERENITY BEHIND HIM, GEORGES STEPS INSIDE!

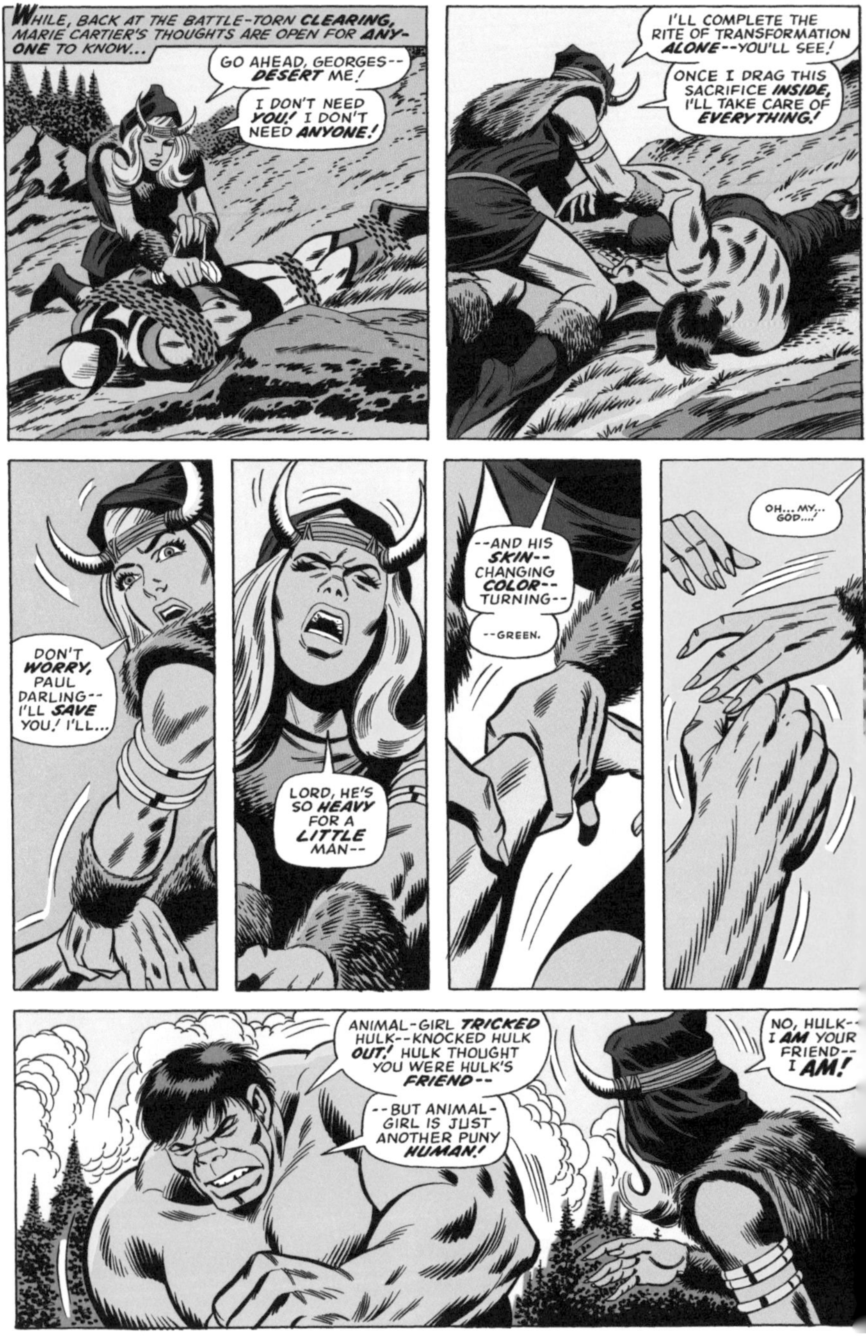
WHILE, BACK AT THE BATTLE-TORN CLEARING, MARIE CARTIER'S THOUGHTS ARE OPEN FOR ANY-ONE TO KNOW...
GO AHEAD, GEORGES--DESERT ME!
I DON'T NEED YOU! I DON'T NEED ANYONE!
I'LL COMPLETE THE RITE OF TRANSFORMATION ALONE--YOU'LL SEE!
ONCE I DRAG THIS SACRIFICE INSIDE, I'LL TAKE CARE OF EVERYTHING!
DON'T WORRY, PAUL DARLING--I'LL SAVE YOU! I'LL...
LORD, HE'S SO HEAVY FOR A LITTLE MAN--
--AND HIS SKIN--CHANGING COLOR--TURNING--
--GREEN.
OH... MY... GOD...!
ANIMAL-GIRL TRICKED HULK--KNOCKED HULK OUT! HULK THOUGHT YOU WERE HULK'S FRIEND--
--BUT ANIMAL-GIRL IS JUST ANOTHER PUNY HUMAN!
NO, HULK--I AM YOUR FRIEND--I AM!

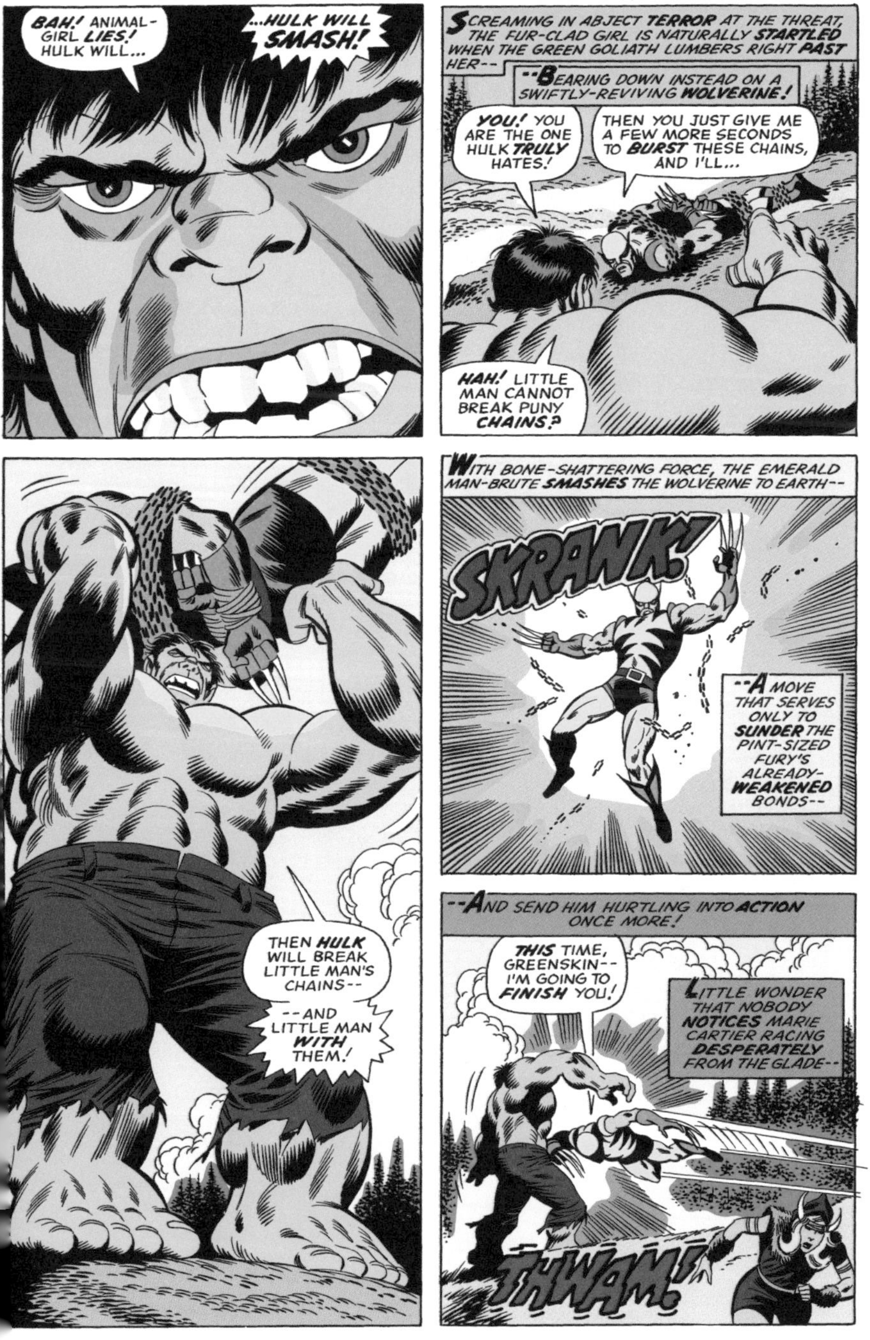
BAH! ANIMAL-GIRL LIES! HULK WILL...
...HULK WILL SMASH!
SCREAMING IN ABJECT TERROR AT THE THREAT, THE FUR-CLAD GIRL IS NATURALLY STARTLED WHEN THE GREEN GOLIATH LUMBERS RIGHT PAST HER--
--BEARING DOWN INSTEAD ON A SWIFTLY-REVIVING WOLVERINE!
YOU! YOU ARE THE ONE HULK TRULY HATES!
THEN YOU JUST GIVE ME A FEW MORE SECONDS TO BURST THESE CHAINS, AND I'LL...
HAH! LITTLE MAN CANNOT BREAK PUNY CHAINS?
THEN HULK WILL BREAK LITTLE MAN'S CHAINS--
--AND LITTLE MAN WITH THEM!
WITH BONE-SHATTERING FORCE, THE EMERALD MAN-BRUTE SMASHES THE WOLVERINE TO EARTH--
SKRANK!
--A MOVE THAT SERVES ONLY TO SUNDER THE PINT-SIZED FURY'S ALREADY-WEAKENED BONDS--
--AND SEND HIM HURTLING INTO ACTION ONCE MORE!
THIS TIME, GREENSKIN-- I'M GOING TO FINISH YOU!
LITTLE WONDER THAT NOBODY NOTICES MARIE CARTIER RACING DESPERATELY FROM THE GLADE--
THWAM!

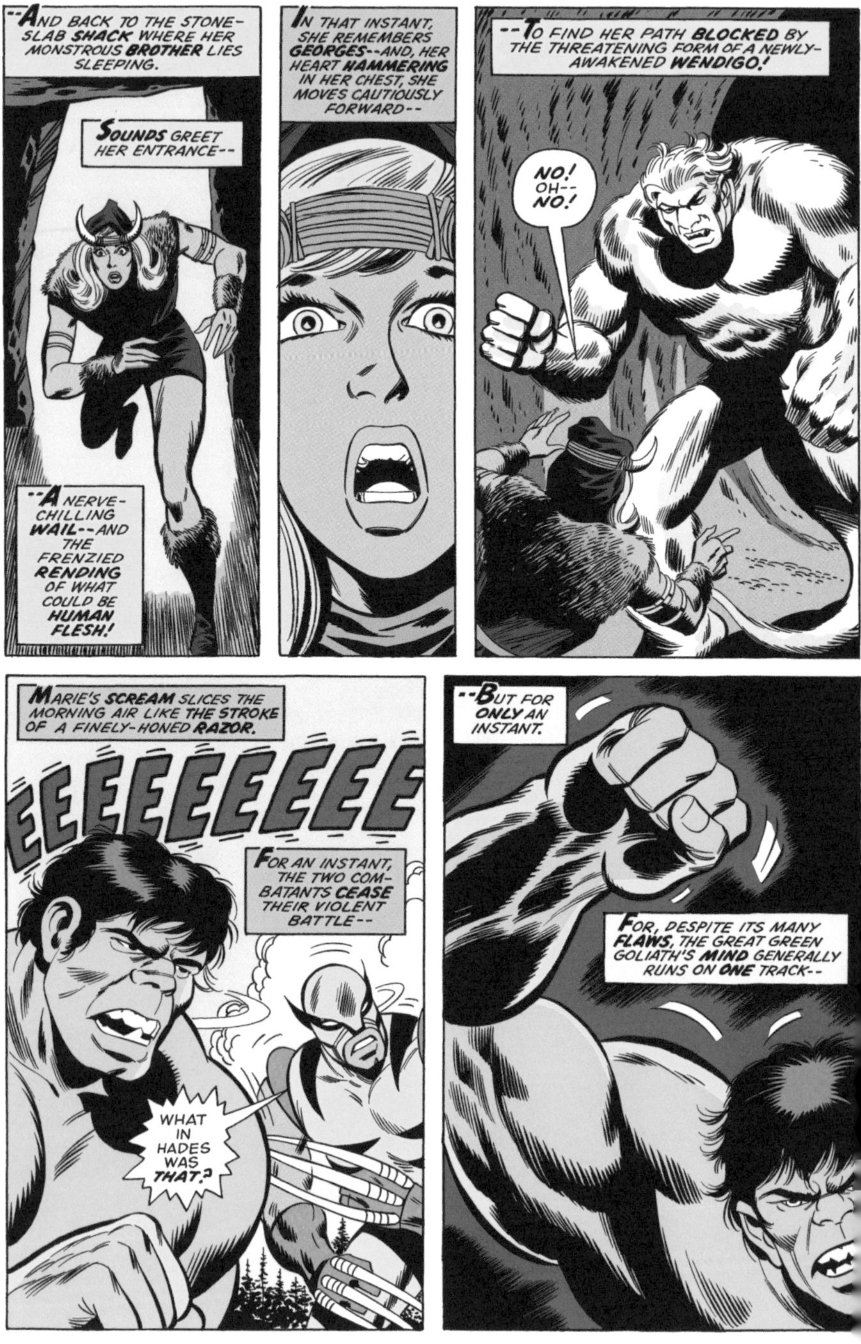
--AND BACK TO THE STONE-SLAB SHACK WHERE HER MONSTROUS BROTHER LIES SLEEPING.
SOUNDS GREET HER ENTRANCE--
--A NERVE-CHILLING WAIL--AND THE FRENZIED RENDING OF WHAT COULD BE HUMAN FLESH!
IN THAT INSTANT, SHE REMEMBERS GEORGES--AND, HER HEART HAMMERING IN HER CHEST, SHE MOVES CAUTIOUSLY FORWARD--
--TO FIND HER PATH BLOCKED BY THE THREATENING FORM OF A NEWLY-AWAKENED WENDIGO!
NO! OH-- NO!
MARIE'S SCREAM SLICES THE MORNING AIR LIKE THE STROKE OF A FINELY-HONED RAZOR.
EEEEEEEEE
FOR AN INSTANT, THE TWO COMBATANTS CEASE THEIR VIOLENT BATTLE--
WHAT IN HADES WAS THAT?
--BUT FOR ONLY AN INSTANT.
FOR, DESPITE ITS MANY FLAWS, THE GREAT GREEN GOLIATH'S MIND GENERALLY RUNS ON ONE TRACK--

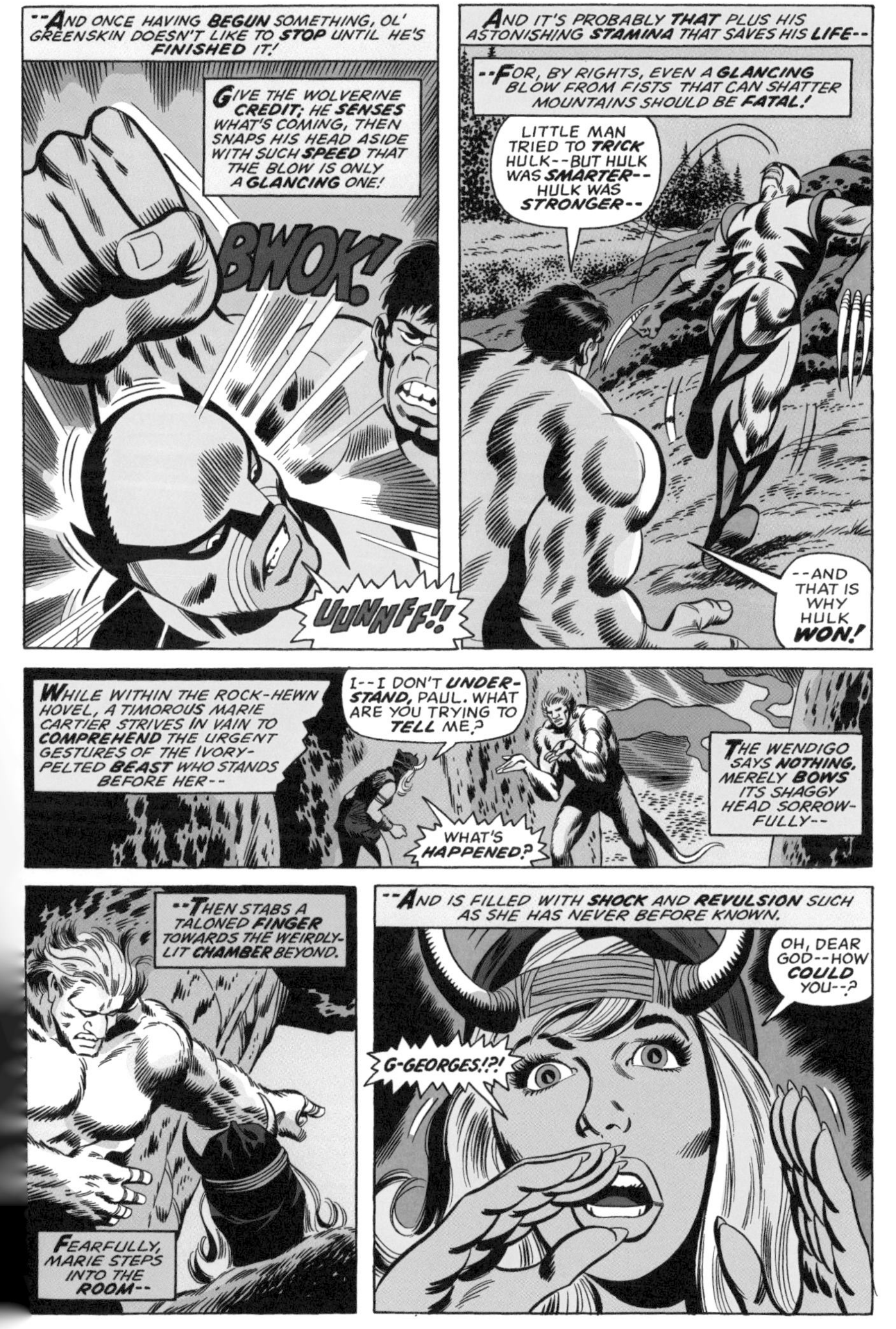
--AND ONCE HAVING BEGUN SOMETHING, OL' GREENSKIN DOESN'T LIKE TO STOP UNTIL HE'S FINISHED IT!
GIVE THE WOLVERINE CREDIT; HE SENSES WHAT'S COMING, THEN SNAPS HIS HEAD ASIDE WITH SUCH SPEED THAT THE BLOW IS ONLY A GLANCING ONE!
BWOK!
UUNNFF!!
AND IT'S PROBABLY THAT PLUS HIS ASTONISHING STAMINA THAT SAVES HIS LIFE--
--FOR, BY RIGHTS, EVEN A GLANCING BLOW FROM FISTS THAT CAN SHATTER MOUNTAINS SHOULD BE FATAL!
LITTLE MAN TRIED TO TRICK HULK--BUT HULK WAS SMARTER--HULK WAS STRONGER--
--AND THAT IS WHY HULK WON!
WHILE WITHIN THE ROCK-HEWN HOVEL, A TIMOROUS MARIE CARTIER STRIVES IN VAIN TO COMPREHEND THE URGENT GESTURES OF THE IVORY-PELTED BEAST WHO STANDS BEFORE HER--
I--I DON'T UNDERSTAND, PAUL. WHAT ARE YOU TRYING TO TELL ME?
WHAT'S HAPPENED?
THE WENDIGO SAYS NOTHING, MERELY BOWS ITS SHAGGY HEAD SORROWFULLY--
--THEN STABS A TALONED FINGER TOWARDS THE WEIRDLY-LIT CHAMBER BEYOND.
FEARFULLY, MARIE STEPS INTO THE ROOM--
--AND IS FILLED WITH SHOCK AND REVULSION SUCH AS SHE HAS NEVER BEFORE KNOWN.
G-GEORGES!?!
OH, DEAR GOD--HOW COULD YOU--?

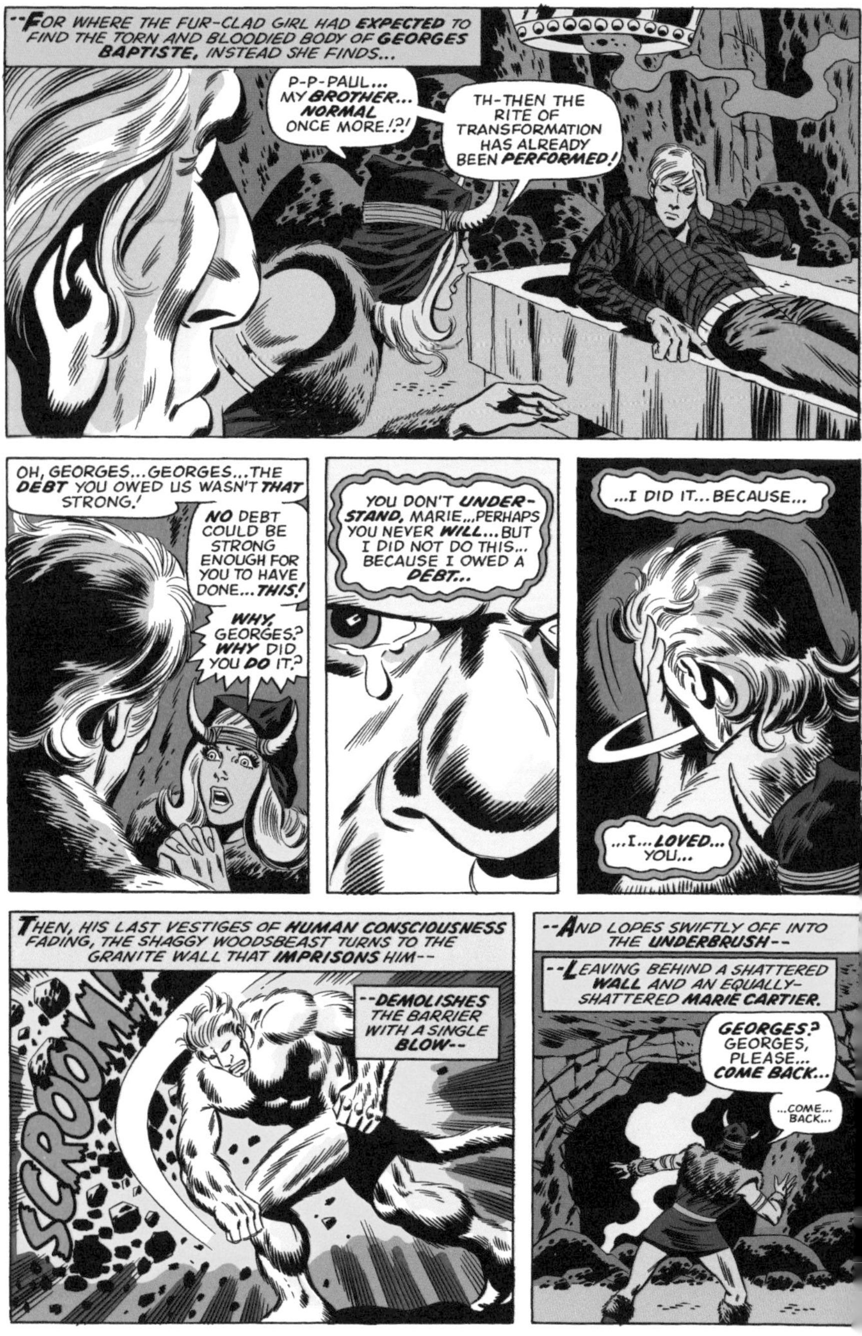
--FOR WHERE THE FUR-CLAD GIRL HAD EXPECTED TO FIND THE TORN AND BLOODIED BODY OF GEORGES BAPTISTE, INSTEAD SHE FINDS...
P-P-PAUL... MY BROTHER... NORMAL ONCE MORE.!?!
TH-THEN THE RITE OF TRANSFORMATION HAS ALREADY BEEN PERFORMED!
OH, GEORGES...GEORGES...THE DEBT YOU OWED US WASN'T THAT STRONG.!
NO DEBT COULD BE STRONG ENOUGH FOR YOU TO HAVE DONE...THIS!
WHY, GEORGES? WHY DID YOU DO IT?
YOU DON'T UNDERSTAND, MARIE...PERHAPS YOU NEVER WILL...BUT I DID NOT DO THIS... BECAUSE I OWED A DEBT...
...I DID IT...BECAUSE...
...I...LOVED... YOU...
THEN, HIS LAST VESTIGES OF HUMAN CONSCIOUSNESS FADING, THE SHAGGY WOODSBEAST TURNS TO THE GRANITE WALL THAT IMPRISONS HIM--
--DEMOLISHES THE BARRIER WITH A SINGLE BLOW--
SCROOM!
--AND LOPES SWIFTLY OFF INTO THE UNDERBRUSH--
--LEAVING BEHIND A SHATTERED WALL AND AN EQUALLY-SHATTERED MARIE CARTIER.
GEORGES? GEORGES, PLEASE... COME BACK...
...COME... BACK...

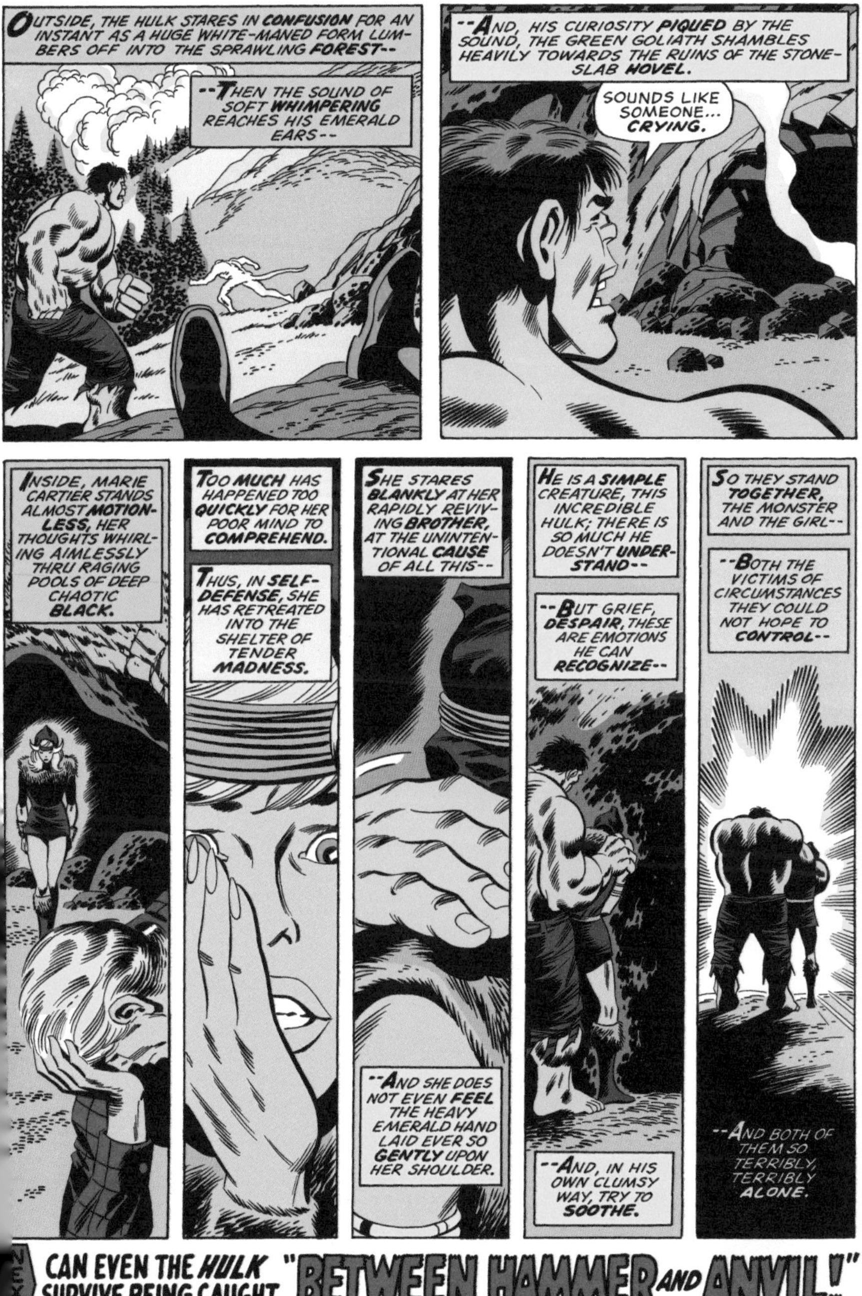
OUTSIDE, THE HULK STARES IN CONFUSION FOR AN INSTANT AS A HUGE WHITE-MANED FORM LUMBERS OFF INTO THE SPRAWLING FOREST--
--THEN THE SOUND OF SOFT WHIMPERING REACHES HIS EMERALD EARS--
--AND, HIS CURIOSITY PIQUED BY THE SOUND, THE GREEN GOLIATH SHAMBLES HEAVILY TOWARDS THE RUINS OF THE STONE-SLAB HOVEL.
SOUNDS LIKE SOMEONE... CRYING.
INSIDE, MARIE CARTIER STANDS ALMOST MOTIONLESS, HER THOUGHTS WHIRLING AIMLESSLY THRU RAGING POOLS OF DEEP CHAOTIC BLACK.
TOO MUCH HAS HAPPENED TOO QUICKLY FOR HER POOR MIND TO COMPREHEND.
THUS, IN SELF-DEFENSE, SHE HAS RETREATED INTO THE SHELTER OF TENDER MADNESS.
SHE STARES BLANKLY AT HER RAPIDLY REVIVING BROTHER, AT THE UNINTENTIONAL CAUSE OF ALL THIS--
--AND SHE DOES NOT EVEN FEEL THE HEAVY EMERALD HAND LAID EVER SO GENTLY UPON HER SHOULDER.
HE IS A SIMPLE CREATURE, THIS INCREDIBLE HULK; THERE IS SO MUCH HE DOESN'T UNDERSTAND--
--BUT GRIEF, DESPAIR, THESE ARE EMOTIONS HE CAN RECOGNIZE--
--AND, IN HIS OWN CLUMSY WAY, TRY TO SOOTHE.
SO THEY STAND TOGETHER, THE MONSTER AND THE GIRL--
--BOTH THE VICTIMS OF CIRCUMSTANCES THEY COULD NOT HOPE TO CONTROL--
--AND BOTH OF THEM SO TERRIBLY, TERRIBLY ALONE.
NEXT
CAN EVEN THE HULK SURVIVE BEING CAUGHT... "BETWEEN HAMMER AND ANVIL!"

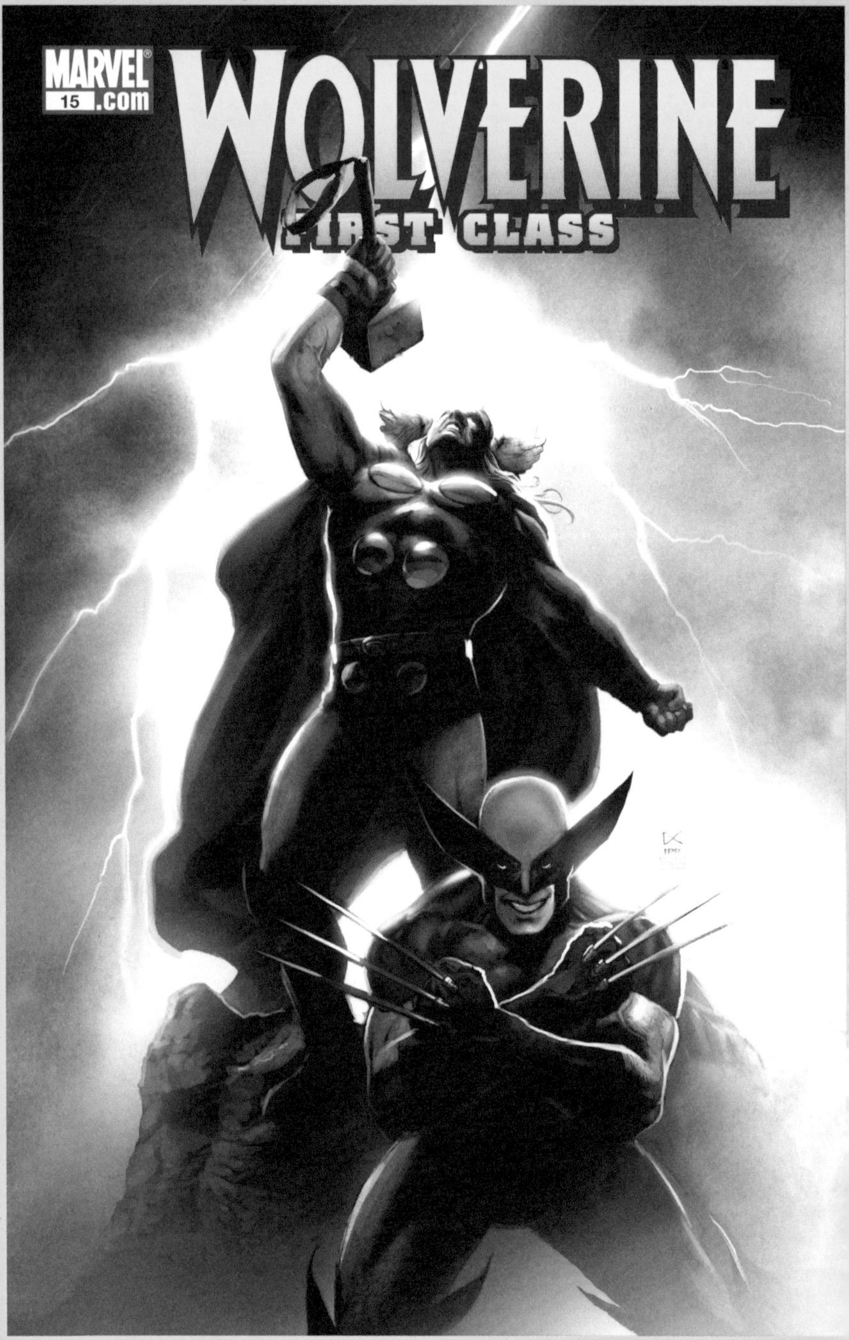
MARVEL
15
.com
WOLVERINE
FIRST CLASS

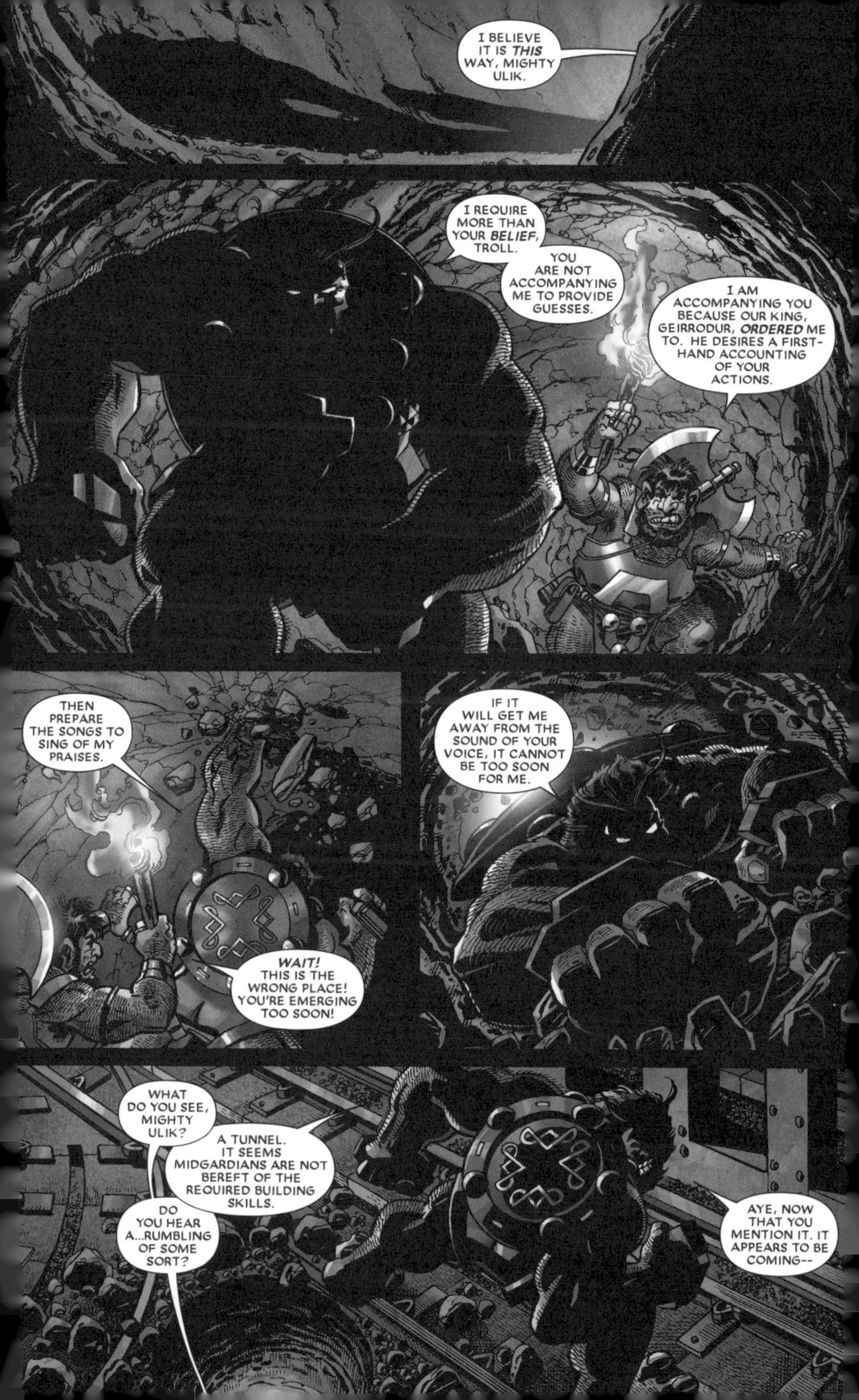
I BELIEVE IT IS *THIS* WAY, MIGHTY ULIK.
I REQUIRE MORE THAN YOUR *BELIEF*, TROLL.
YOU ARE NOT ACCOMPANYING ME TO PROVIDE GUESSES.
I AM ACCOMPANYING YOU BECAUSE OUR KING, GEIRRODUR, *ORDERED* ME TO. HE DESIRES A FIRST-HAND ACCOUNTING OF YOUR ACTIONS.
THEN PREPARE THE SONGS TO SING OF MY PRAISES.
WAIT! THIS IS THE WRONG PLACE! YOU'RE EMERGING TOO SOON!
IF IT WILL GET ME AWAY FROM THE SOUND OF YOUR VOICE, IT CANNOT BE TOO SOON FOR ME.
WHAT DO YOU SEE, MIGHTY ULIK?
A TUNNEL. IT SEEMS MIDGARDIANS ARE NOT BEREFT OF THE REQUIRED BUILDING SKILLS.
DO YOU HEAR A...RUMBLING OF SOME SORT?
AYE, NOW THAT YOU MENTION IT. IT APPEARS TO BE COMING--

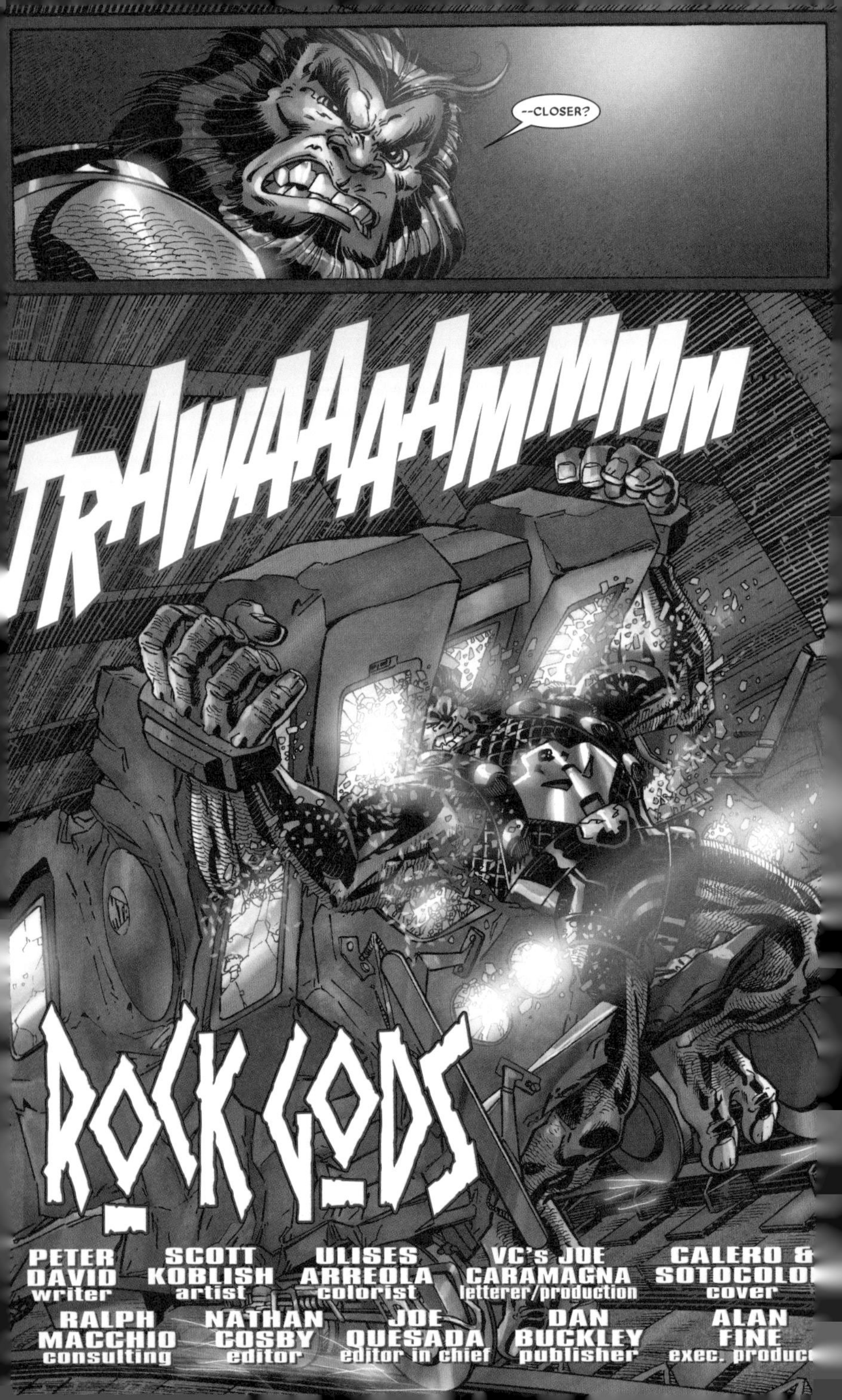
--CLOSER?
TRAWAAAAAMMMMM
ROCK GODS
PETER DAVID writer
SCOTT KOBLISH artist
ULISES ARREOLA colorist
VC's JOE CARAMAGNA letterer/production
CALERO & SOTOCOLOR cover
RALPH MACCHIO consulting
NATHAN COSBY editor
JOE QUESADA editor in chief
DAN BUCKLEY publisher
ALAN FINE exec. producer

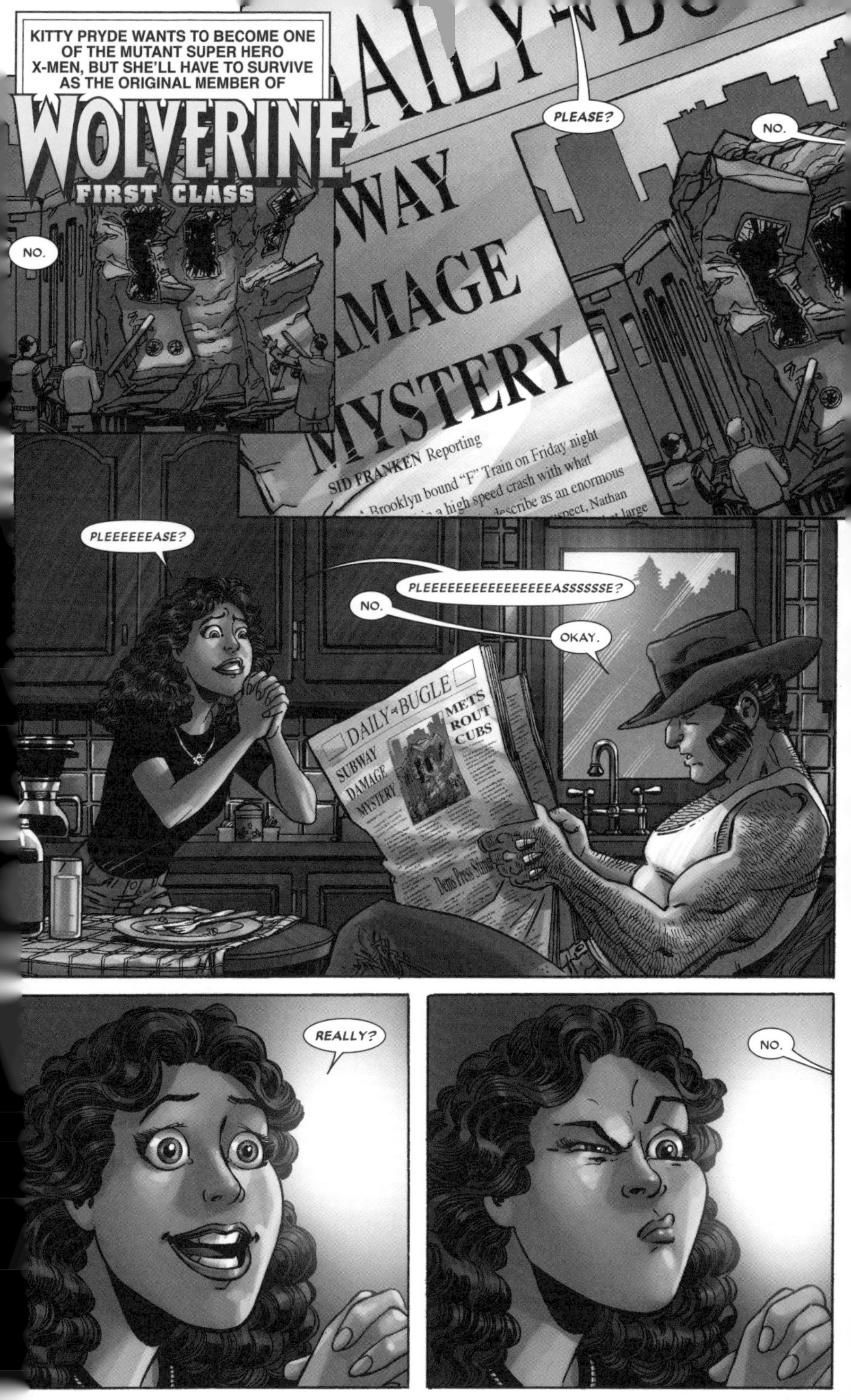
KITTY PRYDE WANTS TO BECOME ONE OF THE MUTANT SUPER HERO X-MEN, BUT SHE'LL HAVE TO SURVIVE AS THE ORIGINAL MEMBER OF
WOLVERINE
FIRST CLASS
PLEASE?
NO.
NO.
SUBWAY DAMAGE MYSTERY
SID FRANKEN Reporting
PLEEEEEEASE?
PLEEEEEEEEEEEEEEEEASSSSSSE?
NO.
OKAY.
DAILY BUGLE
SUBWAY DAMAGE MYSTERY
METS ROUT CUBS
REALLY?
NO.

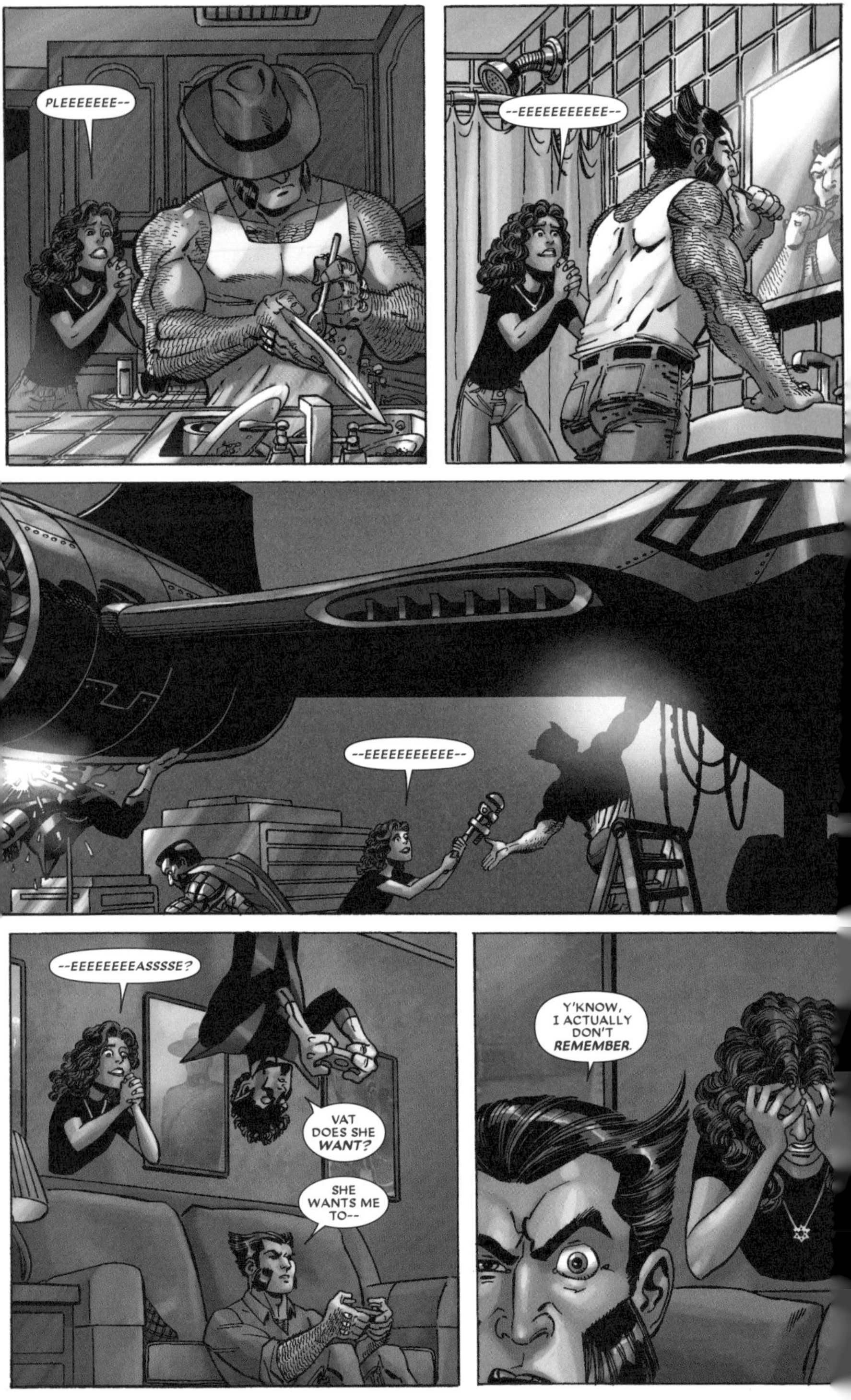
PLEEEEEEE--
--EEEEEEEEEEE--
--EEEEEEEEEEE--
--EEEEEEEEASSSSE?
VAT DOES SHE WANT?
SHE WANTS ME TO--
Y'KNOW, I ACTUALLY DON'T REMEMBER.

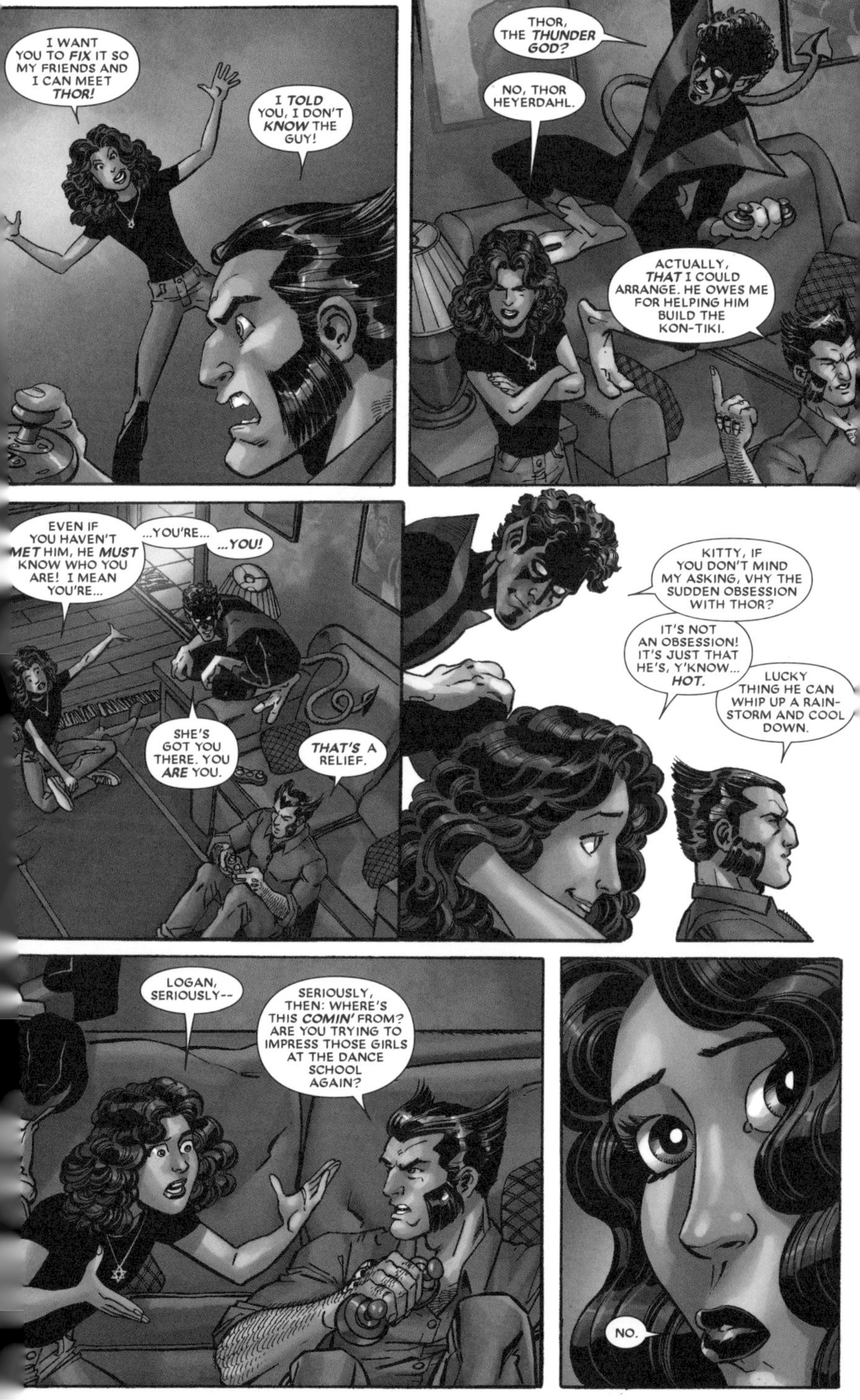

I WANT YOU TO *FIX* IT SO MY FRIENDS AND I CAN MEET *THOR!*
I *TOLD* YOU, I DON'T *KNOW* THE GUY!
THOR, THE *THUNDER GOD?*
NO, THOR HEYERDAHL.
ACTUALLY, *THAT* I COULD ARRANGE. HE OWES ME FOR HELPING HIM BUILD THE KON-TIKI.
EVEN IF YOU HAVEN'T *MET* HIM, HE *MUST* KNOW WHO YOU ARE! I MEAN YOU'RE...
...YOU'RE...
...*YOU!*
SHE'S GOT YOU THERE. YOU *ARE* YOU.
THAT'S A RELIEF.
KITTY, IF YOU DON'T MIND MY ASKING, VHY THE SUDDEN OBSESSION WITH THOR?
IT'S NOT AN OBSESSION! IT'S JUST THAT HE'S, Y'KNOW... *HOT.*
LUCKY THING HE CAN WHIP UP A RAIN-STORM AND COOL DOWN.
LOGAN, SERIOUSLY--
SERIOUSLY, THEN: WHERE'S THIS *COMIN'* FROM? ARE YOU TRYING TO IMPRESS THOSE GIRLS AT THE DANCE SCHOOL AGAIN?
NO.

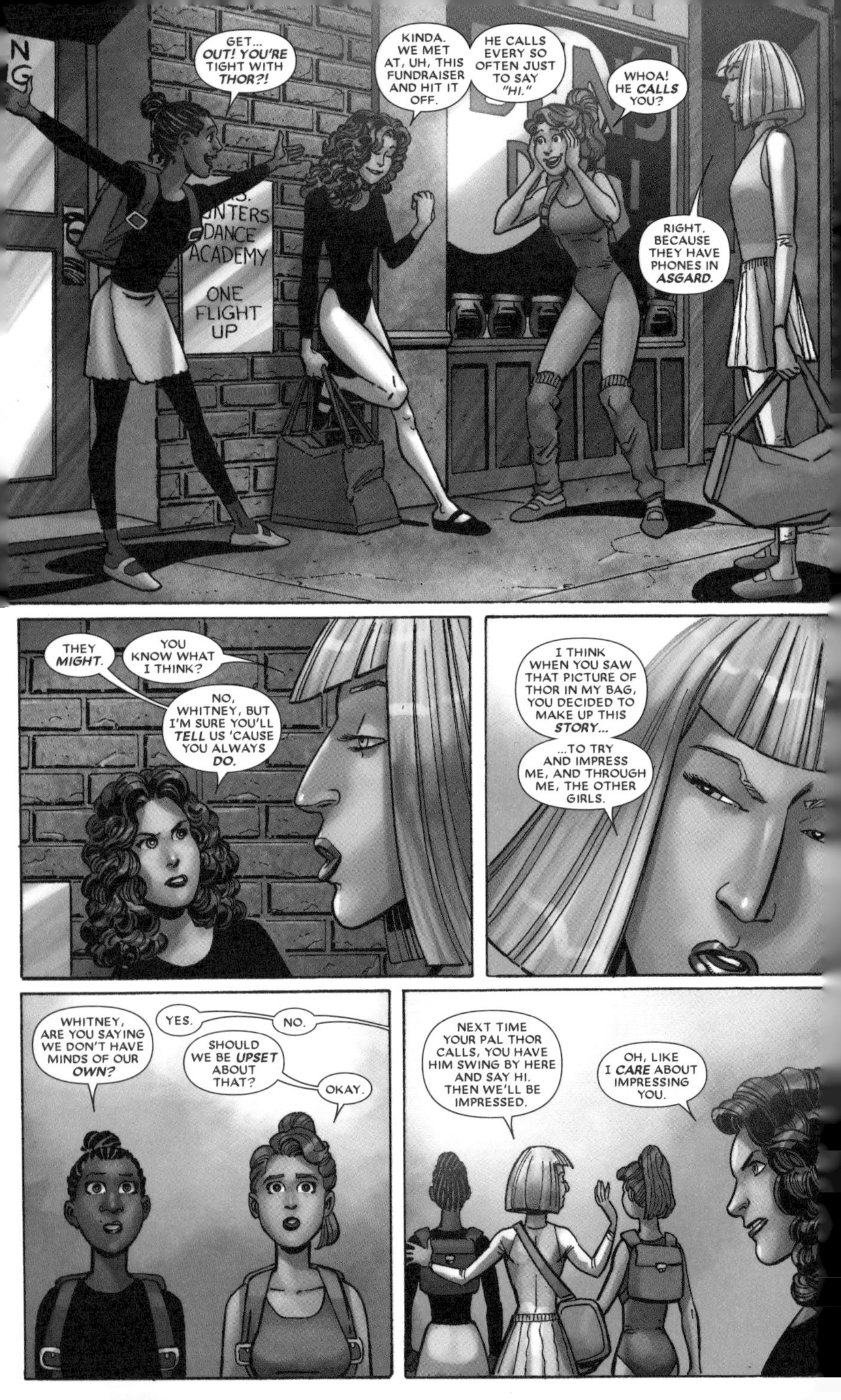

NG
GET... OUT! YOU'RE TIGHT WITH THOR?!
KINDA. WE MET AT, UH, THIS FUNDRAISER AND HIT IT OFF.
HE CALLS EVERY SO OFTEN JUST TO SAY "HI."
WHOA! HE CALLS YOU?
RIGHT. BECAUSE THEY HAVE PHONES IN ASGARD.
NTERS DANCE ACADEMY
ONE FLIGHT UP
THEY MIGHT.
YOU KNOW WHAT I THINK?
NO, WHITNEY, BUT I'M SURE YOU'LL TELL US 'CAUSE YOU ALWAYS DO.
I THINK WHEN YOU SAW THAT PICTURE OF THOR IN MY BAG, YOU DECIDED TO MAKE UP THIS STORY...
...TO TRY AND IMPRESS ME, AND THROUGH ME, THE OTHER GIRLS.
WHITNEY, ARE YOU SAYING WE DON'T HAVE MINDS OF OUR OWN?
YES.
NO.
SHOULD WE BE UPSET ABOUT THAT?
OKAY.
NEXT TIME YOUR PAL THOR CALLS, YOU HAVE HIM SWING BY HERE AND SAY HI. THEN WE'LL BE IMPRESSED.
OH, LIKE I CARE ABOUT IMPRESSING YOU.

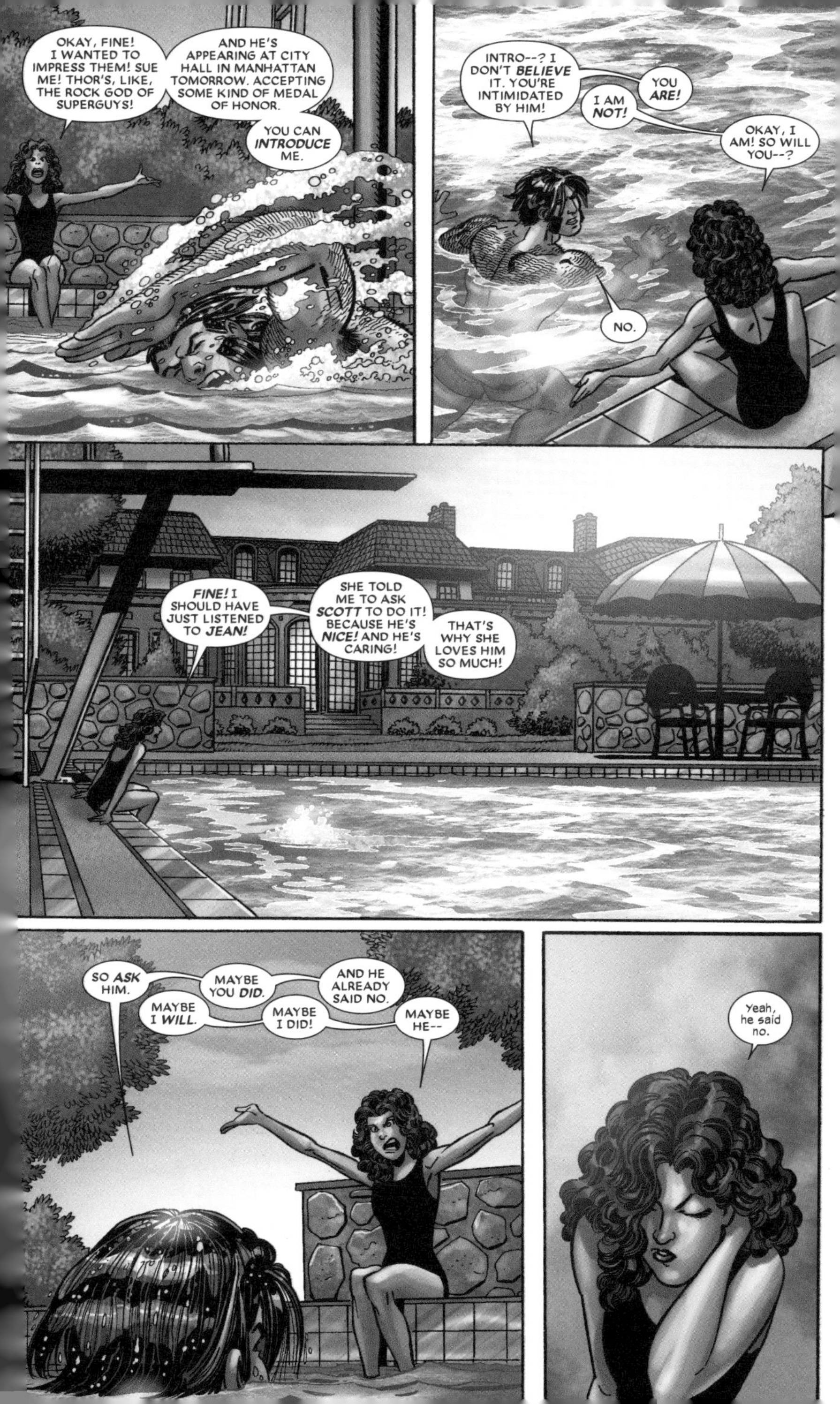
OKAY, FINE! I WANTED TO IMPRESS THEM! SUE ME! THOR'S, LIKE, THE ROCK GOD OF SUPERGUYS!
AND HE'S APPEARING AT CITY HALL IN MANHATTAN TOMORROW. ACCEPTING SOME KIND OF MEDAL OF HONOR.
YOU CAN INTRODUCE ME.
INTRO--? I DON'T BELIEVE IT. YOU'RE INTIMIDATED BY HIM!
YOU ARE!
I AM NOT!
OKAY, I AM! SO WILL YOU--?
NO.
FINE! I SHOULD HAVE JUST LISTENED TO JEAN!
SHE TOLD ME TO ASK SCOTT TO DO IT! BECAUSE HE'S NICE! AND HE'S CARING!
THAT'S WHY SHE LOVES HIM SO MUCH!
SO ASK HIM.
MAYBE I WILL.
MAYBE YOU DID.
MAYBE I DID!
AND HE ALREADY SAID NO.
MAYBE HE--
Yeah, he said no.

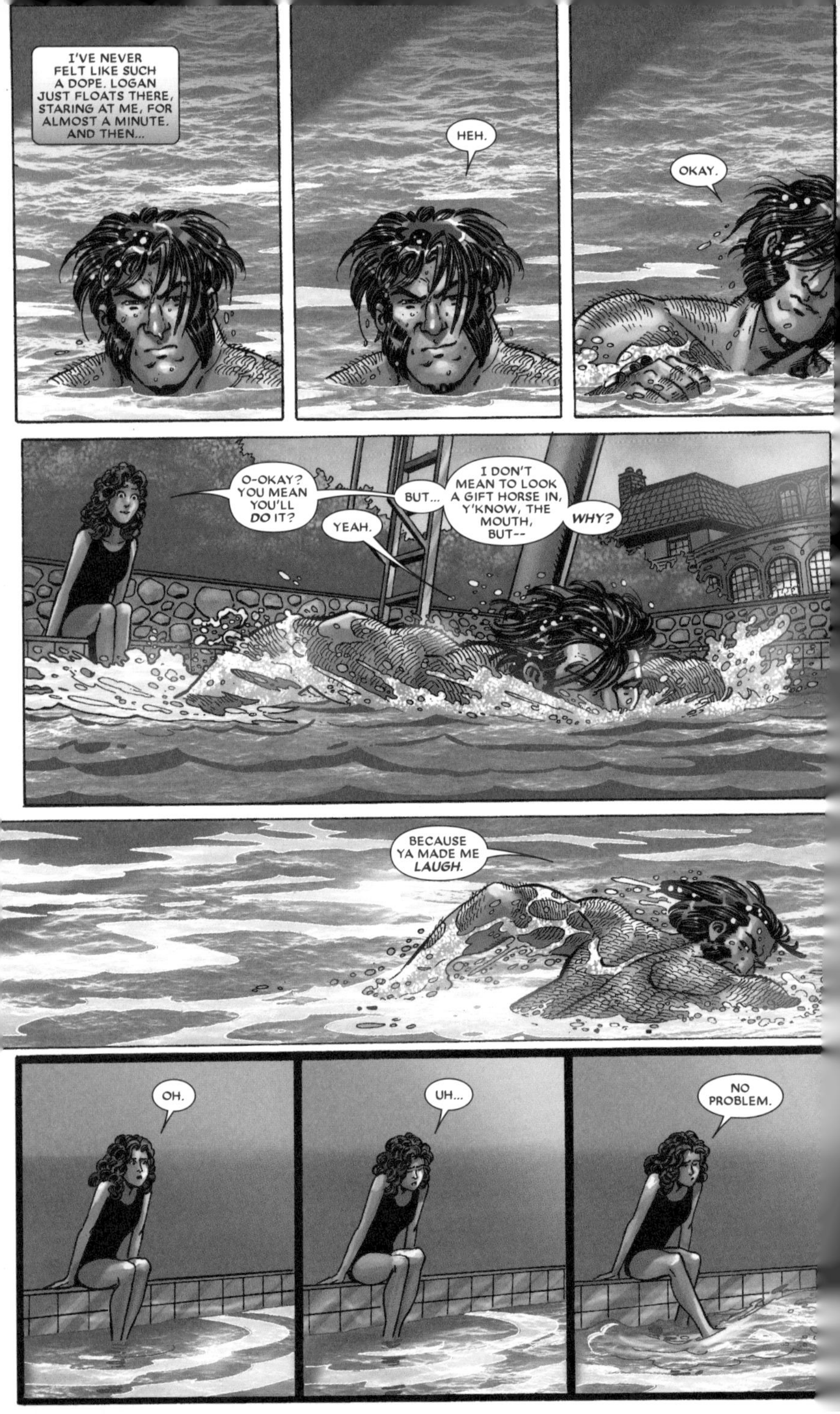
I'VE NEVER FELT LIKE SUCH A DOPE. LOGAN JUST FLOATS THERE, STARING AT ME, FOR ALMOST A MINUTE. AND THEN...
HEH.
OKAY.
O-OKAY? YOU MEAN YOU'LL *DO* IT?
YEAH.
BUT...
I DON'T MEAN TO LOOK A GIFT HORSE IN, Y'KNOW, THE MOUTH, BUT--
WHY?
BECAUSE YA MADE ME *LAUGH.*
OH.
UH...
NO PROBLEM.

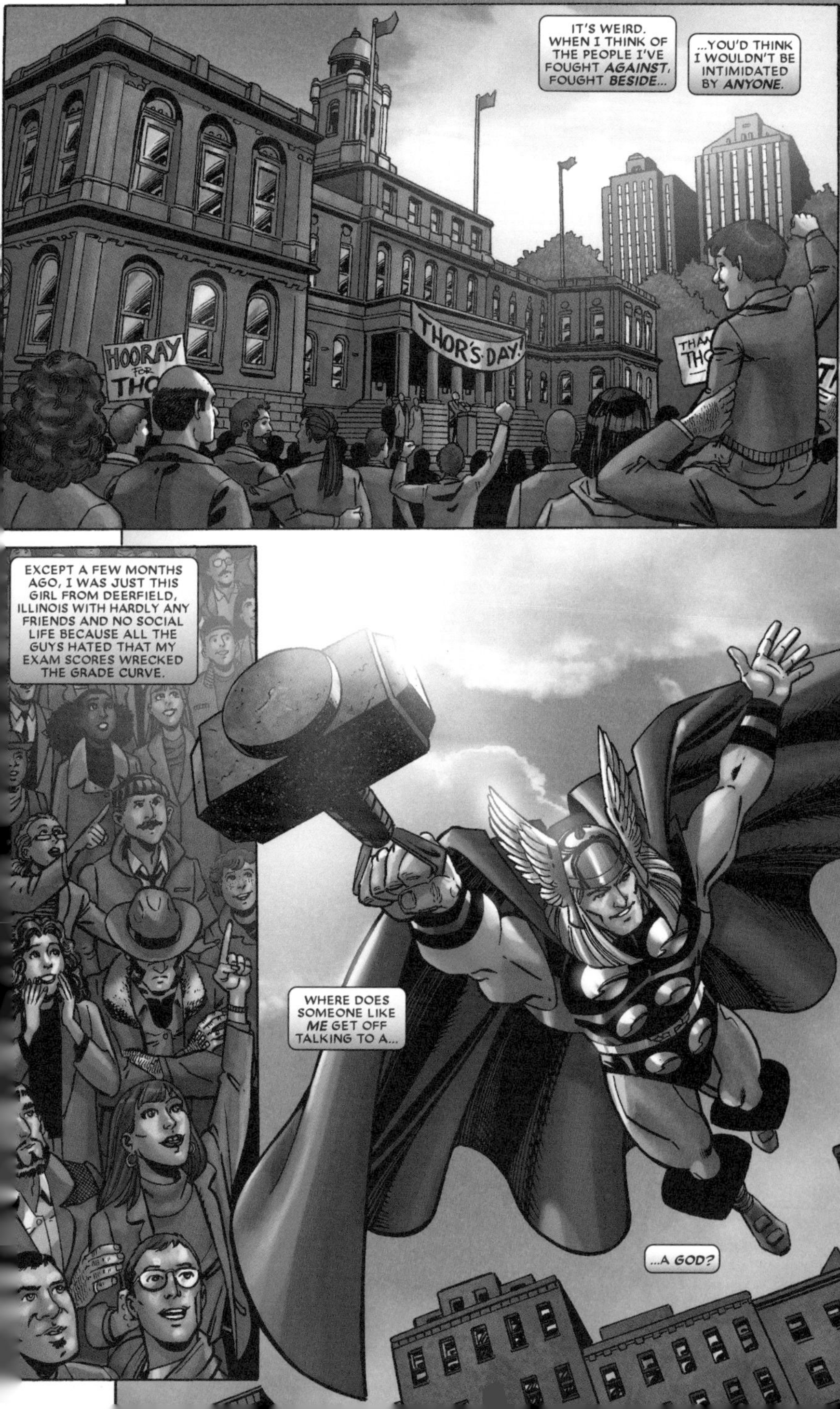
IT'S WEIRD. WHEN I THINK OF THE PEOPLE I'VE FOUGHT *AGAINST*, FOUGHT *BESIDE*...
...YOU'D THINK I WOULDN'T BE INTIMIDATED BY *ANYONE*.
HOORAY FOR THO
THOR'S DAY!
EXCEPT A FEW MONTHS AGO, I WAS JUST THIS GIRL FROM DEERFIELD, ILLINOIS WITH HARDLY ANY FRIENDS AND NO SOCIAL LIFE BECAUSE ALL THE GUYS HATED THAT MY EXAM SCORES WRECKED THE GRADE CURVE.
WHERE DOES SOMEONE LIKE *ME* GET OFF TALKING TO A...
...A *GOD?*

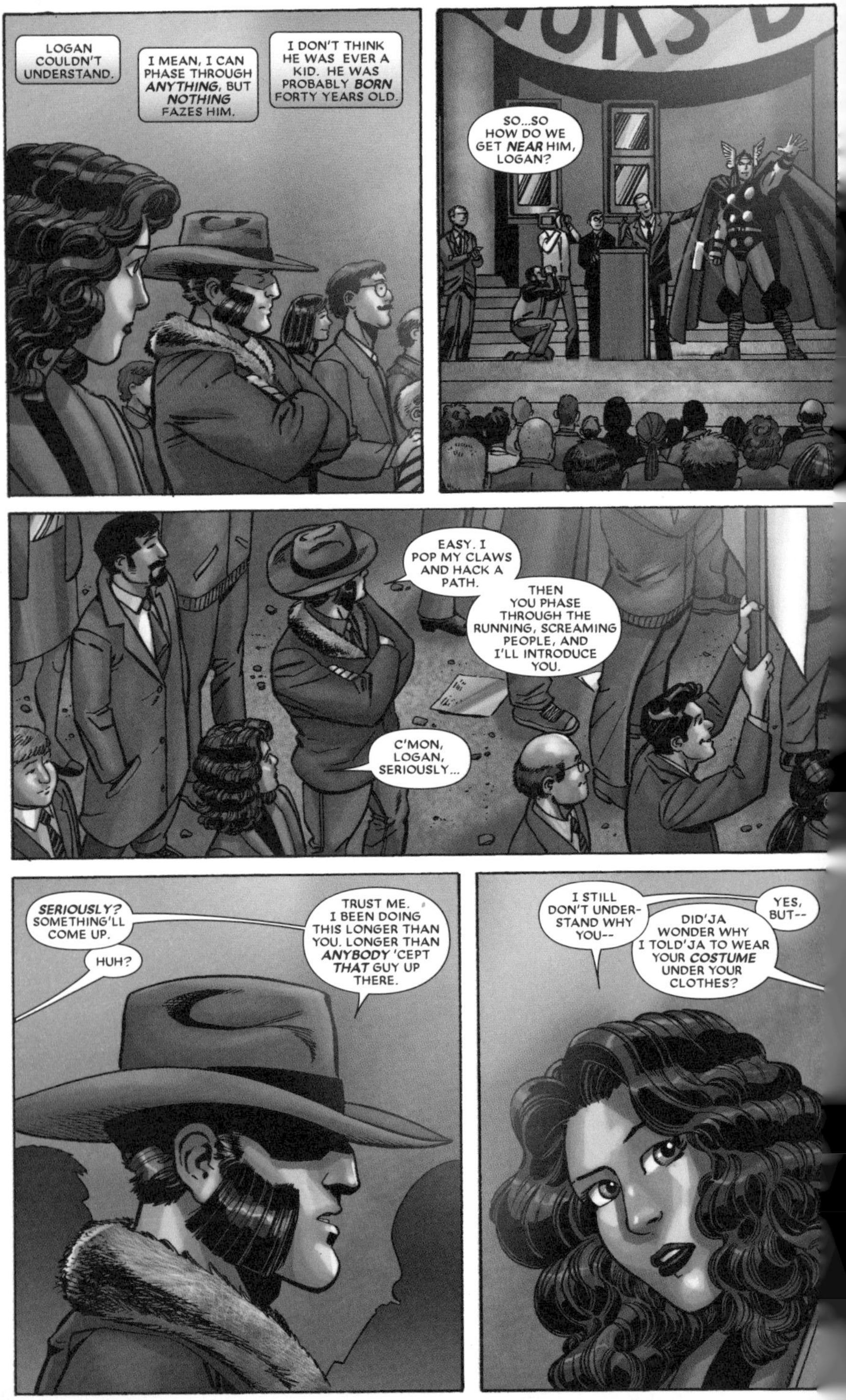

LOGAN COULDN'T UNDERSTAND.
I MEAN, I CAN PHASE THROUGH ***ANYTHING***, BUT ***NOTHING*** FAZES HIM.
I DON'T THINK HE WAS EVER A KID. HE WAS PROBABLY ***BORN*** FORTY YEARS OLD.
SO...SO HOW DO WE GET ***NEAR*** HIM, LOGAN?
EASY. I POP MY CLAWS AND HACK A PATH.
THEN YOU PHASE THROUGH THE RUNNING, SCREAMING PEOPLE, AND I'LL INTRODUCE YOU.
C'MON, LOGAN, SERIOUSLY...
SERIOUSLY? SOMETHING'LL COME UP.
HUH?
TRUST ME. I BEEN DOING THIS LONGER THAN YOU. LONGER THAN ***ANYBODY*** 'CEPT ***THAT*** GUY UP THERE.
I STILL DON'T UNDER-STAND WHY YOU--
YES, BUT--
DID'JA WONDER WHY I TOLD'JA TO WEAR YOUR ***COSTUME*** UNDER YOUR CLOTHES?

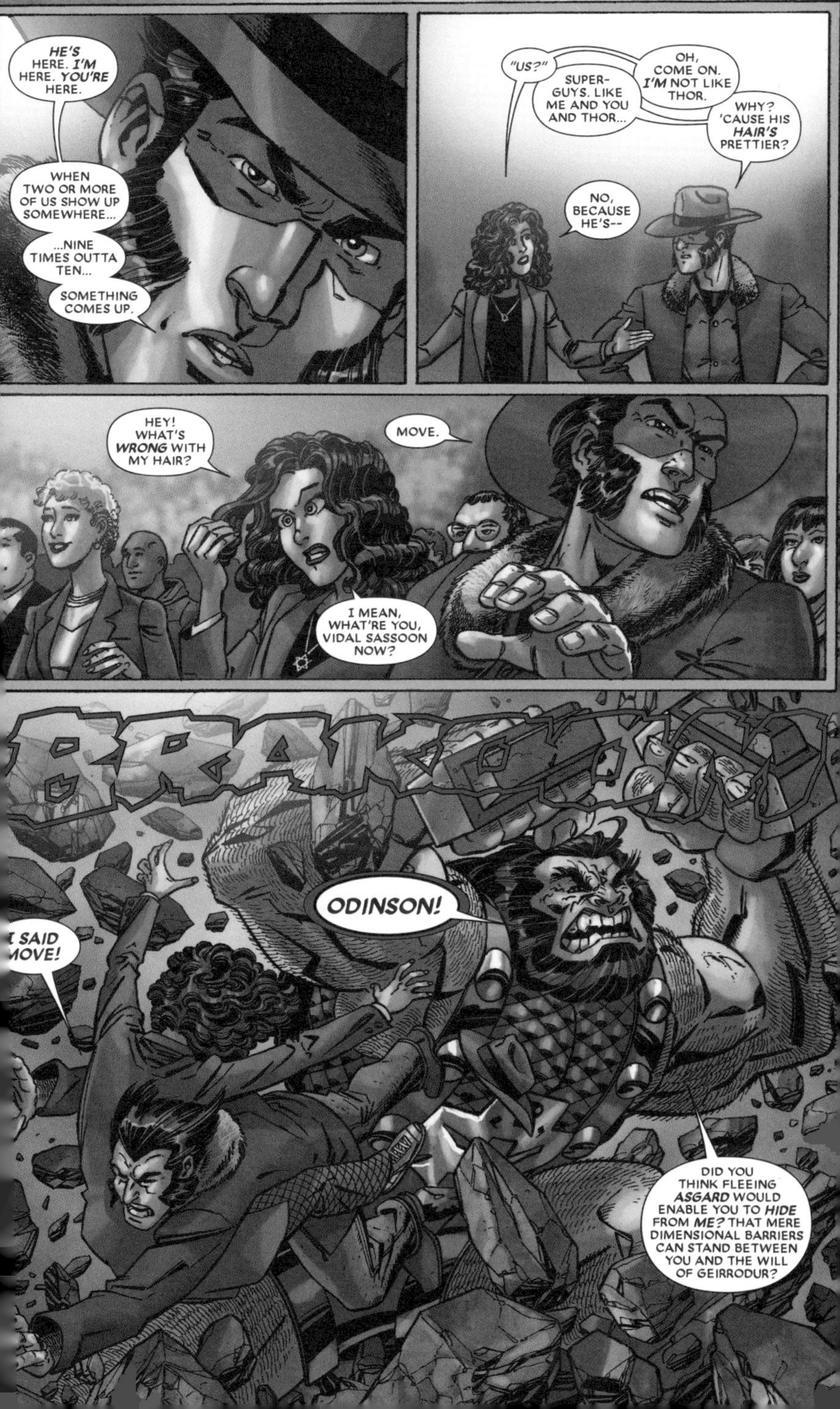

HE'S HERE. I'M HERE. YOU'RE HERE.
WHEN TWO OR MORE OF US SHOW UP SOMEWHERE...
...NINE TIMES OUTTA TEN...
SOMETHING COMES UP.
"US?"
SUPER-GUYS. LIKE ME AND YOU AND THOR...
OH, COME ON. I'M NOT LIKE THOR.
WHY? 'CAUSE HIS HAIR'S PRETTIER?
NO, BECAUSE HE'S--
HEY! WHAT'S WRONG WITH MY HAIR?
MOVE.
I MEAN, WHAT'RE YOU, VIDAL SASSOON NOW?
I SAID MOVE!
ODINSON!
DID YOU THINK FLEEING ASGARD WOULD ENABLE YOU TO HIDE FROM ME? THAT MERE DIMENSIONAL BARRIERS CAN STAND BETWEEN YOU AND THE WILL OF GEIRRODUR?

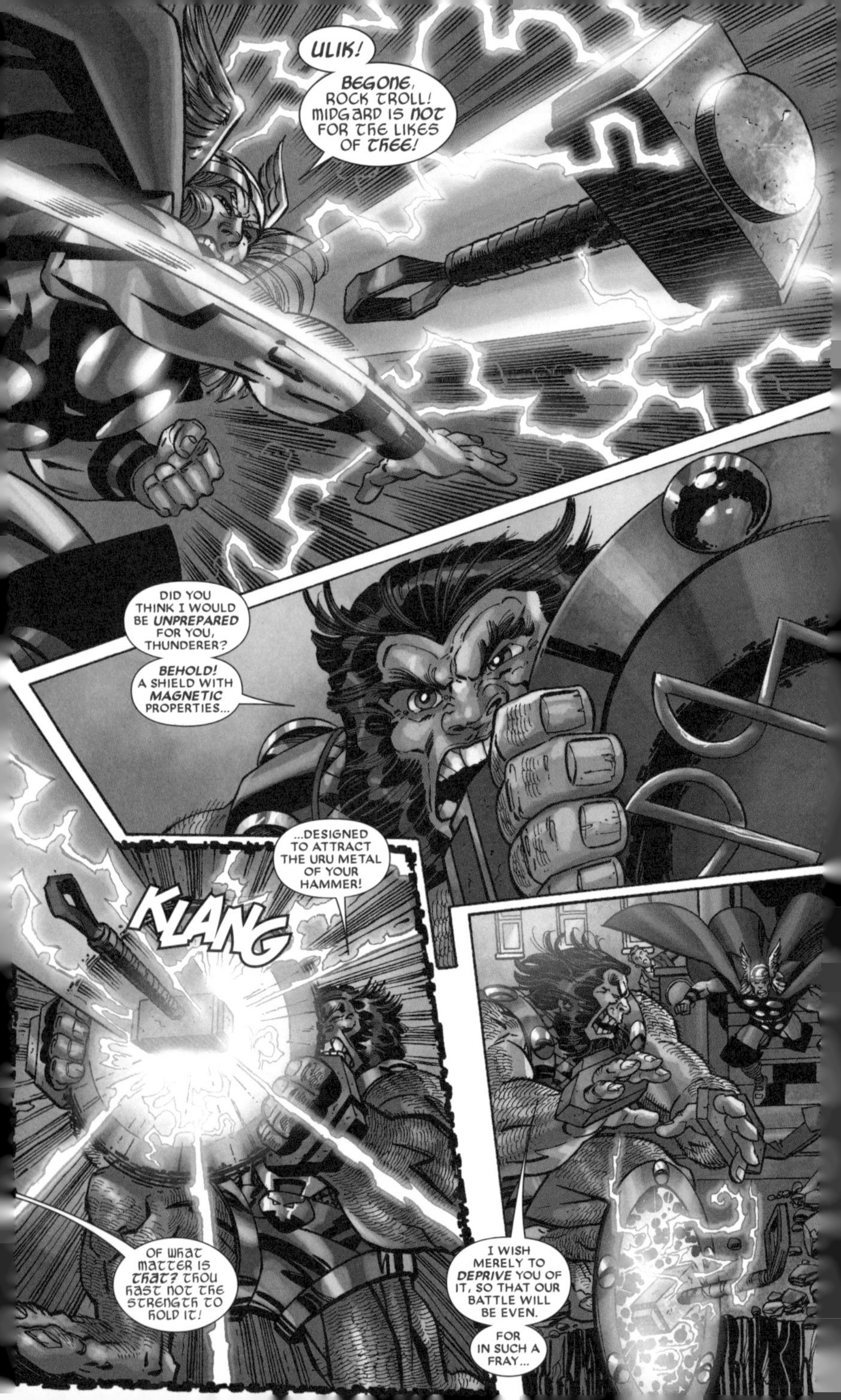
ULIK!
BEGONE, ROCK TROLL! MIDGARD IS NOT FOR THE LIKES OF THEE!
DID YOU THINK I WOULD BE UNPREPARED FOR YOU, THUNDERER?
BEHOLD! A SHIELD WITH MAGNETIC PROPERTIES...
...DESIGNED TO ATTRACT THE URU METAL OF YOUR HAMMER!
KLANG
OF WHAT MATTER IS THAT? THOU HAST NOT THE STRENGTH TO HOLD IT!
I WISH MERELY TO DEPRIVE YOU OF IT, SO THAT OUR BATTLE WILL BE EVEN.
FOR IN SUCH A FRAY...

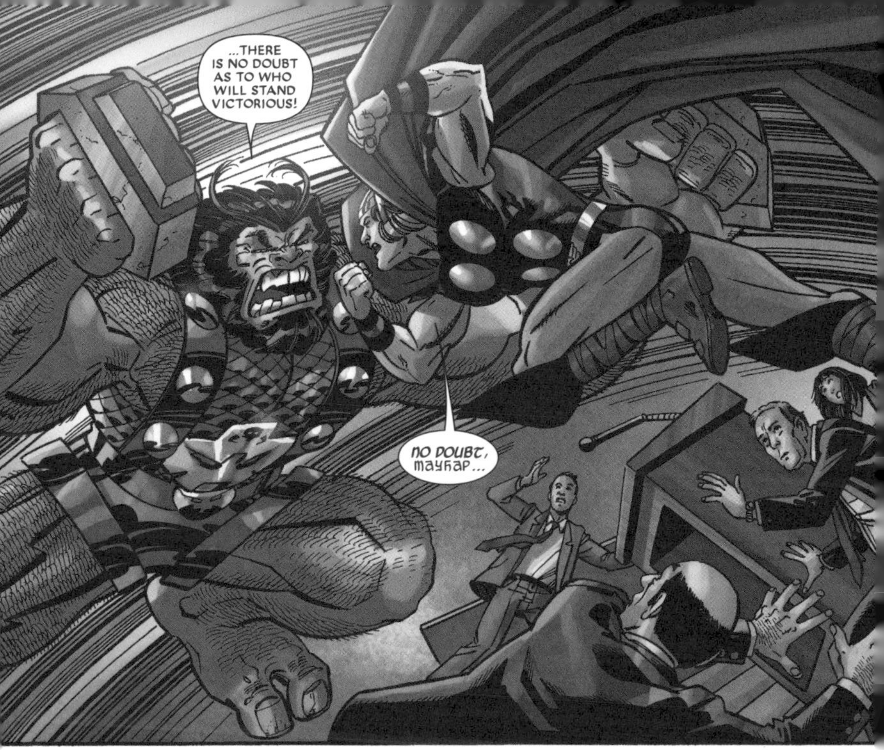
...THERE IS NO DOUBT AS TO WHO WILL STAND VICTORIOUS!
NO DOUBT, MAYHAP...

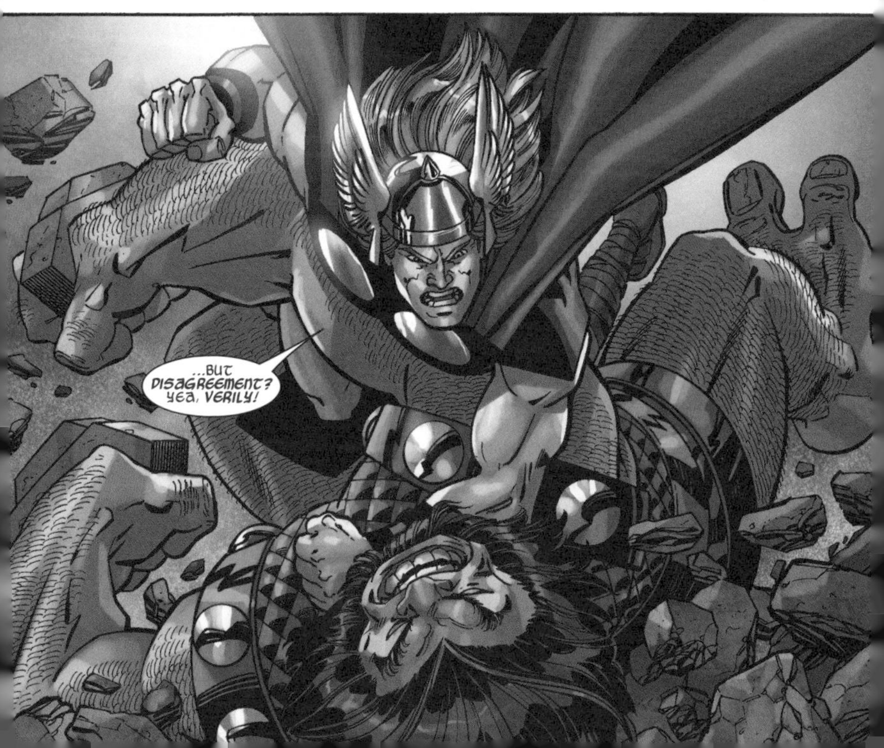
...BUT DISAGREEMENT? YEA, VERILY!

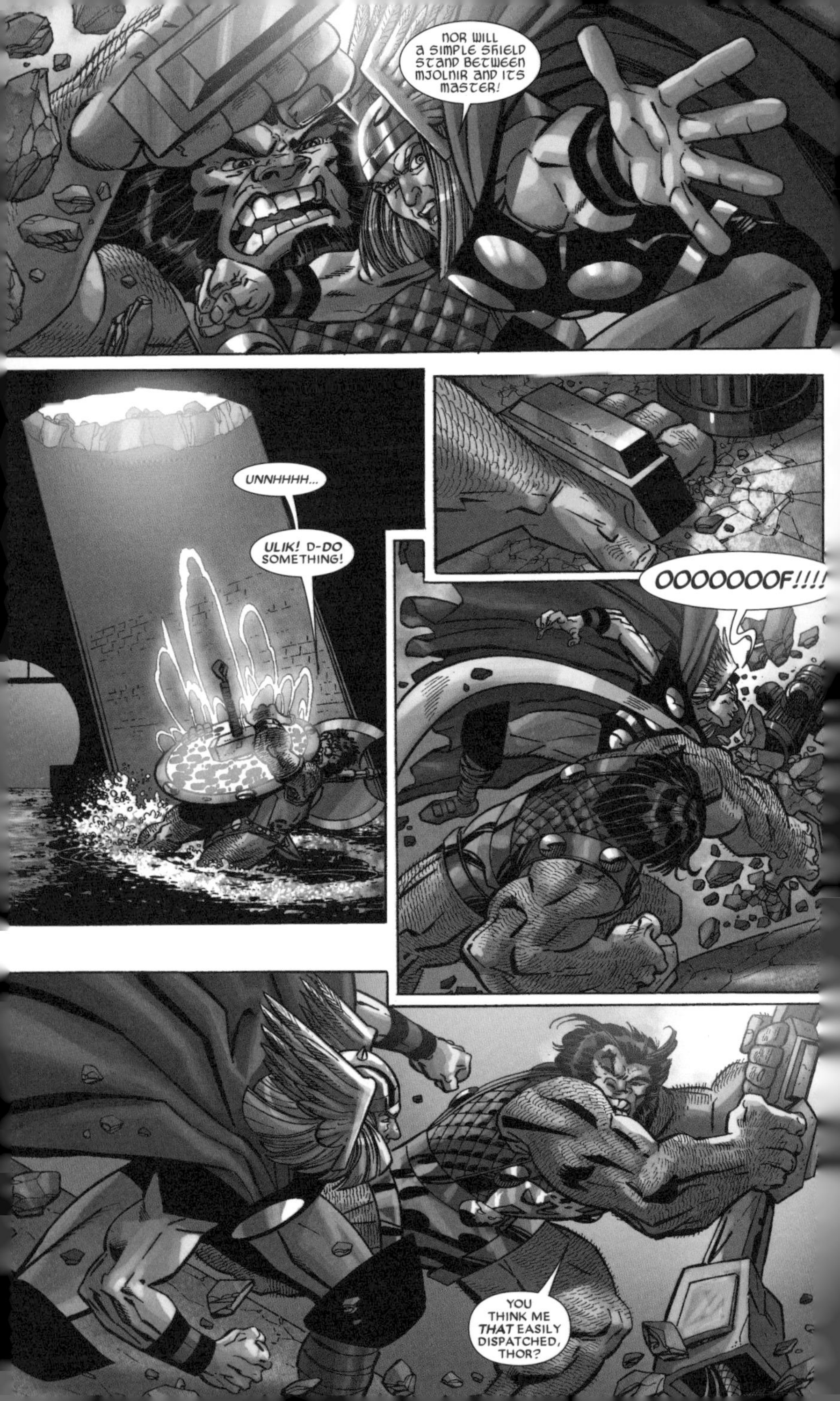
NOR WILL A SIMPLE SHIELD STAND BETWEEN MJOLNIR AND ITS MASTER!
UNNHHHH...
ULIK! D-DO SOMETHING!
OOOOOOOF!!!!
YOU THINK ME THAT EASILY DISPATCHED, THOR?

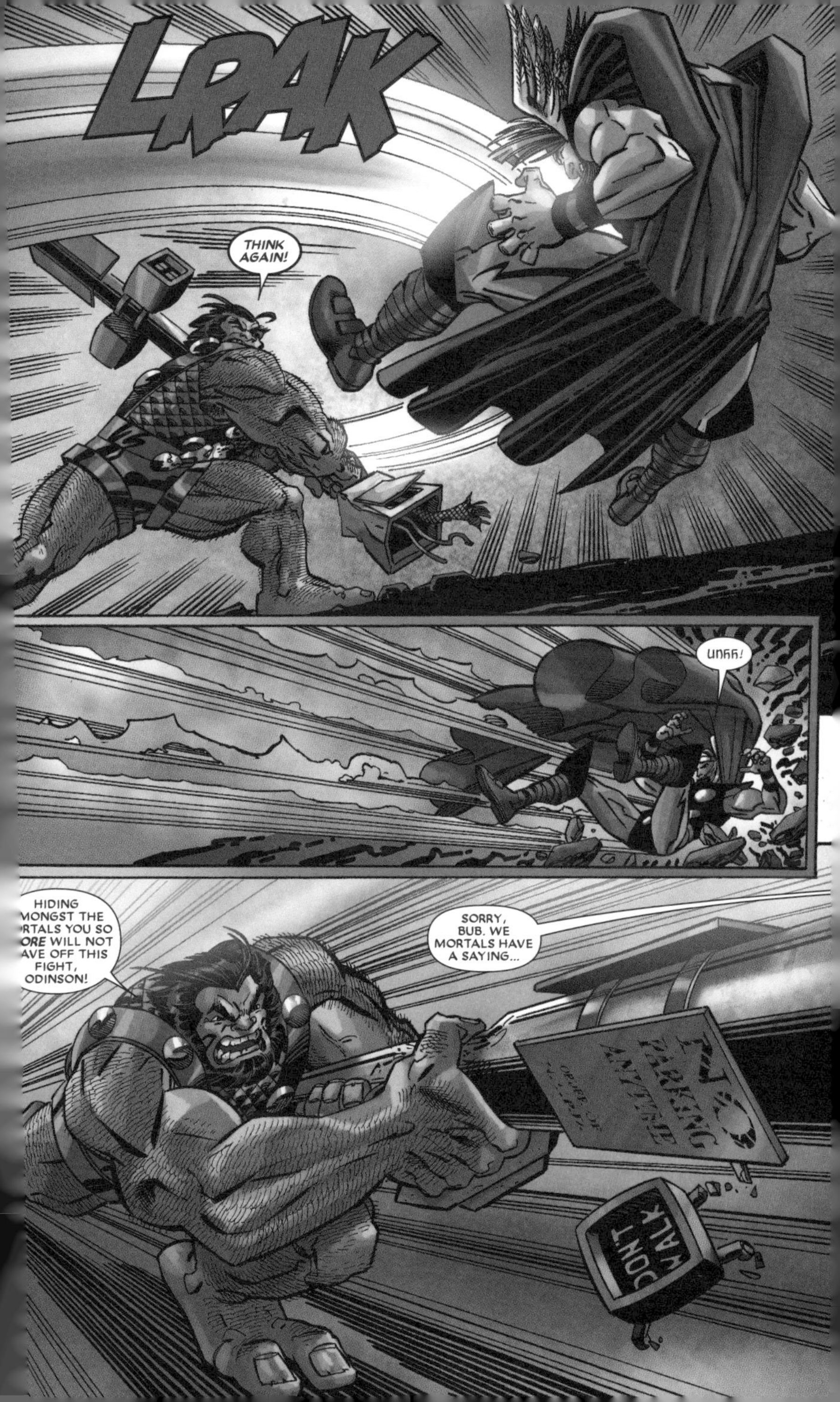
LRAAK
THINK AGAIN!
UNGG!
HIDING MONGST THE MORTALS YOU SO ORE WILL NOT AVE OFF THIS FIGHT, ODINSON!
SORRY, BUB. WE MORTALS HAVE A SAYING...
DON'T WALK

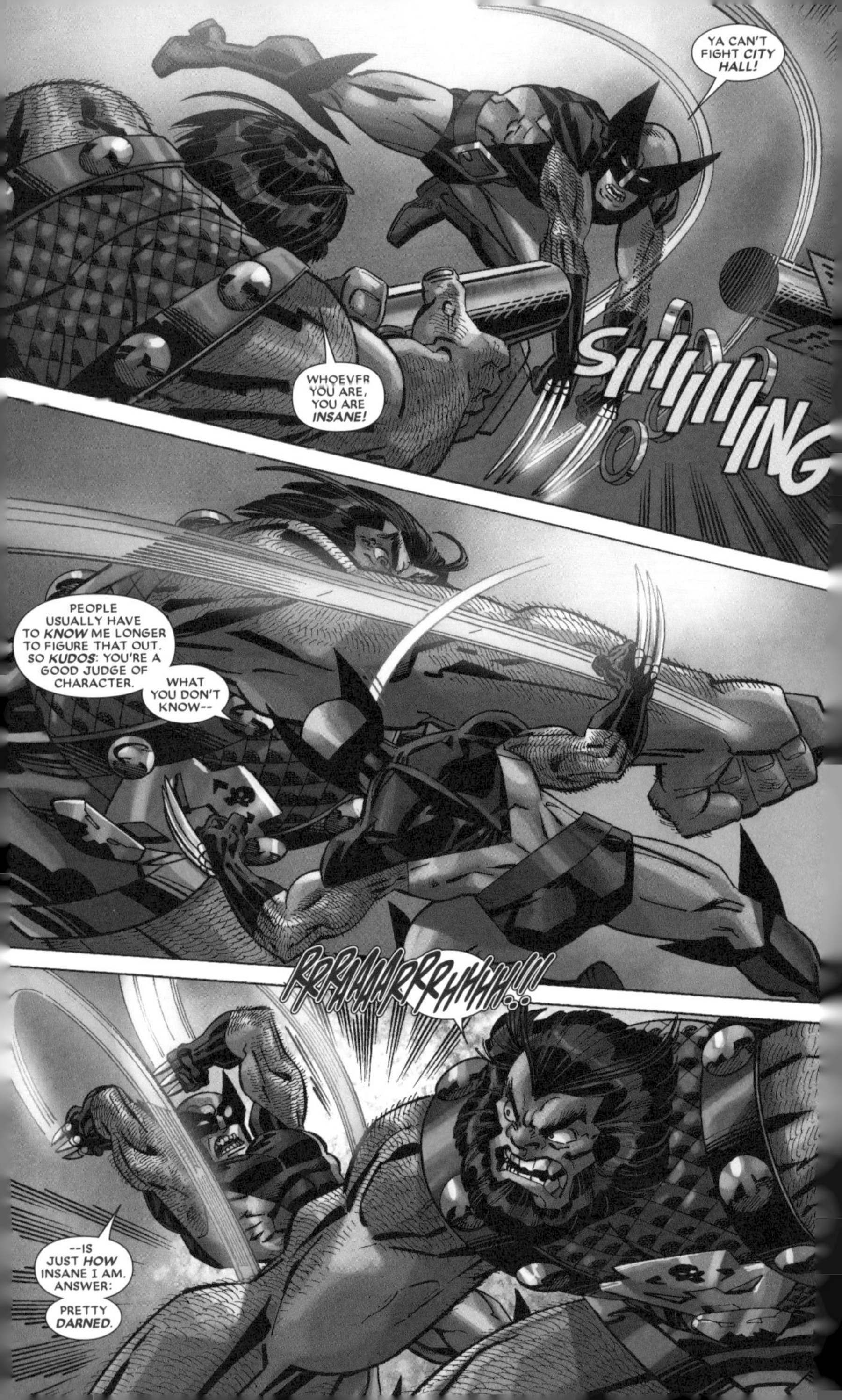

YA CAN'T FIGHT *CITY HALL!*
WHOEVFR YOU ARE, YOU ARE *INSANE!*
SIIIIIIIIING
PEOPLE USUALLY HAVE TO *KNOW* ME LONGER TO FIGURE THAT OUT. SO *KUDOS*: YOU'RE A GOOD JUDGE OF CHARACTER.
WHAT YOU DON'T KNOW--
RRRAAAARRRHHHH!!!
--IS JUST *HOW* INSANE I AM. ANSWER:
PRETTY *DARNED.*

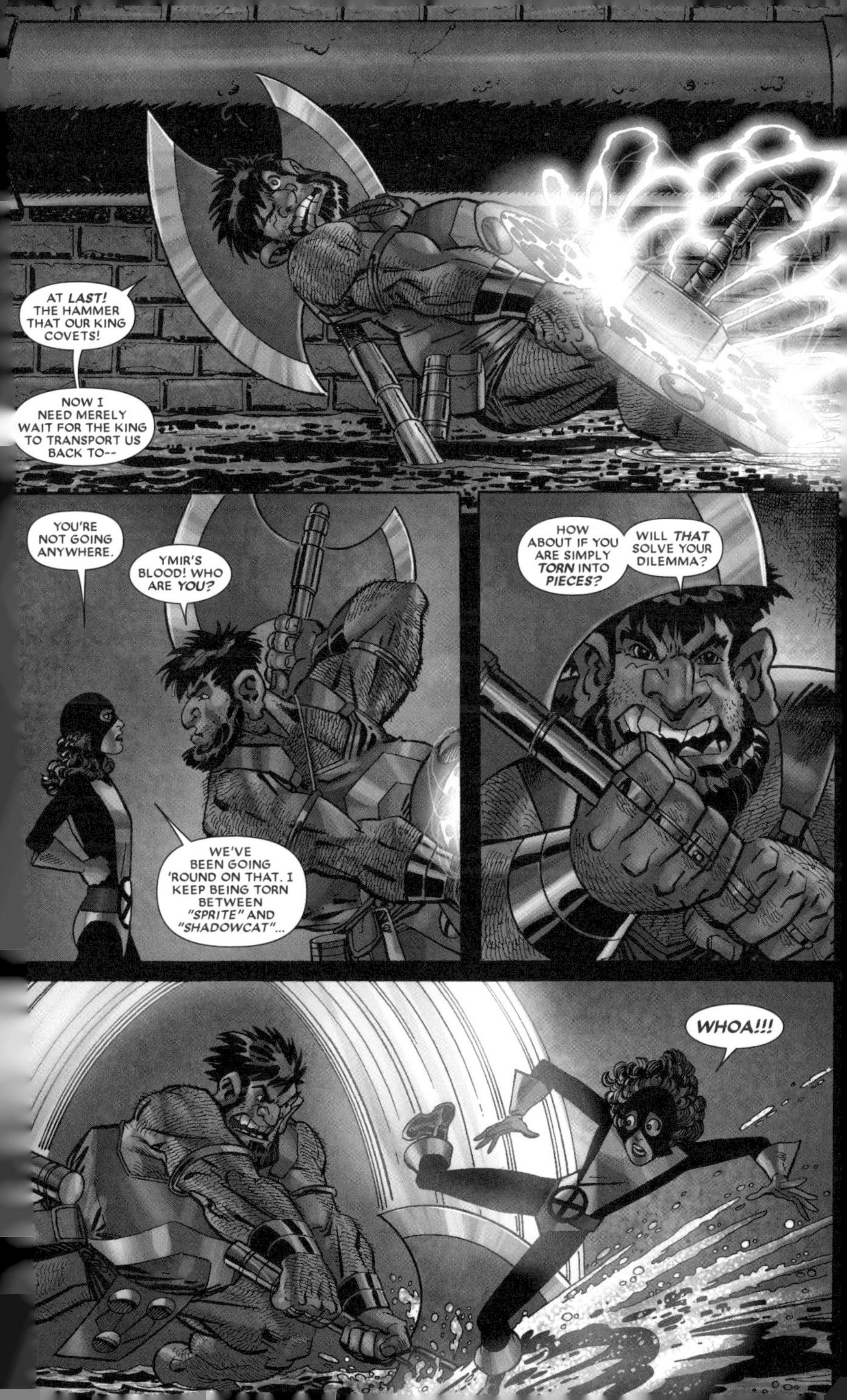
AT LAST! THE HAMMER THAT OUR KING COVETS!
NOW I NEED MERELY WAIT FOR THE KING TO TRANSPORT US BACK TO--
YOU'RE NOT GOING ANYWHERE.
YMIR'S BLOOD! WHO ARE YOU?
WE'VE BEEN GOING 'ROUND ON THAT. I KEEP BEING TORN BETWEEN "SPRITE" AND "SHADOWCAT"...
HOW ABOUT IF YOU ARE SIMPLY TORN INTO PIECES?
WILL THAT SOLVE YOUR DILEMMA?
WHOA!!!

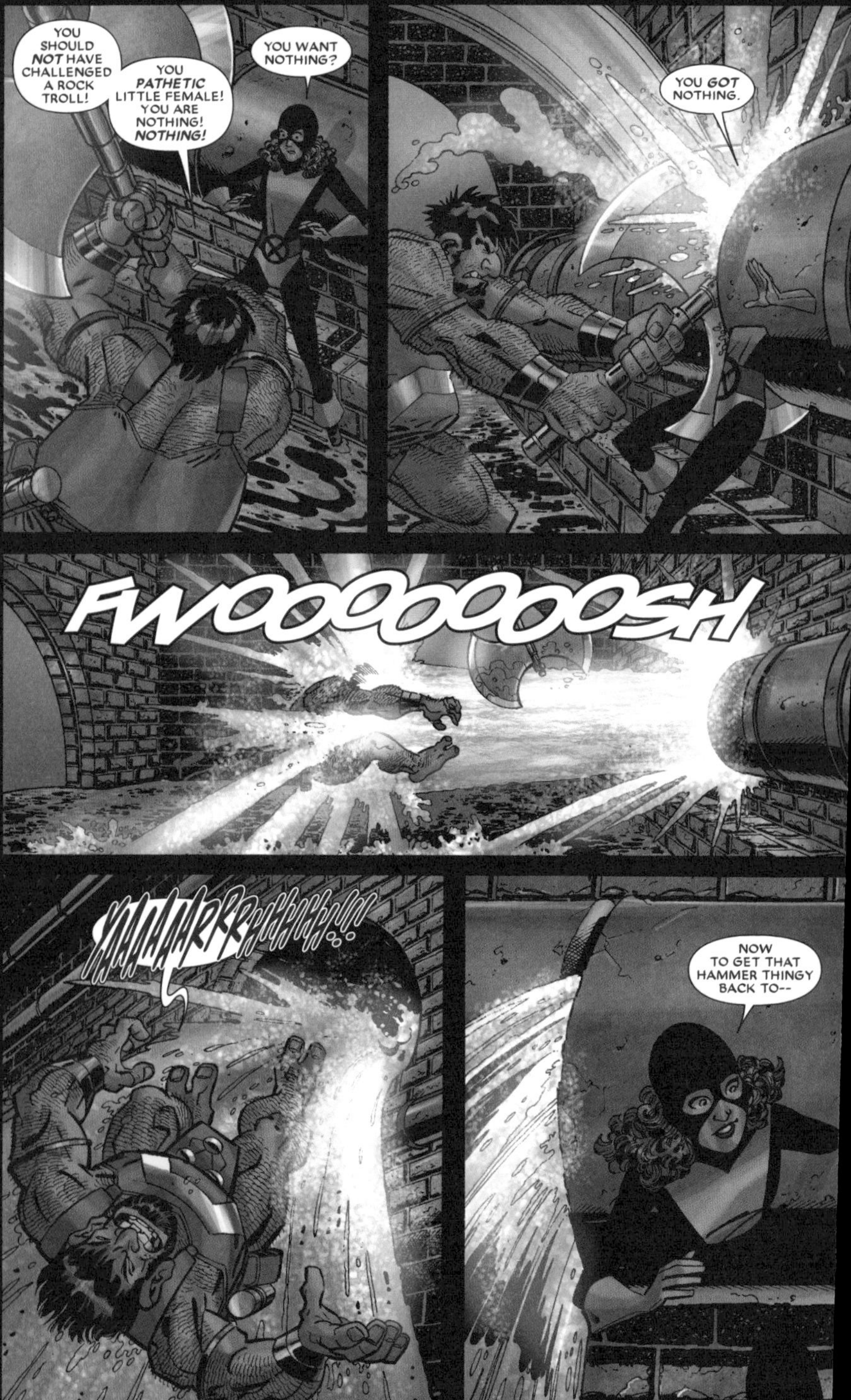
YOU SHOULD **NOT** HAVE CHALLENGED A ROCK TROLL!
YOU **PATHETIC** LITTLE FEMALE! YOU ARE NOTHING! ***NOTHING!***
YOU WANT NOTHING?
YOU **GOT** NOTHING.
FWOOOOOOOOSH
NOW TO GET THAT HAMMER THINGY BACK TO--

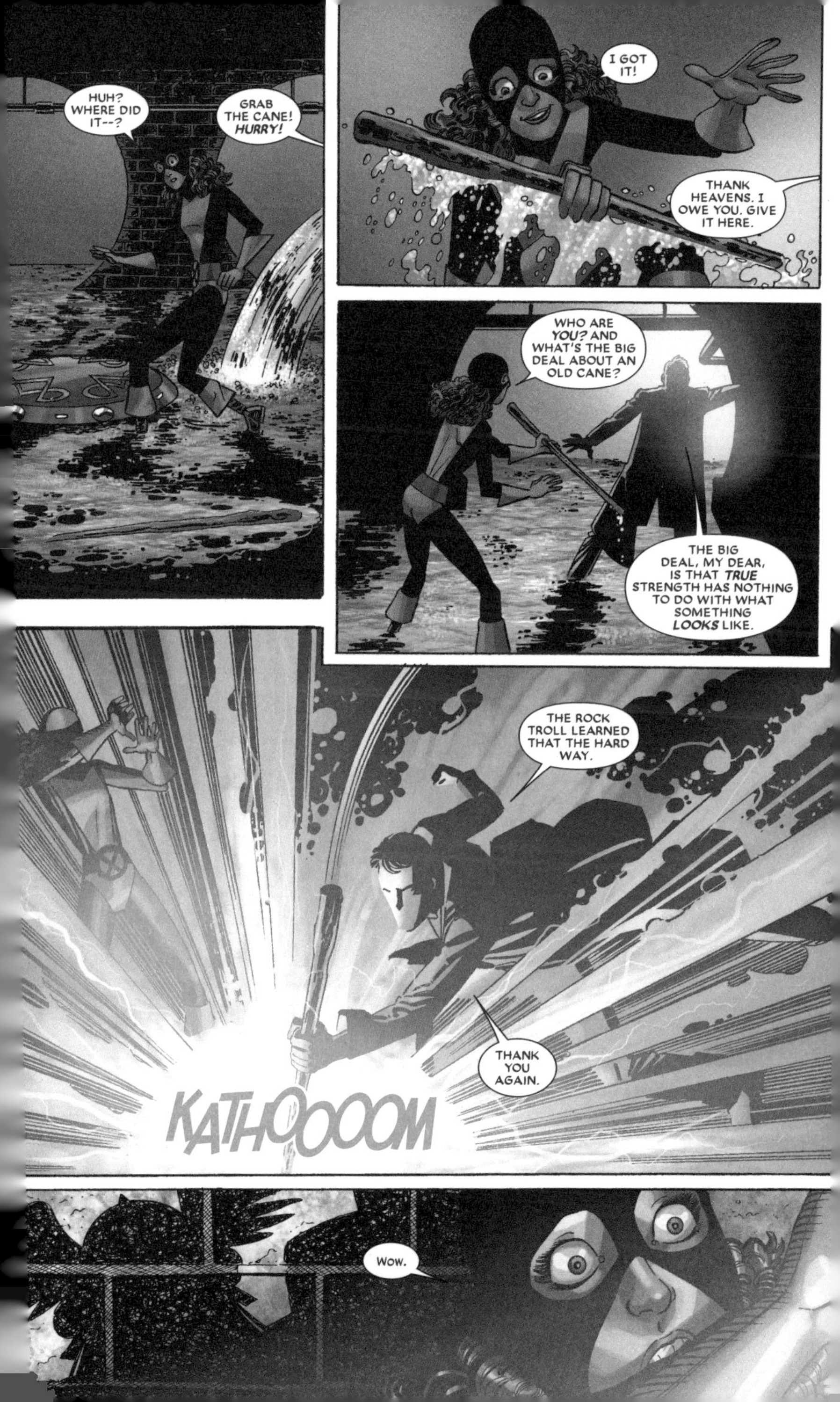
HUH? WHERE DID IT--?
GRAB THE CANE! HURRY!
I GOT IT!
THANK HEAVENS. I OWE YOU. GIVE IT HERE.
WHO ARE YOU? AND WHAT'S THE BIG DEAL ABOUT AN OLD CANE?
THE BIG DEAL, MY DEAR, IS THAT TRUE STRENGTH HAS NOTHING TO DO WITH WHAT SOMETHING LOOKS LIKE.
THE ROCK TROLL LEARNED THAT THE HARD WAY.
THANK YOU AGAIN.
KATHOOOOM
WOW.

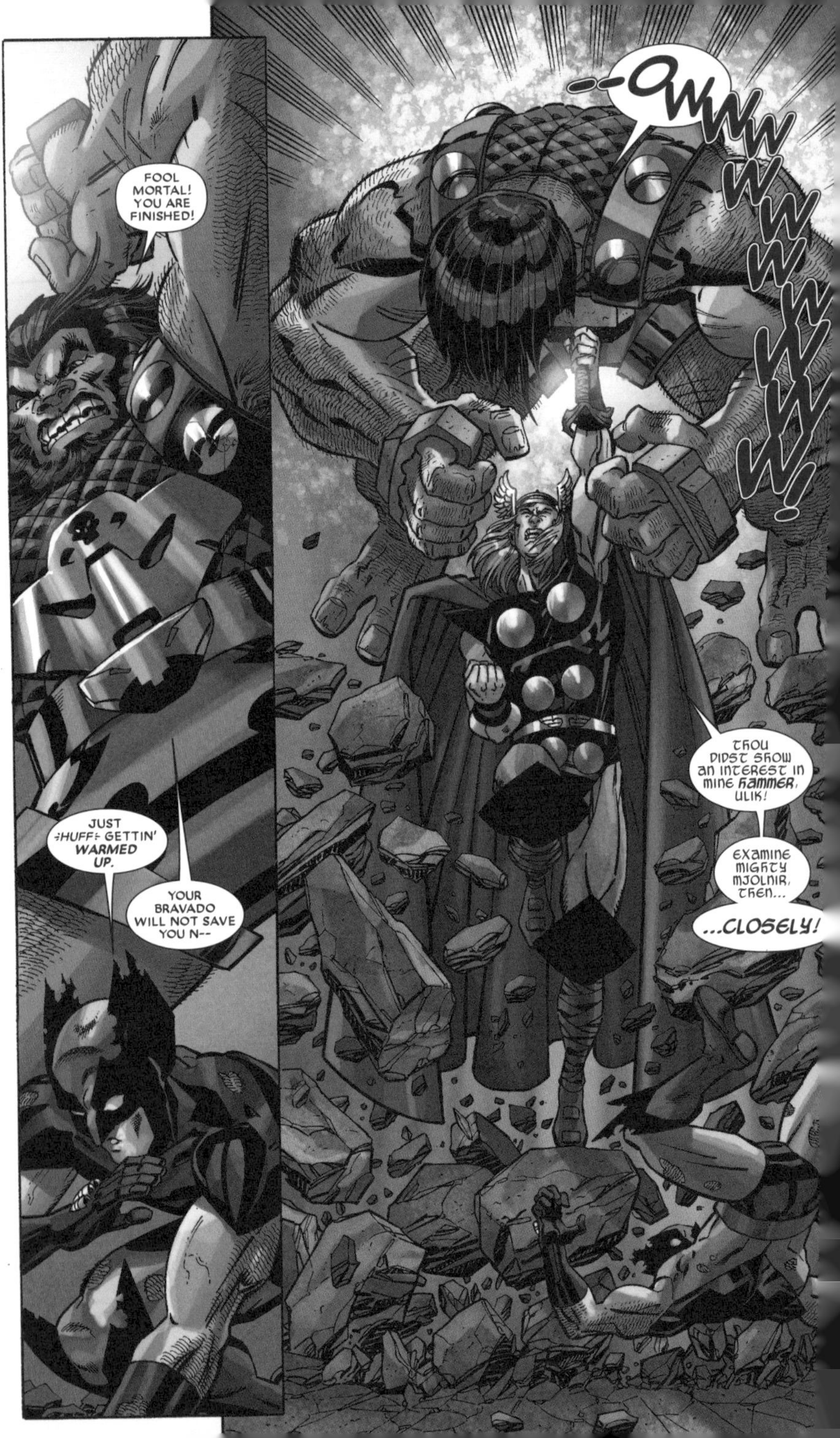
FOOL MORTAL! YOU ARE FINISHED!
JUST -HUFF- GETTIN' WARMED UP.
YOUR BRAVADO WILL NOT SAVE YOU N--
--OWWWWWWWWW!
THOU DIDST SHOW AN INTEREST IN MINE HAMMER, ULIK!
EXAMINE MIGHTY MJOLNIR, THEN...
...CLOSELY!

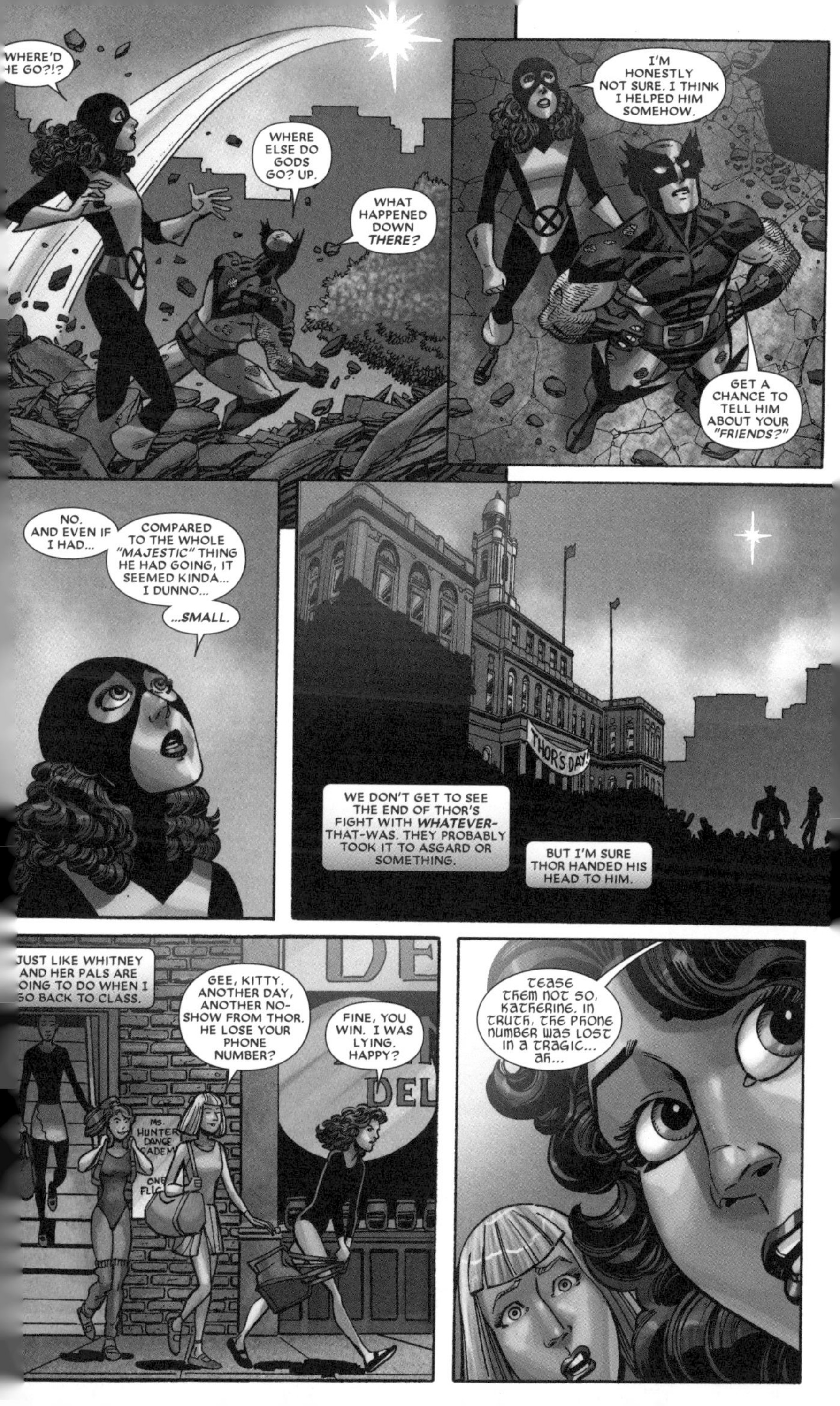

WHERE'D HE GO?!?
WHERE ELSE DO GODS GO? UP.
WHAT HAPPENED DOWN *THERE?*
I'M HONESTLY NOT SURE. I THINK I HELPED HIM SOMEHOW.
GET A CHANCE TO TELL HIM ABOUT YOUR *"FRIENDS?"*
NO. AND EVEN IF I HAD...
COMPARED TO THE WHOLE *"MAJESTIC"* THING HE HAD GOING, IT SEEMED KINDA... I DUNNO...
...SMALL.
THOR'S DAY!
WE DON'T GET TO SEE THE END OF THOR'S FIGHT WITH *WHATEVER*-THAT-WAS. THEY PROBABLY TOOK IT TO ASGARD OR SOMETHING.
BUT I'M SURE THOR HANDED HIS HEAD TO HIM.
JUST LIKE WHITNEY AND HER PALS ARE GOING TO DO WHEN I GO BACK TO CLASS.
GEE, KITTY. ANOTHER DAY, ANOTHER NO-SHOW FROM THOR. HE LOSE YOUR PHONE NUMBER?
FINE, YOU WIN. I WAS LYING. HAPPY?
TEASE THEM NOT SO, KATHERINE. IN TRUTH, THE PHONE NUMBER WAS LOST IN A TRAGIC... AH...

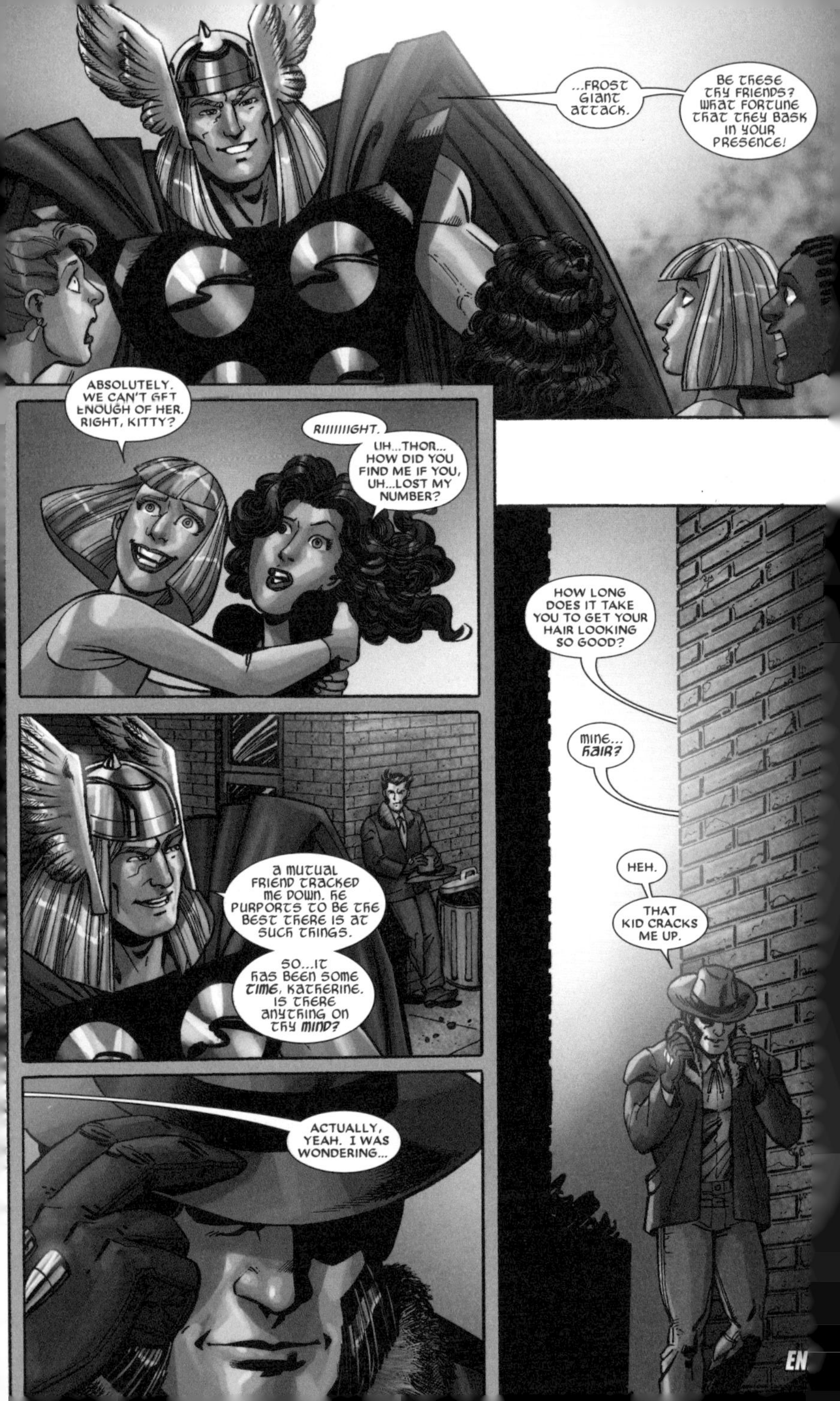
...FROST GIANT ATTACK.
BE THESE THY FRIENDS? WHAT FORTUNE THAT THEY BASK IN YOUR PRESENCE!
ABSOLUTELY. WE CAN'T GET ENOUGH OF HER. RIGHT, KITTY?
RIIIIIIGHT.
UH...THOR... HOW DID YOU FIND ME IF YOU, UH...LOST MY NUMBER?
A MUTUAL FRIEND TRACKED ME DOWN. HE PURPORTS TO BE THE BEST THERE IS AT SUCH THINGS.
SO...IT HAS BEEN SOME TIME, KATHERINE. IS THERE ANYTHING ON THY MIND?
ACTUALLY, YEAH. I WAS WONDERING...
HOW LONG DOES IT TAKE YOU TO GET YOUR HAIR LOOKING SO GOOD?
MINE... HAIR?
HEH.
THAT KID CRACKS ME UP.
EN

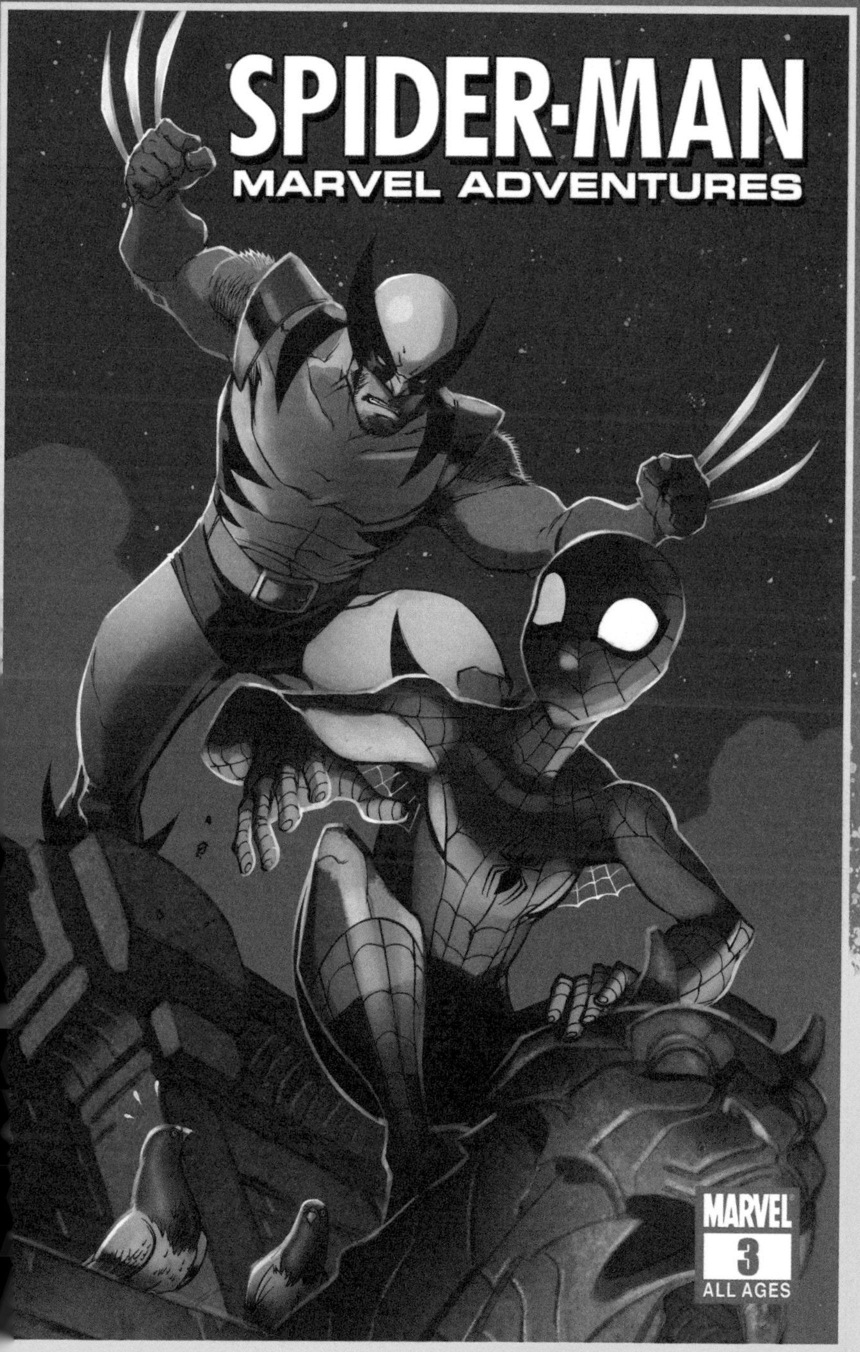

SPIDER-MAN
MARVEL ADVENTURES
MARVEL
3
ALL AGES

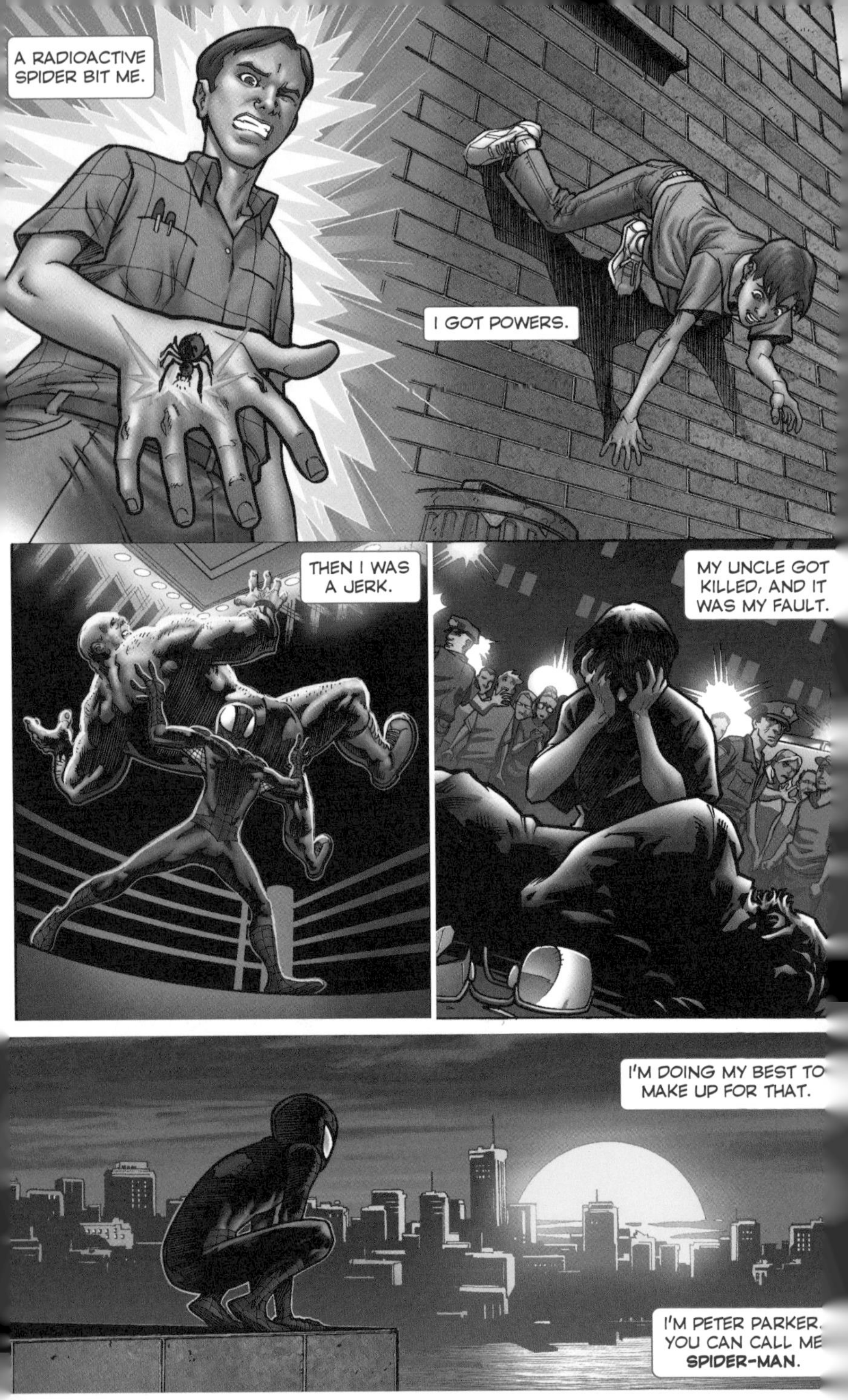
A RADIOACTIVE SPIDER BIT ME.
I GOT POWERS.
THEN I WAS A JERK.
MY UNCLE GOT KILLED, AND IT WAS MY FAULT.
I'M DOING MY BEST TO MAKE UP FOR THAT.
I'M PETER PARKER. YOU CAN CALL ME SPIDER-MAN.

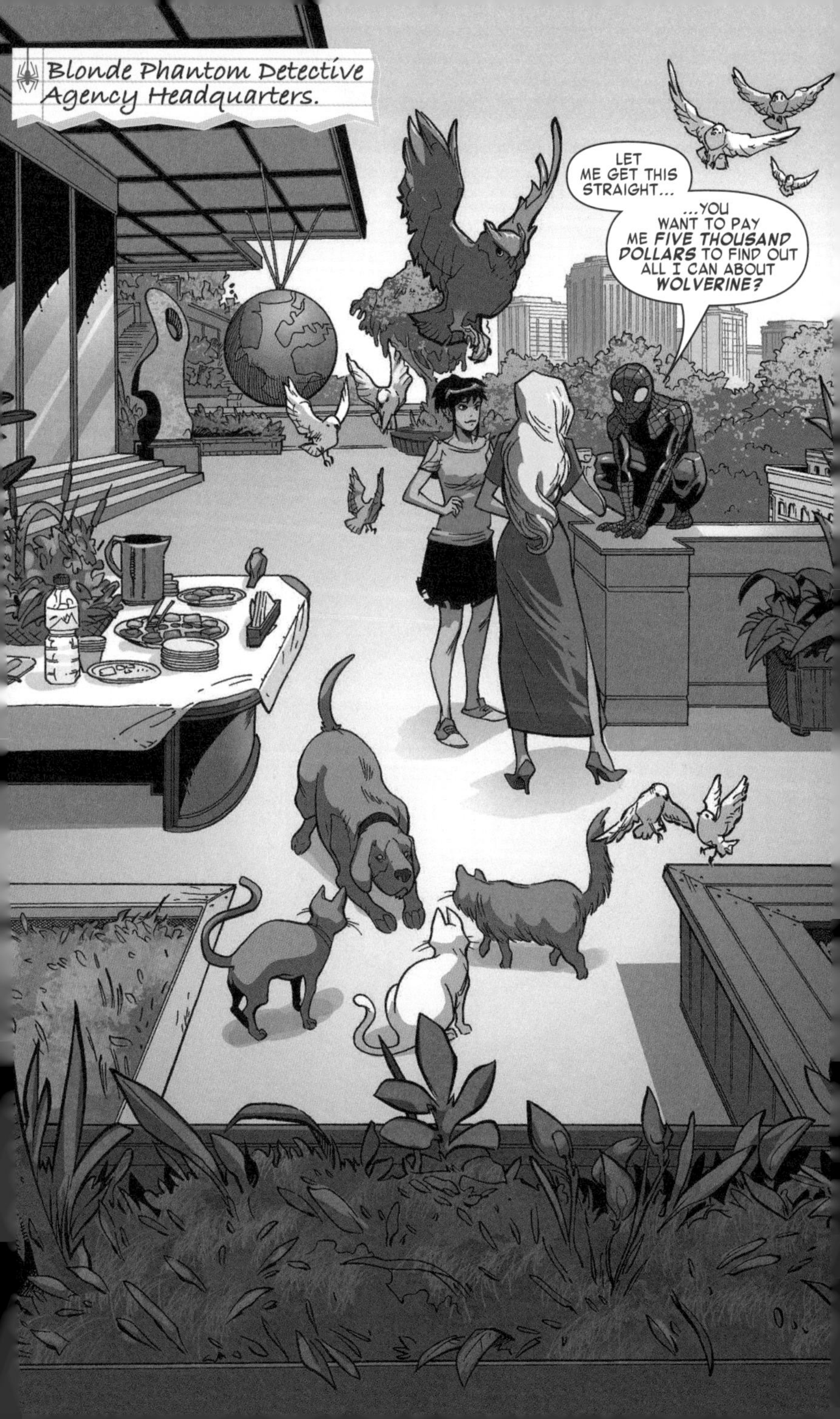
Blonde Phantom Detective Agency Headquarters.
LET ME GET THIS STRAIGHT...
...YOU WANT TO PAY ME **FIVE THOUSAND DOLLARS** TO FIND OUT ALL I CAN ABOUT **WOLVERINE?**

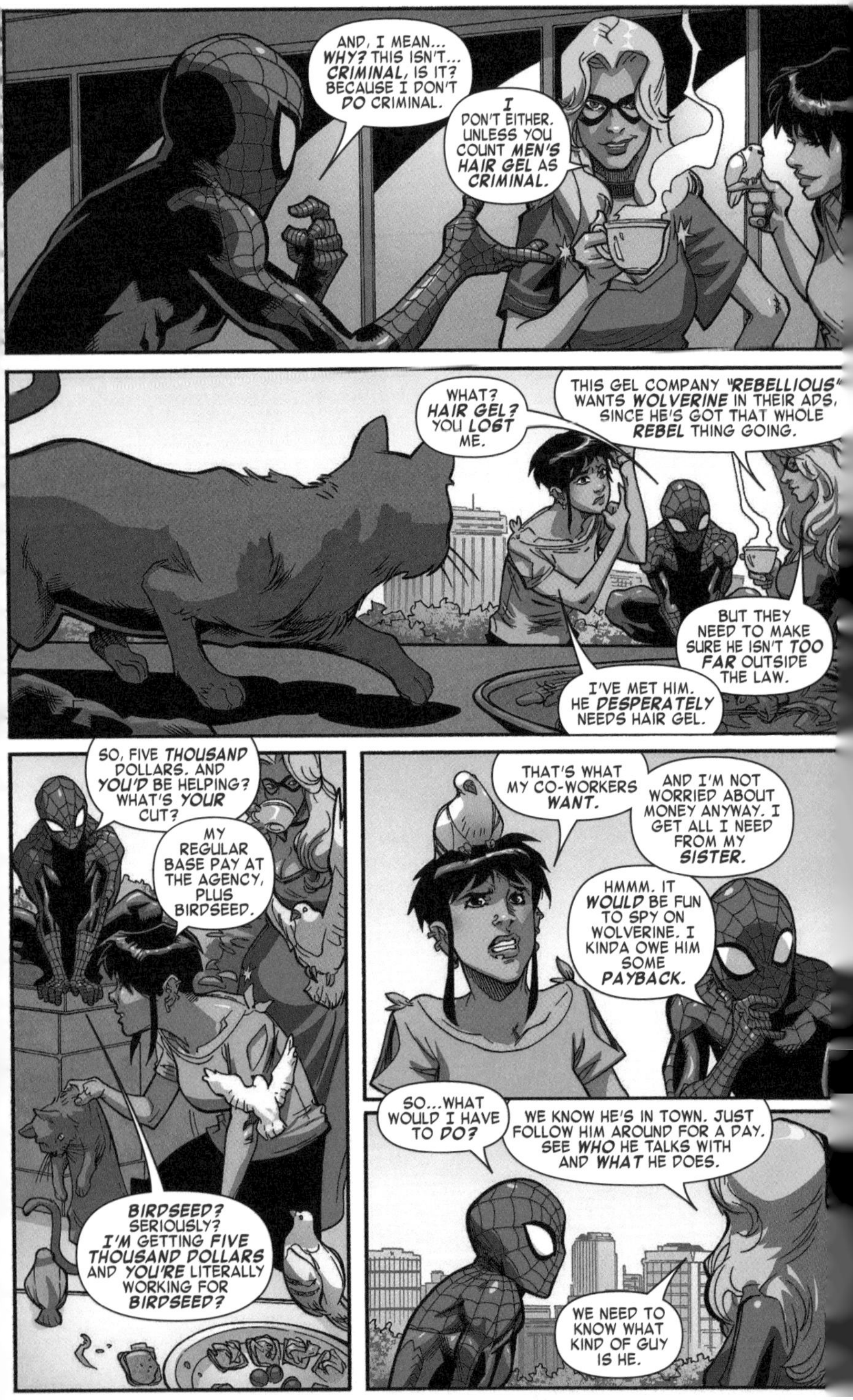
AND, I MEAN... WHY? THIS ISN'T... CRIMINAL, IS IT? BECAUSE I DON'T DO CRIMINAL.
I DON'T EITHER. UNLESS YOU COUNT MEN'S HAIR GEL AS CRIMINAL.
WHAT? HAIR GEL? YOU LOST ME.
THIS GEL COMPANY "REBELLIOUS" WANTS WOLVERINE IN THEIR ADS, SINCE HE'S GOT THAT WHOLE REBEL THING GOING.
BUT THEY NEED TO MAKE SURE HE ISN'T TOO FAR OUTSIDE THE LAW.
I'VE MET HIM. HE DESPERATELY NEEDS HAIR GEL.
SO, FIVE THOUSAND DOLLARS. AND YOU'D BE HELPING? WHAT'S YOUR CUT?
MY REGULAR BASE PAY AT THE AGENCY, PLUS BIRDSEED.
BIRDSEED? SERIOUSLY? I'M GETTING FIVE THOUSAND DOLLARS AND YOU'RE LITERALLY WORKING FOR BIRDSEED?
THAT'S WHAT MY CO-WORKERS WANT.
AND I'M NOT WORRIED ABOUT MONEY ANYWAY. I GET ALL I NEED FROM MY SISTER.
HMMM. IT WOULD BE FUN TO SPY ON WOLVERINE. I KINDA OWE HIM SOME PAYBACK.
SO...WHAT WOULD I HAVE TO DO?
WE KNOW HE'S IN TOWN. JUST FOLLOW HIM AROUND FOR A DAY. SEE WHO HE TALKS WITH AND WHAT HE DOES.
WE NEED TO KNOW WHAT KIND OF GUY IS HE.

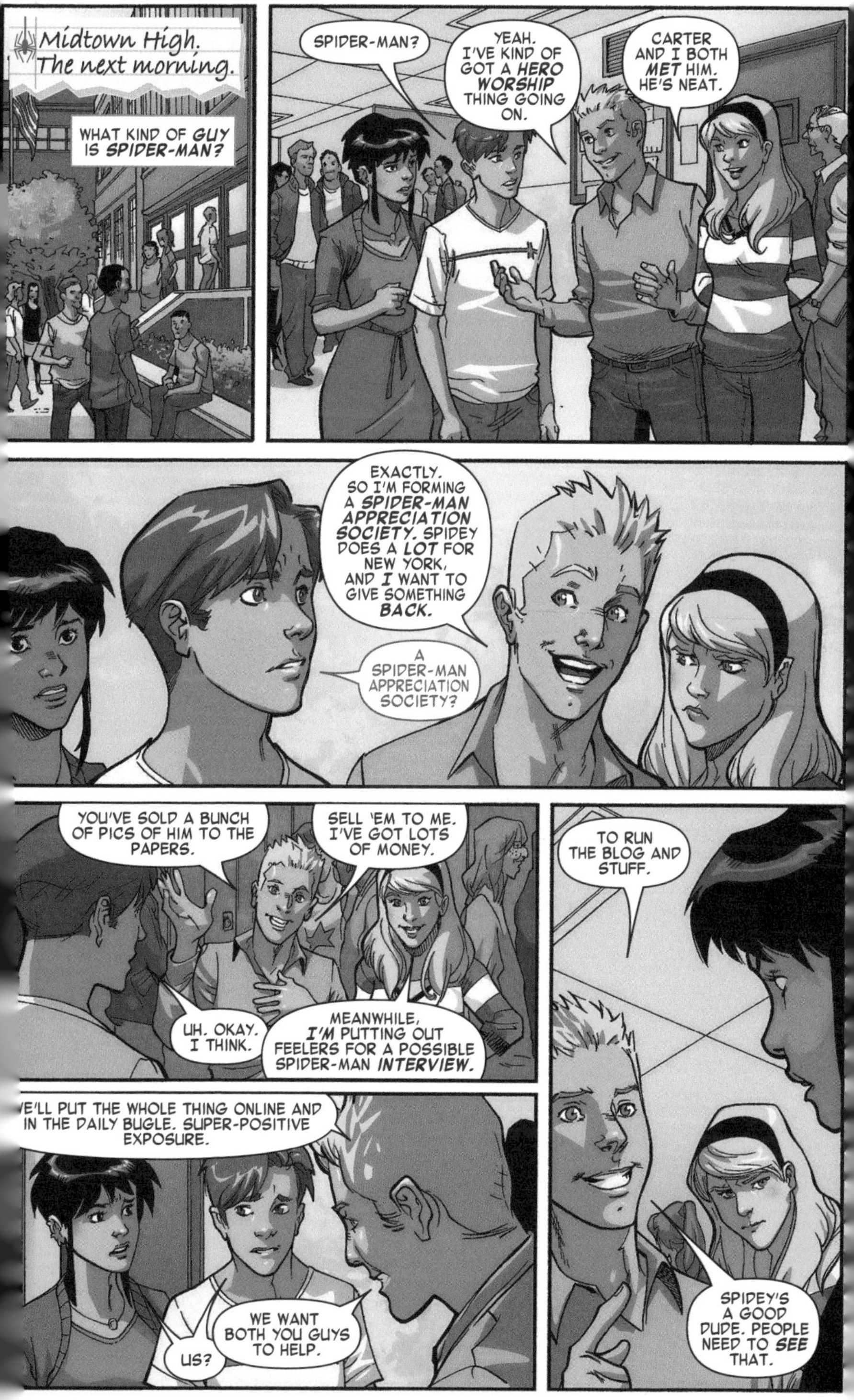

Midtown High. The next morning.
WHAT KIND OF GUY IS SPIDER-MAN?
SPIDER-MAN?
YEAH. I'VE KIND OF GOT A HERO WORSHIP THING GOING ON.
CARTER AND I BOTH MET HIM. HE'S NEAT.
EXACTLY. SO I'M FORMING A SPIDER-MAN APPRECIATION SOCIETY. SPIDEY DOES A LOT FOR NEW YORK, AND I WANT TO GIVE SOMETHING BACK.
A SPIDER-MAN APPRECIATION SOCIETY?
YOU'VE SOLD A BUNCH OF PICS OF HIM TO THE PAPERS.
SELL 'EM TO ME. I'VE GOT LOTS OF MONEY.
UH. OKAY. I THINK.
MEANWHILE, I'M PUTTING OUT FEELERS FOR A POSSIBLE SPIDER-MAN INTERVIEW.
WE'LL PUT THE WHOLE THING ONLINE AND IN THE DAILY BUGLE. SUPER-POSITIVE EXPOSURE.
US?
WE WANT BOTH YOU GUYS TO HELP.
TO RUN THE BLOG AND STUFF.
SPIDEY'S A GOOD DUDE. PEOPLE NEED TO SEE THAT.

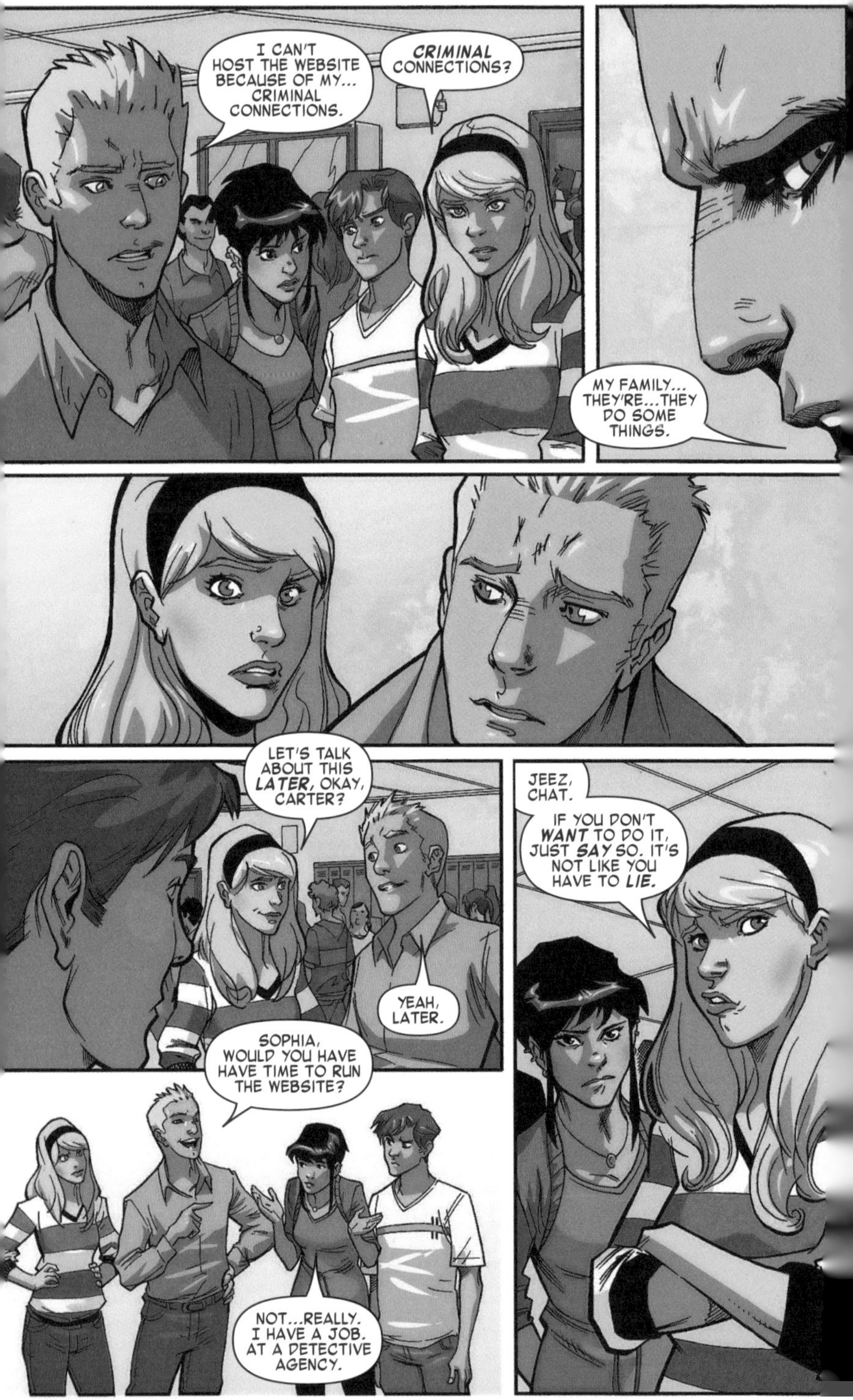
I CAN'T HOST THE WEBSITE BECAUSE OF MY... CRIMINAL CONNECTIONS.
CRIMINAL CONNECTIONS?
MY FAMILY... THEY'RE...THEY DO SOME THINGS.
LET'S TALK ABOUT THIS *LATER,* OKAY, CARTER?
YEAH, LATER.
SOPHIA, WOULD YOU HAVE HAVE TIME TO RUN THE WEBSITE?
NOT...REALLY. I HAVE A JOB. AT A DETECTIVE AGENCY.
JEEZ, CHAT.
IF YOU DON'T *WANT* TO DO IT, JUST *SAY* SO. IT'S NOT LIKE YOU HAVE TO *LIE.*

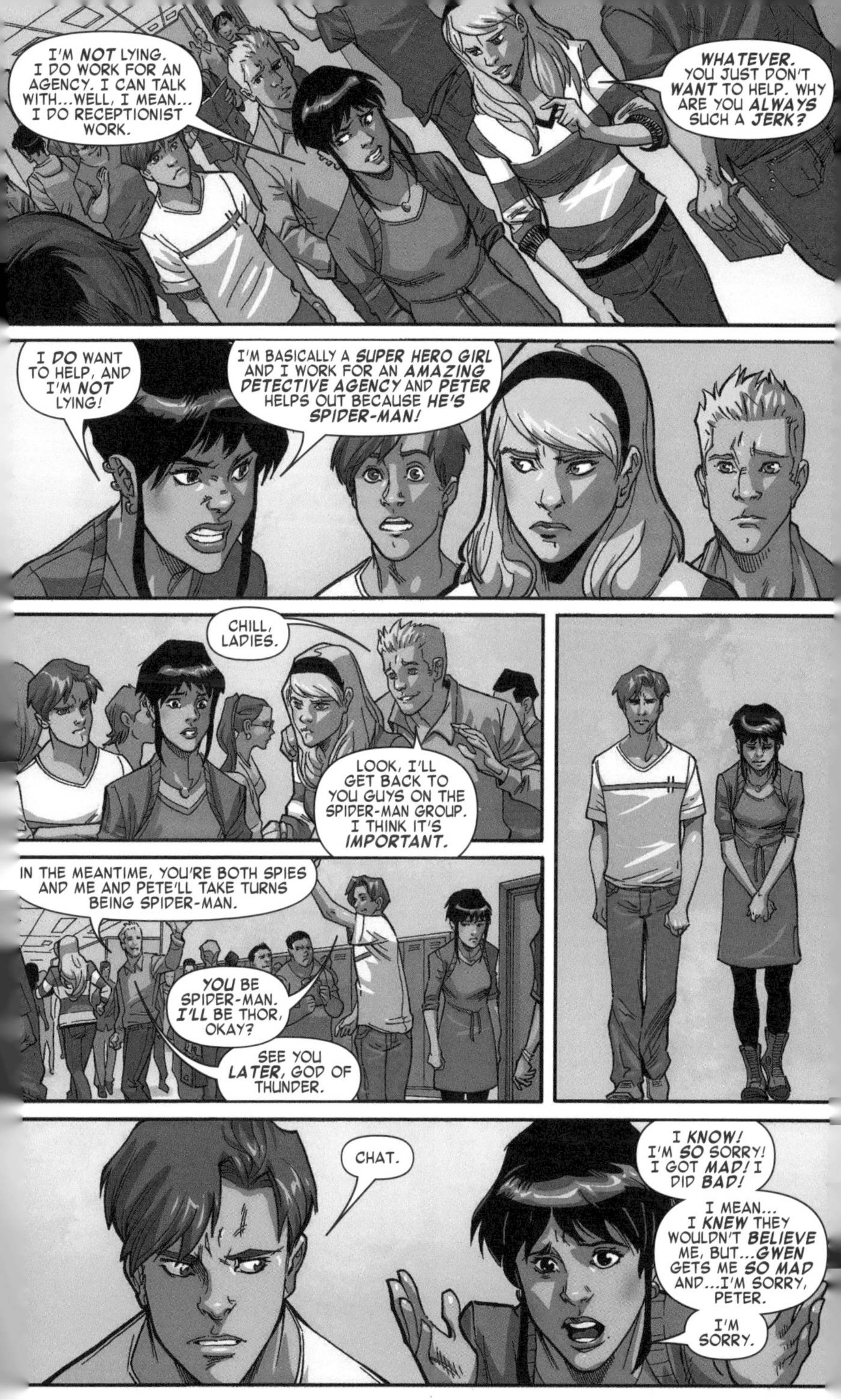
I'M NOT LYING. I DO WORK FOR AN AGENCY. I CAN TALK WITH...WELL, I MEAN... I DO RECEPTIONIST WORK.
WHATEVER. YOU JUST DON'T WANT TO HELP. WHY ARE YOU ALWAYS SUCH A JERK?
I DO WANT TO HELP, AND I'M NOT LYING!
I'M BASICALLY A SUPER HERO GIRL AND I WORK FOR AN AMAZING DETECTIVE AGENCY AND PETER HELPS OUT BECAUSE HE'S SPIDER-MAN!
CHILL, LADIES.
LOOK, I'LL GET BACK TO YOU GUYS ON THE SPIDER-MAN GROUP. I THINK IT'S IMPORTANT.
IN THE MEANTIME, YOU'RE BOTH SPIES AND ME AND PETE'LL TAKE TURNS BEING SPIDER-MAN.
YOU BE SPIDER-MAN. I'LL BE THOR, OKAY?
SEE YOU LATER, GOD OF THUNDER.
CHAT.
I KNOW! I'M SO SORRY! I GOT MAD! I DID BAD!
I MEAN... I KNEW THEY WOULDN'T BELIEVE ME, BUT...GWEN GETS ME SO MAD AND...I'M SORRY, PETER.
I'M SORRY.

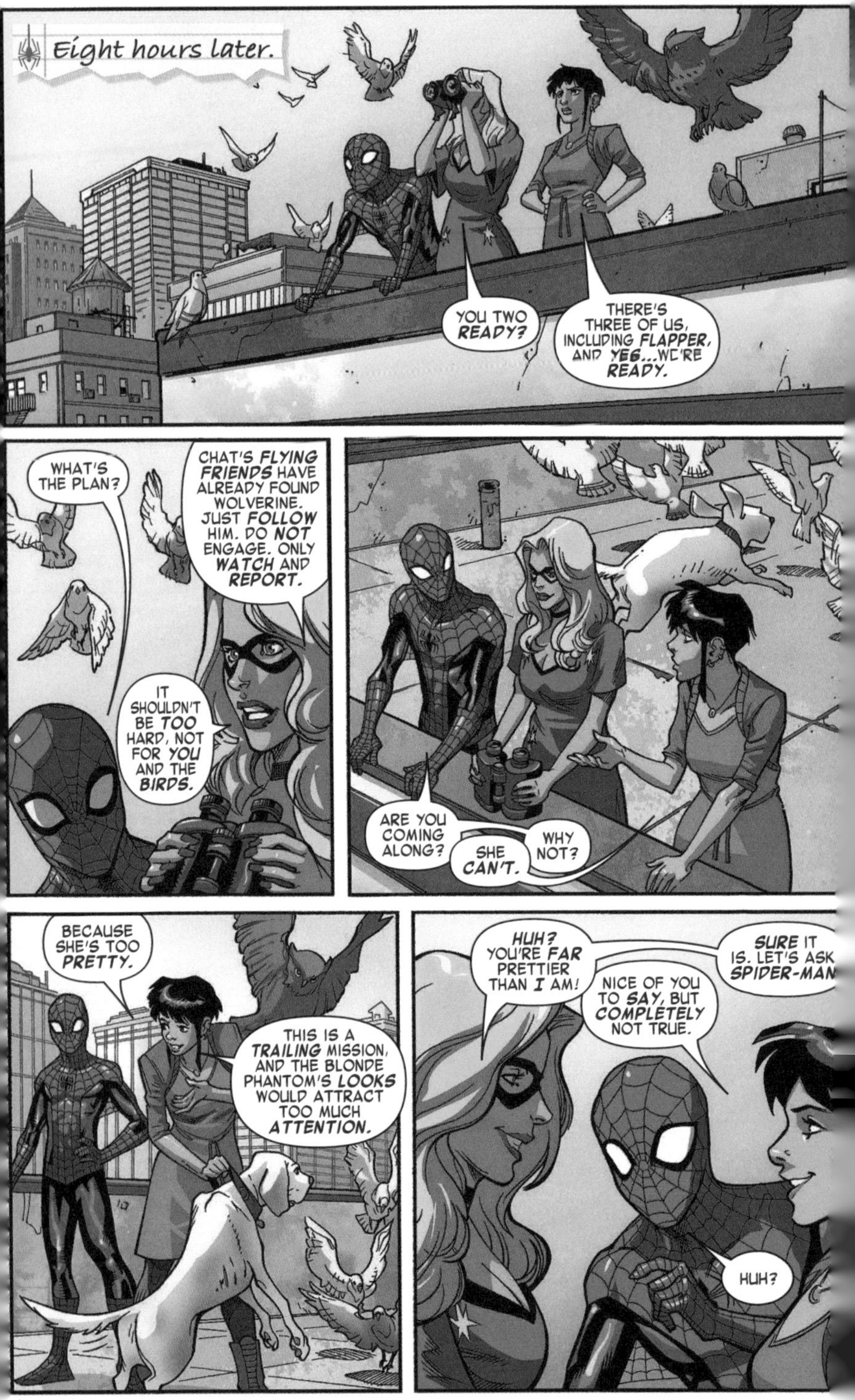

Eight hours later.
YOU TWO READY?
THERE'S THREE OF US, INCLUDING FLAPPER, AND YES...WE'RE READY.
WHAT'S THE PLAN?
CHAT'S FLYING FRIENDS HAVE ALREADY FOUND WOLVERINE. JUST FOLLOW HIM. DO NOT ENGAGE. ONLY WATCH AND REPORT.
IT SHOULDN'T BE TOO HARD, NOT FOR YOU AND THE BIRDS.
ARE YOU COMING ALONG?
SHE CAN'T.
WHY NOT?
BECAUSE SHE'S TOO PRETTY.
THIS IS A TRAILING MISSION, AND THE BLONDE PHANTOM'S LOOKS WOULD ATTRACT TOO MUCH ATTENTION.
HUH? YOU'RE FAR PRETTIER THAN I AM!
NICE OF YOU TO SAY, BUT COMPLETELY NOT TRUE.
SURE IT IS. LET'S ASK SPIDER-MAN
HUH?

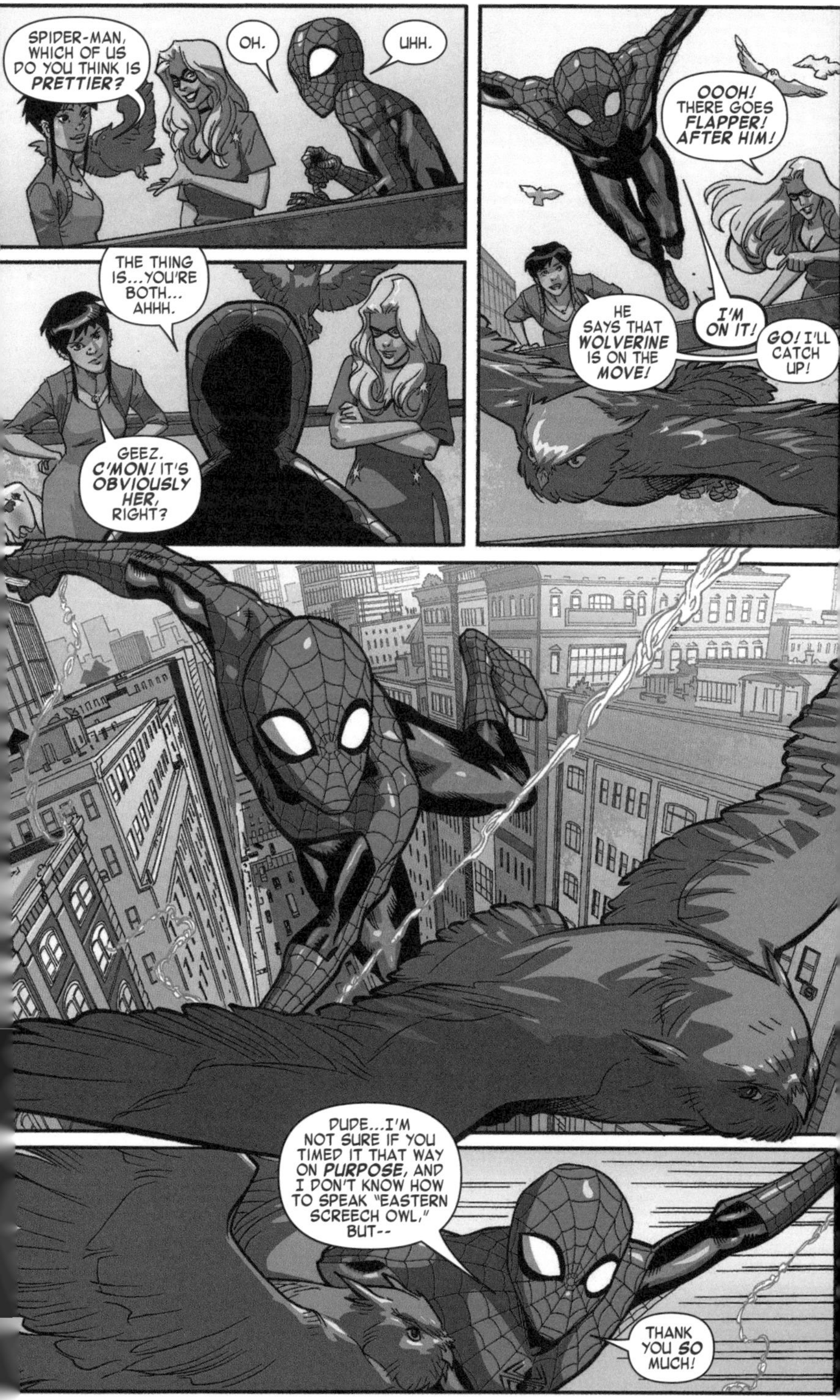
SPIDER-MAN, WHICH OF US DO YOU THINK IS PRETTIER?
OH.
UHH.
OOOH! THERE GOES FLAPPER! AFTER HIM!
THE THING IS...YOU'RE BOTH... AHHH.
GEEZ. C'MON! IT'S OBVIOUSLY HER, RIGHT?
HE SAYS THAT WOLVERINE IS ON THE MOVE!
I'M ON IT!
GO! I'LL CATCH UP!
DUDE...I'M NOT SURE IF YOU TIMED IT THAT WAY ON PURPOSE, AND I DON'T KNOW HOW TO SPEAK "EASTERN SCREECH OWL," BUT--
THANK YOU SO MUCH!

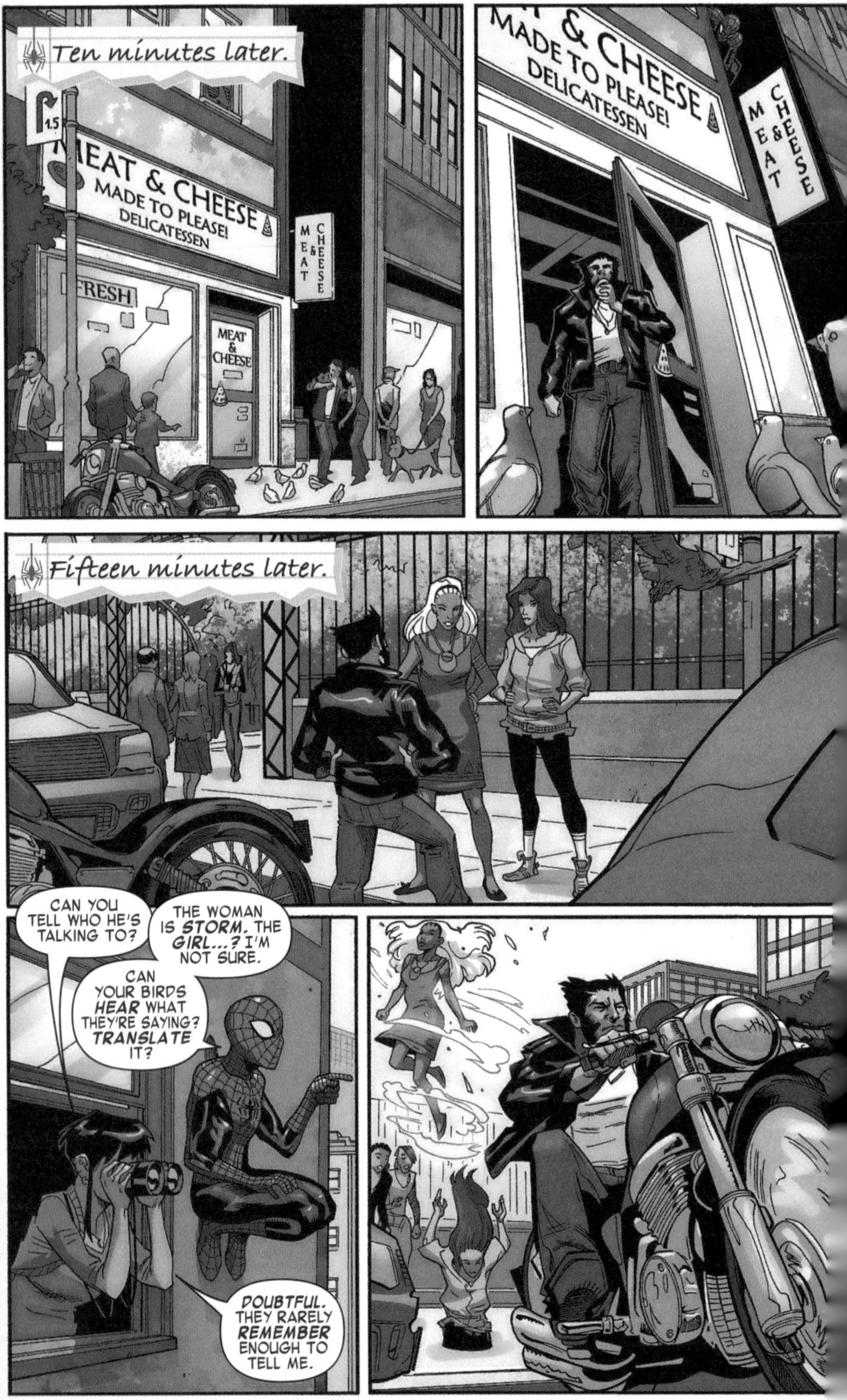

Ten minutes later.
MEAT & CHEESE
MADE TO PLEASE!
DELICATESSEN
FRESH
MEAT & CHEESE
Fifteen minutes later.
CAN YOU TELL WHO HE'S TALKING TO?
THE WOMAN IS STORM. THE GIRL...? I'M NOT SURE.
CAN YOUR BIRDS HEAR WHAT THEY'RE SAYING? TRANSLATE IT?
DOUBTFUL. THEY RARELY REMEMBER ENOUGH TO TELL ME.

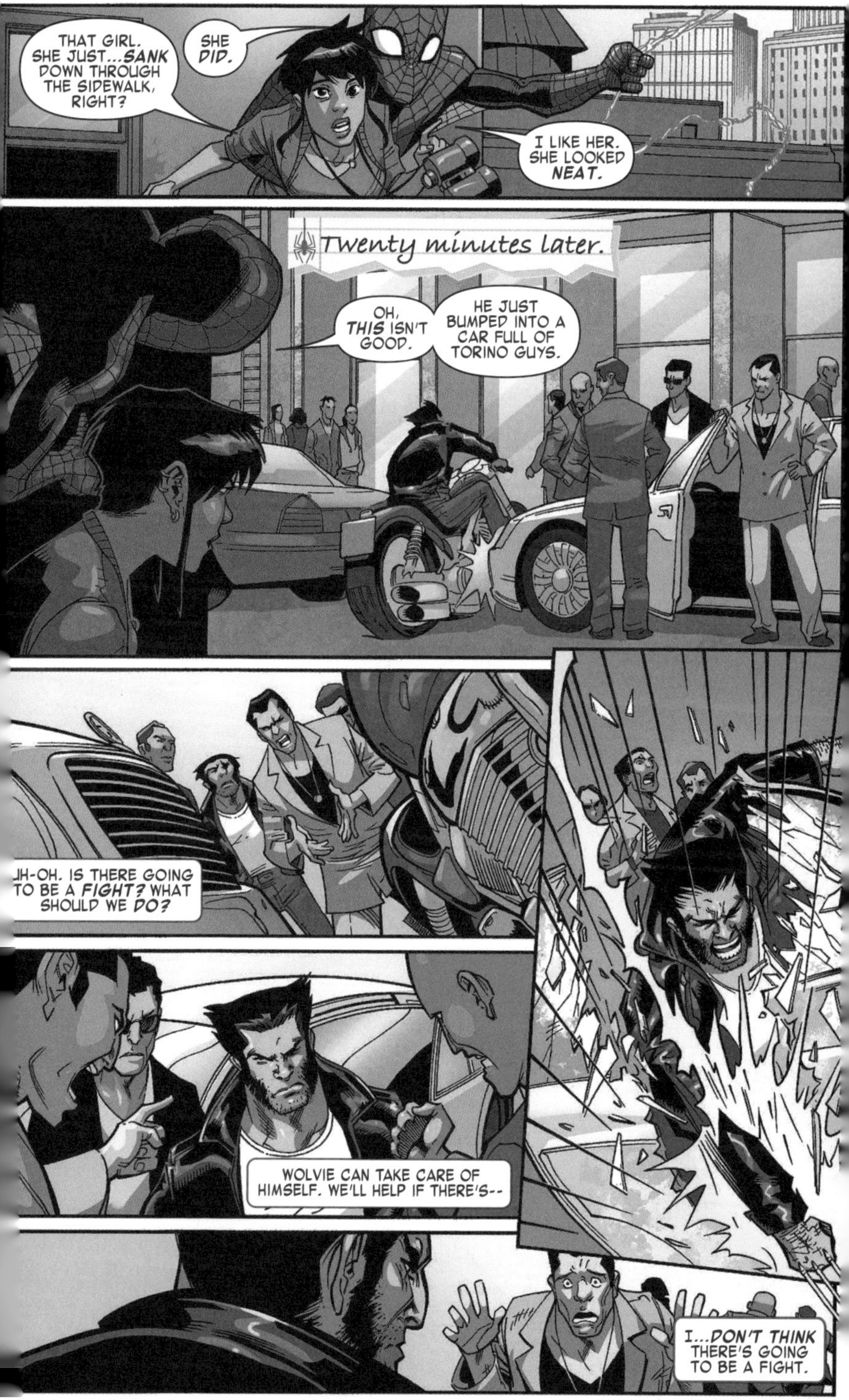

THAT GIRL. SHE JUST...SANK DOWN THROUGH THE SIDEWALK, RIGHT?
SHE DID.
I LIKE HER. SHE LOOKED NEAT.
Twenty minutes later.
OH, THIS ISN'T GOOD.
HE JUST BUMPED INTO A CAR FULL OF TORINO GUYS.
UH-OH. IS THERE GOING TO BE A FIGHT? WHAT SHOULD WE DO?
WOLVIE CAN TAKE CARE OF HIMSELF. WE'LL HELP IF THERE'S--
I...DON'T THINK THERE'S GOING TO BE A FIGHT.

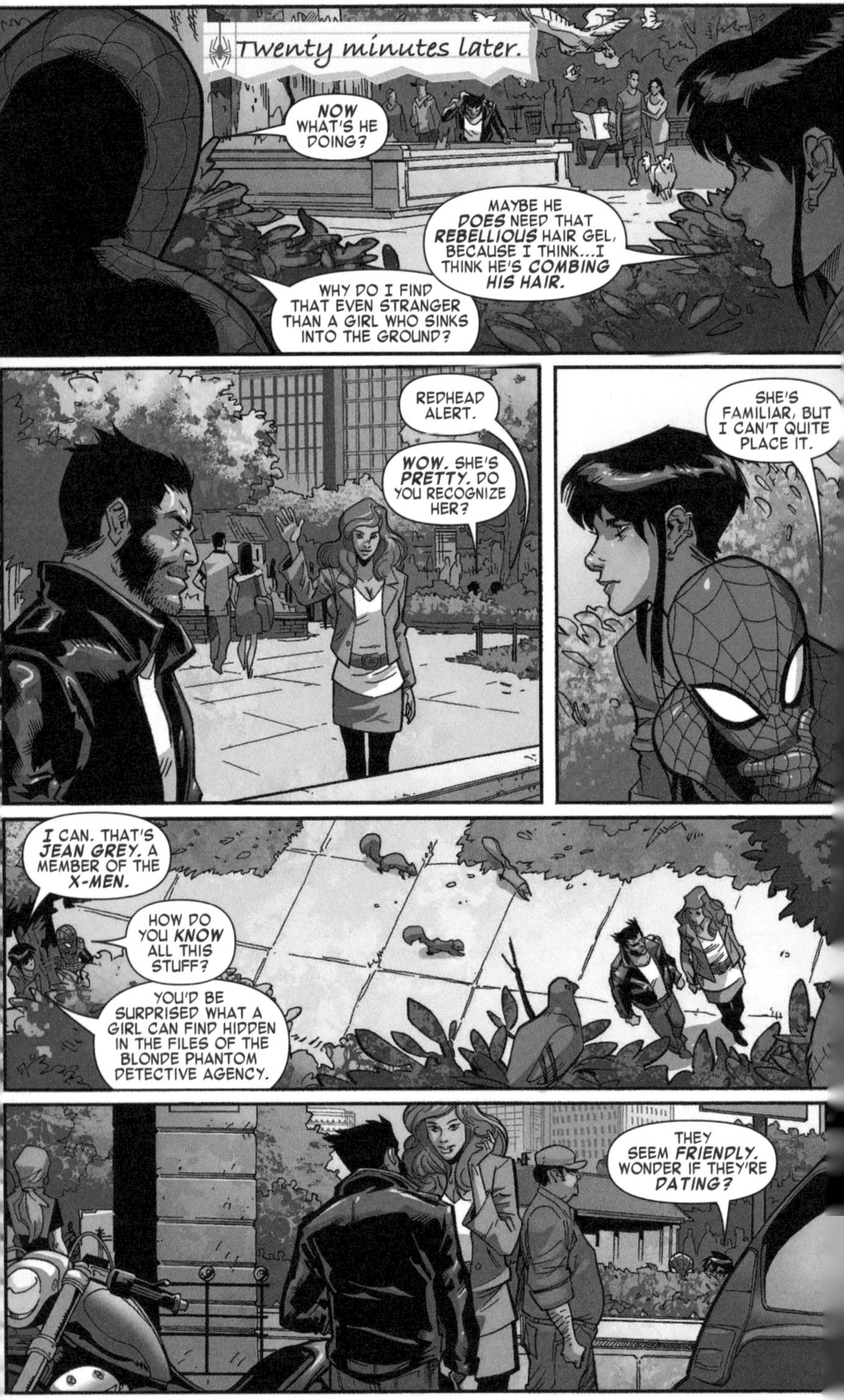
Twenty minutes later.
NOW WHAT'S HE DOING?
MAYBE HE DOES NEED THAT REBELLIOUS HAIR GEL, BECAUSE I THINK...I THINK HE'S COMBING HIS HAIR.
WHY DO I FIND THAT EVEN STRANGER THAN A GIRL WHO SINKS INTO THE GROUND?
REDHEAD ALERT.
WOW. SHE'S PRETTY. DO YOU RECOGNIZE HER?
SHE'S FAMILIAR, BUT I CAN'T QUITE PLACE IT.
I CAN. THAT'S JEAN GREY. A MEMBER OF THE X-MEN.
HOW DO YOU KNOW ALL THIS STUFF?
YOU'D BE SURPRISED WHAT A GIRL CAN FIND HIDDEN IN THE FILES OF THE BLONDE PHANTOM DETECTIVE AGENCY.
THEY SEEM FRIENDLY. WONDER IF THEY'RE DATING?

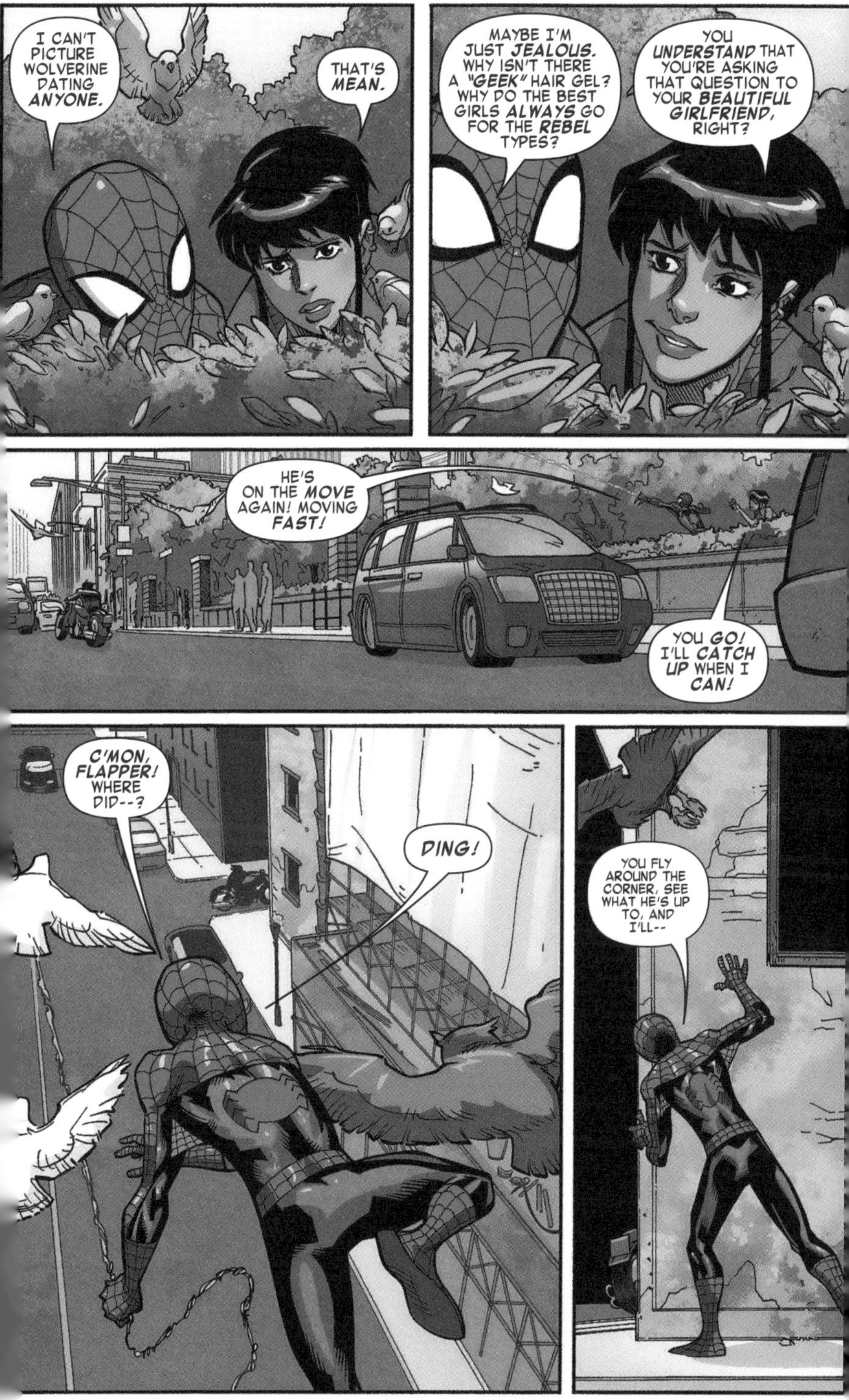
I CAN'T PICTURE WOLVERINE DATING ANYONE.
THAT'S MEAN.
MAYBE I'M JUST JEALOUS. WHY ISN'T THERE A "GEEK" HAIR GEL? WHY DO THE BEST GIRLS ALWAYS GO FOR THE REBEL TYPES?
YOU UNDERSTAND THAT YOU'RE ASKING THAT QUESTION TO YOUR BEAUTIFUL GIRLFRIEND, RIGHT?
HE'S ON THE MOVE AGAIN! MOVING FAST!
YOU GO! I'LL CATCH UP WHEN I CAN!
C'MON, FLAPPER! WHERE DID--?
DING!
YOU FLY AROUND THE CORNER, SEE WHAT HE'S UP TO, AND I'LL--

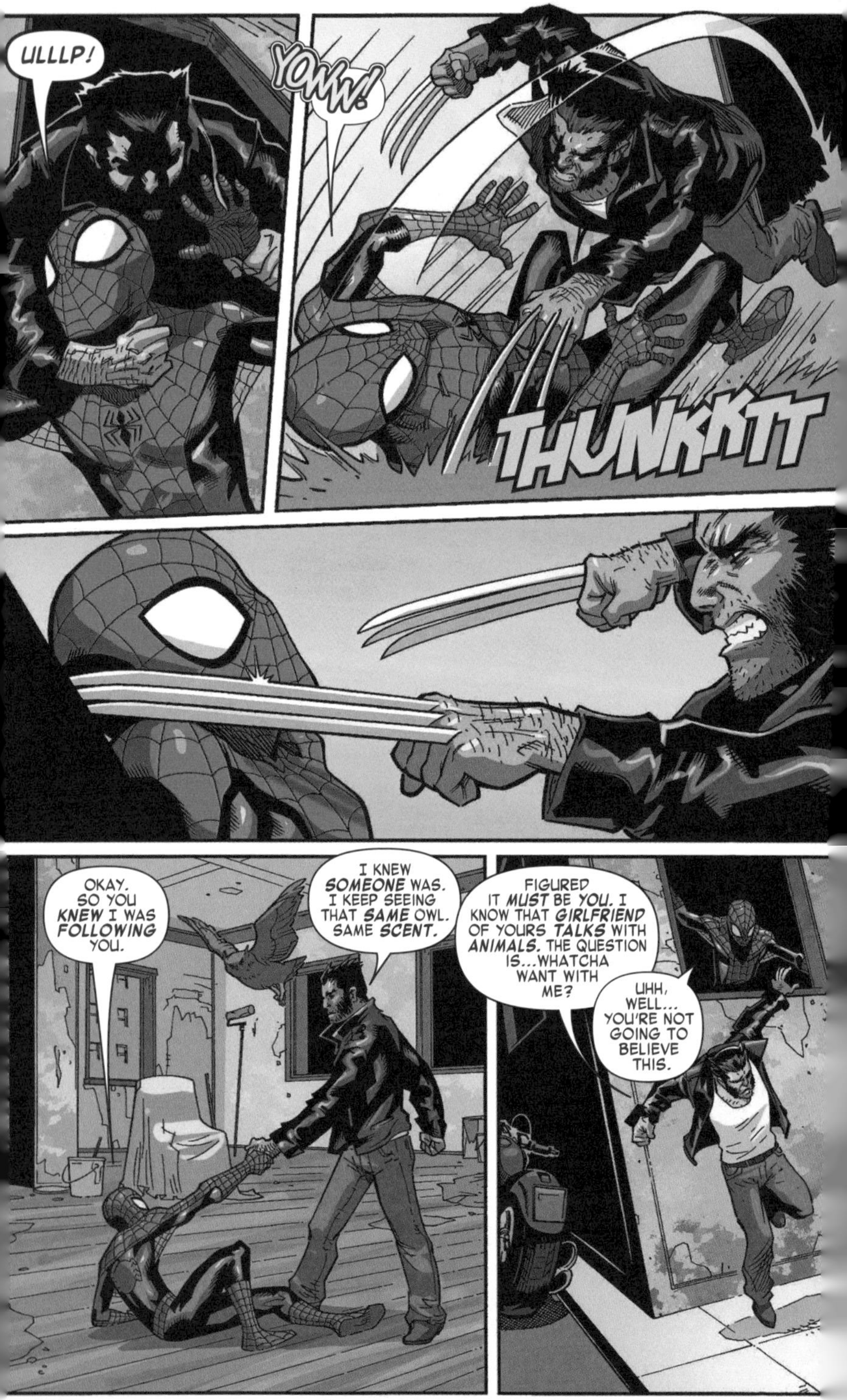
ULLLP!
YOWW!
THUNKKTT
OKAY. SO YOU KNEW I WAS FOLLOWING YOU.
I KNEW SOMEONE WAS. I KEEP SEEING THAT SAME OWL. SAME SCENT.
FIGURED IT MUST BE YOU. I KNOW THAT GIRLFRIEND OF YOURS TALKS WITH ANIMALS. THE QUESTION IS...WHATCHA WANT WITH ME?
UHH, WELL... YOU'RE NOT GOING TO BELIEVE THIS.

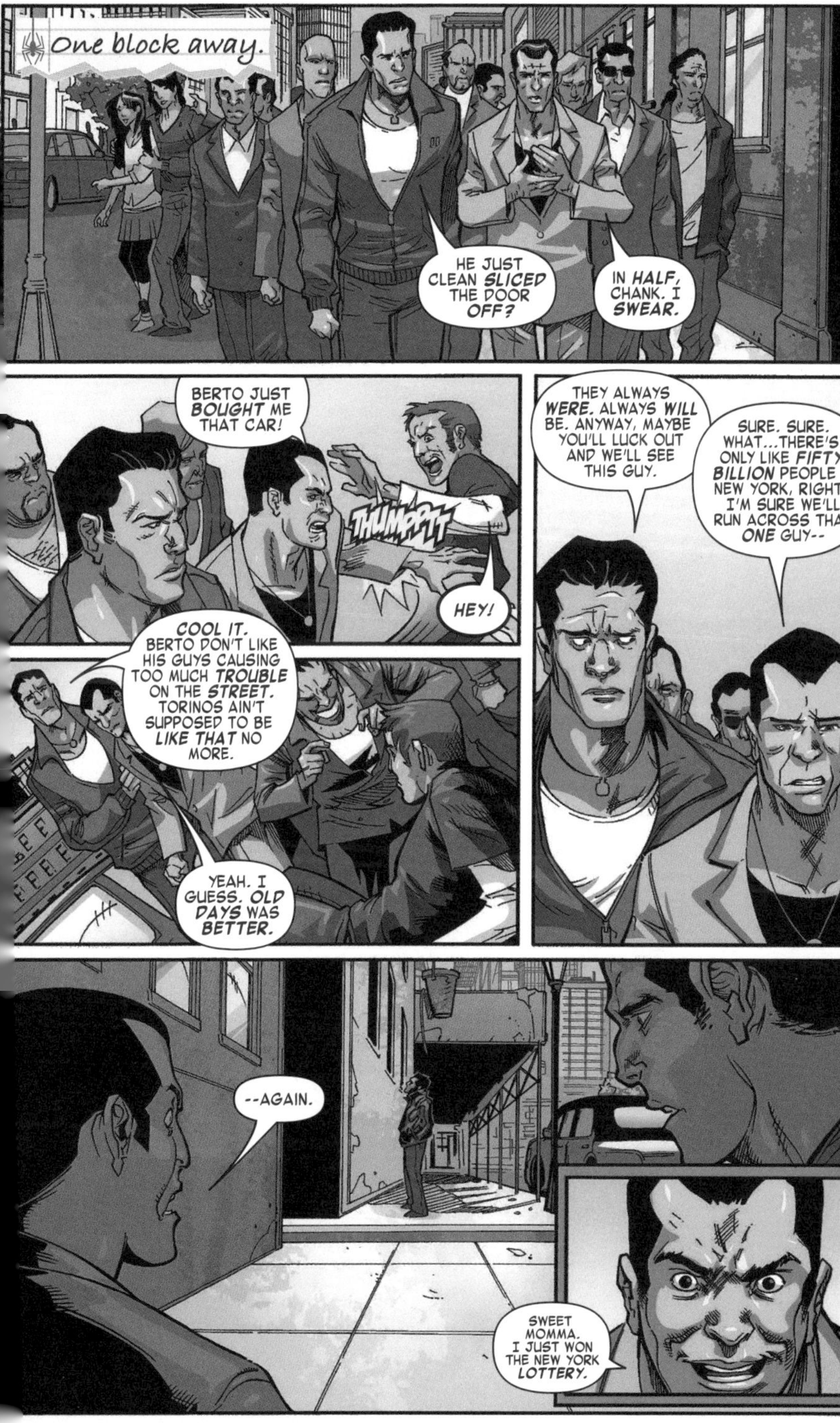
One block away.
HE JUST CLEAN SLICED THE DOOR OFF?
IN HALF, CHANK. I SWEAR.
BERTO JUST BOUGHT ME THAT CAR!
THUMPPT
HEY!
COOL IT. BERTO DON'T LIKE HIS GUYS CAUSING TOO MUCH TROUBLE ON THE STREET. TORINOS AIN'T SUPPOSED TO BE LIKE THAT NO MORE.
YEAH. I GUESS. OLD DAYS WAS BETTER.
THEY ALWAYS WERE. ALWAYS WILL BE. ANYWAY, MAYBE YOU'LL LUCK OUT AND WE'LL SEE THIS GUY.
SURE. SURE. WHAT...THERE'S ONLY LIKE FIFTY BILLION PEOPLE IN NEW YORK, RIGHT? I'M SURE WE'LL RUN ACROSS THAT ONE GUY--
--AGAIN.
SWEET MOMMA. I JUST WON THE NEW YORK LOTTERY.

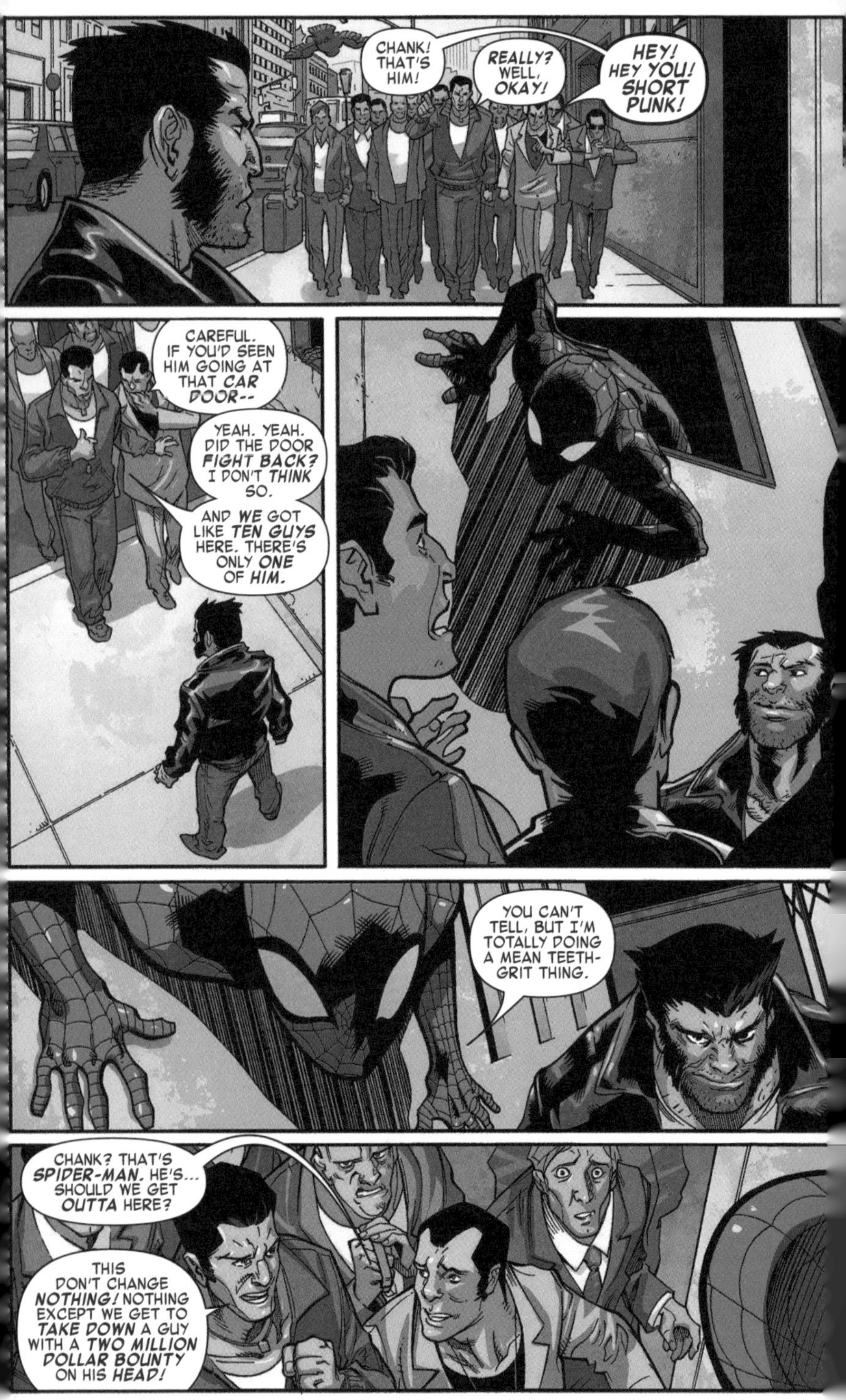

CHANK! THAT'S HIM!
REALLY? WELL, OKAY!
HEY! HEY YOU! SHORT PUNK!
CAREFUL. IF YOU'D SEEN HIM GOING AT THAT CAR DOOR--
YEAH. YEAH. DID THE DOOR FIGHT BACK? I DON'T THINK SO.
AND WE GOT LIKE TEN GUYS HERE. THERE'S ONLY ONE OF HIM.
YOU CAN'T TELL, BUT I'M TOTALLY DOING A MEAN TEETH-GRIT THING.
CHANK? THAT'S SPIDER-MAN. HE'S... SHOULD WE GET OUTTA HERE?
THIS DON'T CHANGE NOTHING! NOTHING EXCEPT WE GET TO TAKE DOWN A GUY WITH A TWO MILLION DOLLAR BOUNTY ON HIS HEAD!

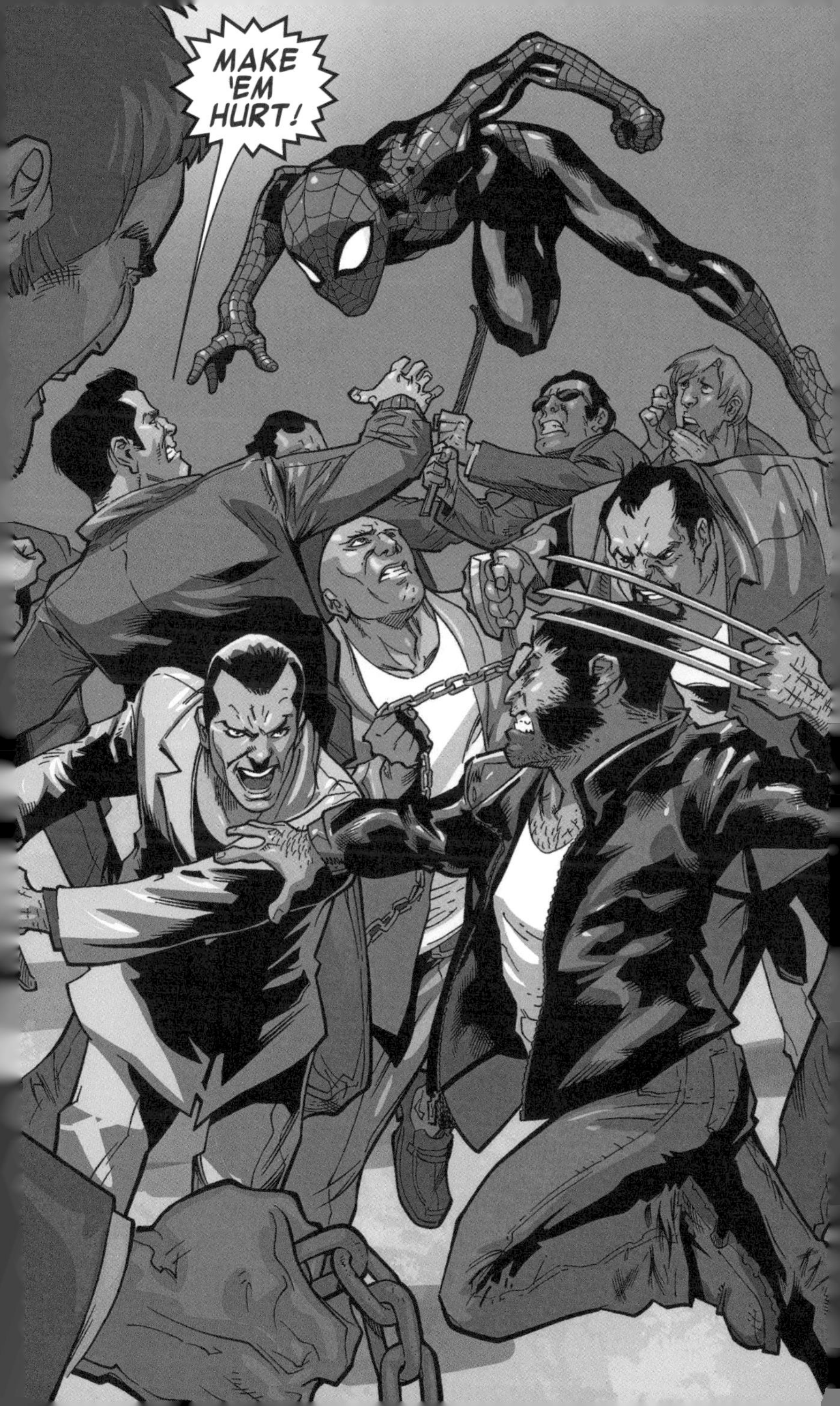
MAKE 'EM HURT!

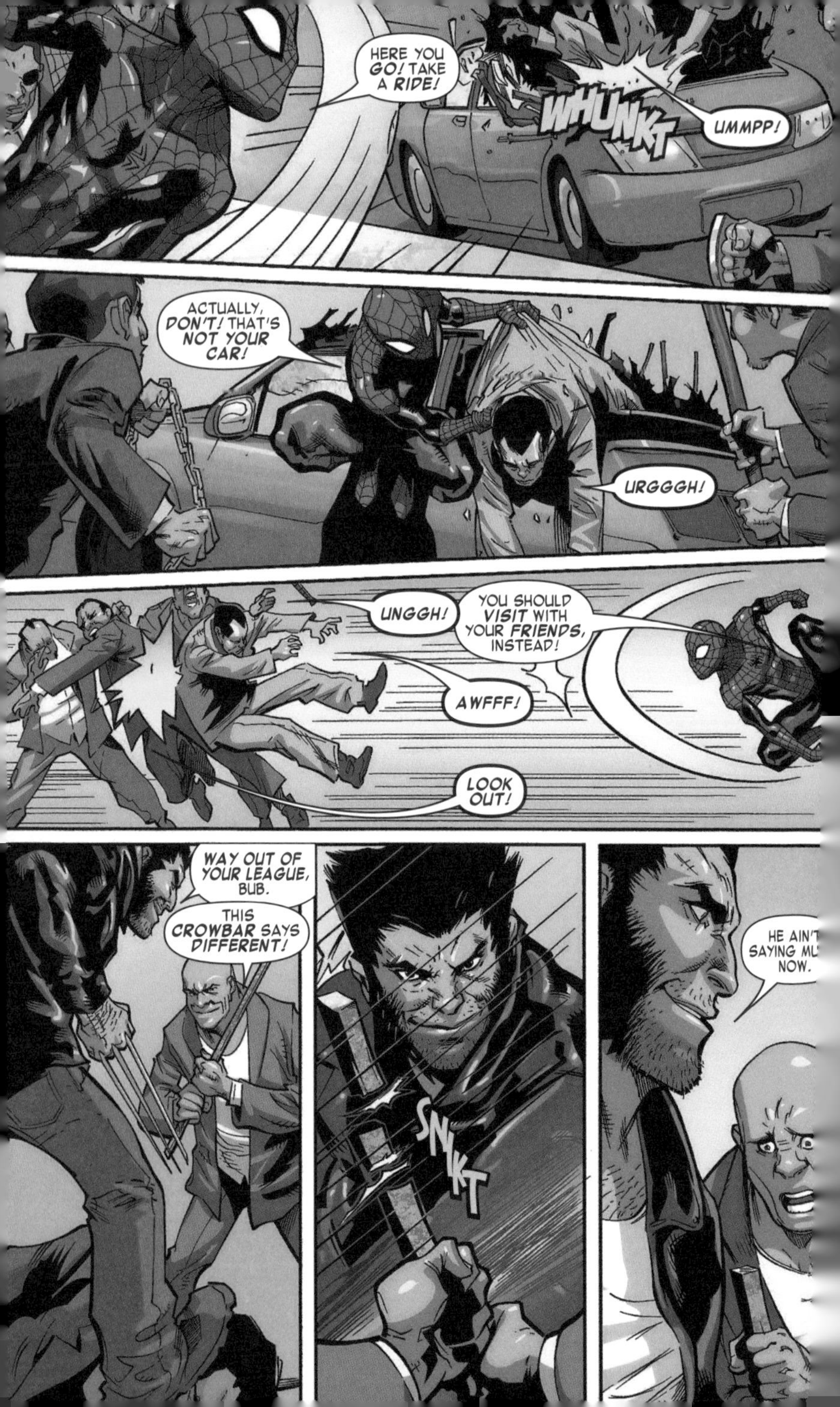
HERE YOU GO! TAKE A RIDE!
WHUNKT
UMMPP!
ACTUALLY, DON'T! THAT'S NOT YOUR CAR!
URGGGH!
UNGGH!
YOU SHOULD VISIT WITH YOUR FRIENDS, INSTEAD!
AWFFF!
LOOK OUT!
WAY OUT OF YOUR LEAGUE, BUB.
THIS CROWBAR SAYS DIFFERENT!
SNIKT
HE AIN'T SAYING MU
NOW.

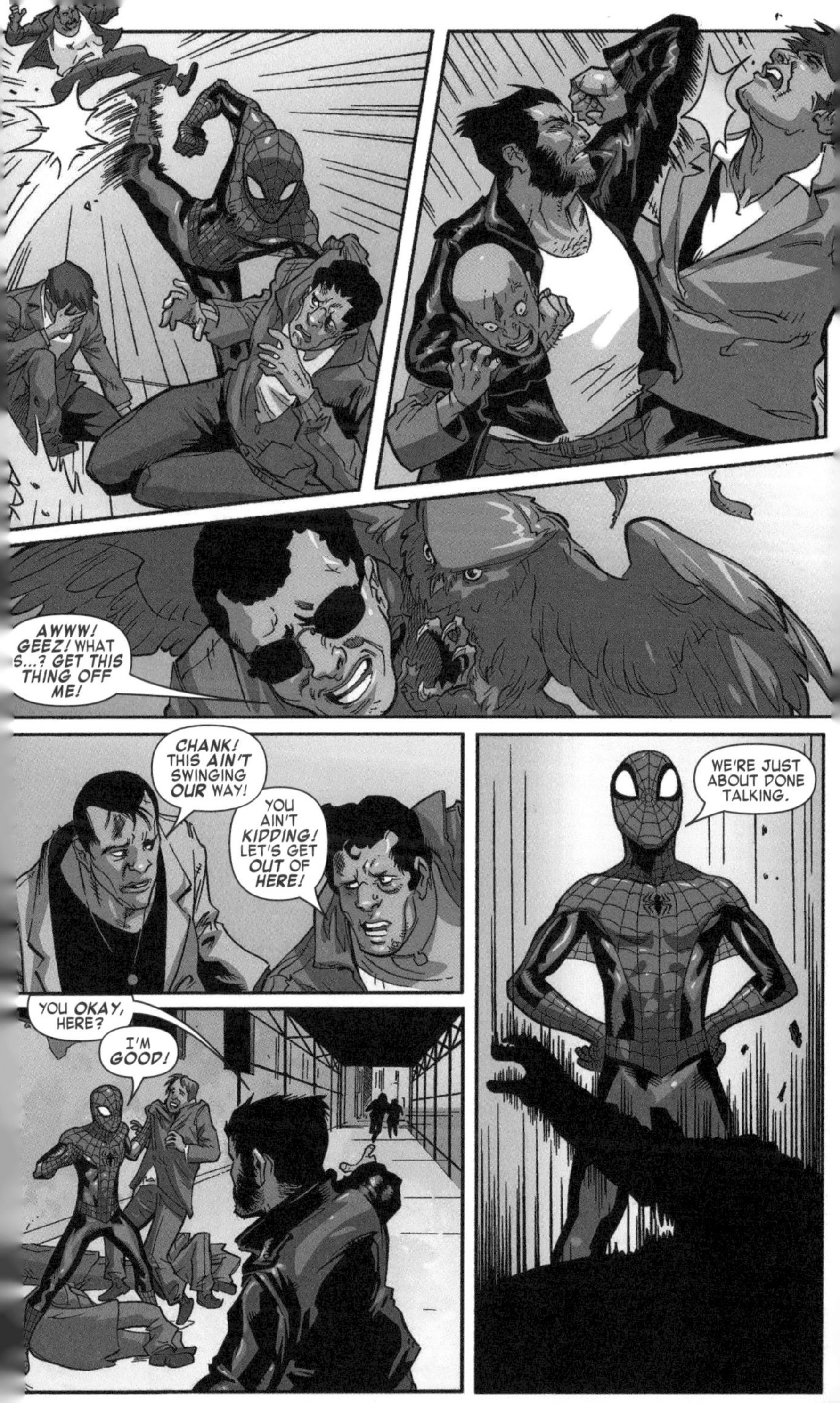
AWWW! GEEZ! WHAT S...? GET THIS THING OFF ME!
CHANK! THIS AIN'T SWINGING OUR WAY!
YOU AIN'T KIDDING! LET'S GET OUT OF HERE!
WE'RE JUST ABOUT DONE TALKING.
YOU OKAY, HERE?
I'M GOOD!

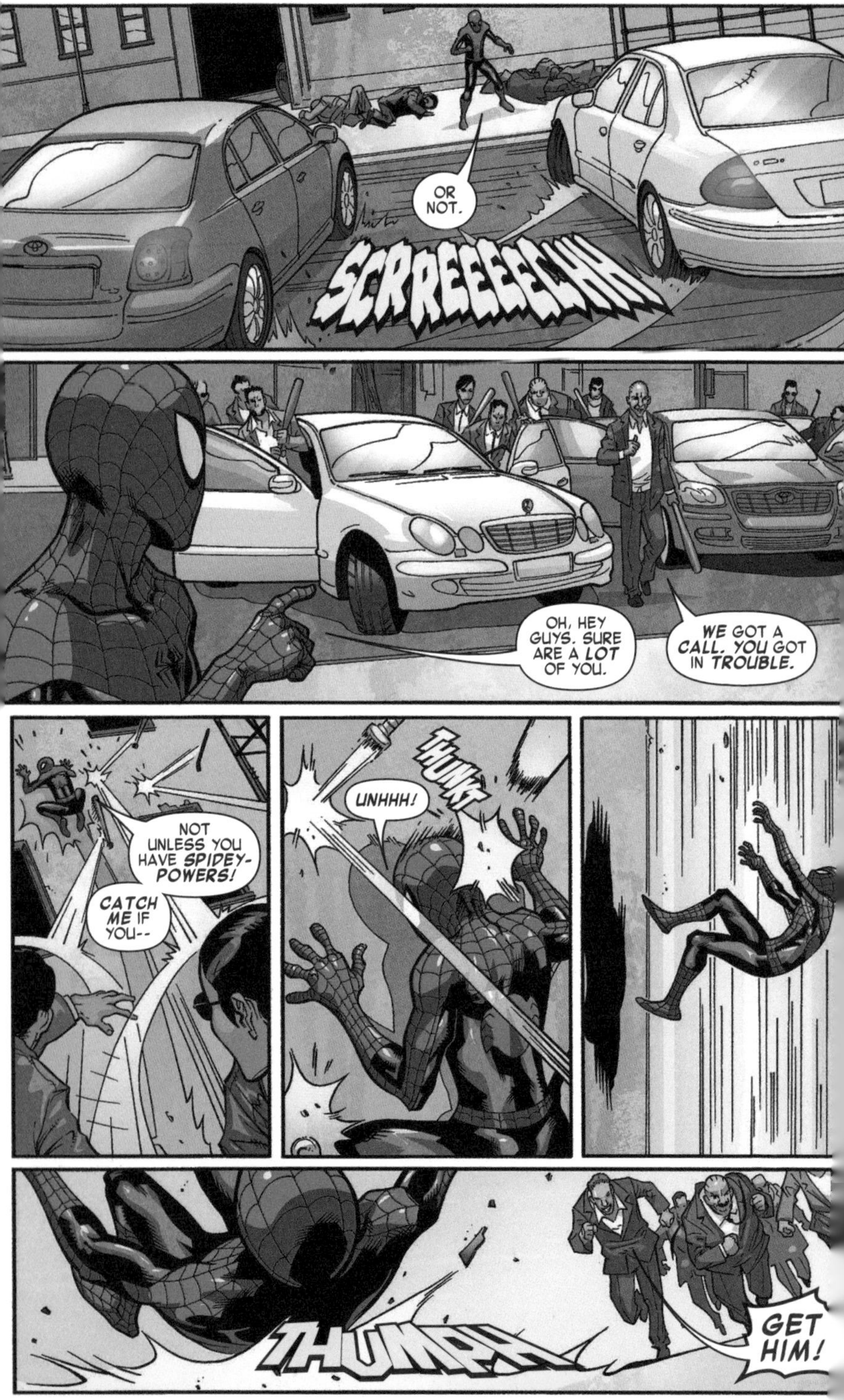
OR NOT.
SCRREEEECHH
OH, HEY GUYS. SURE ARE A LOT OF YOU.
WE GOT A CALL. YOU GOT IN TROUBLE.
NOT UNLESS YOU HAVE SPIDEY-POWERS!
CATCH ME IF YOU--
UNHHH!
THUNK
THUMPH
GET HIM!

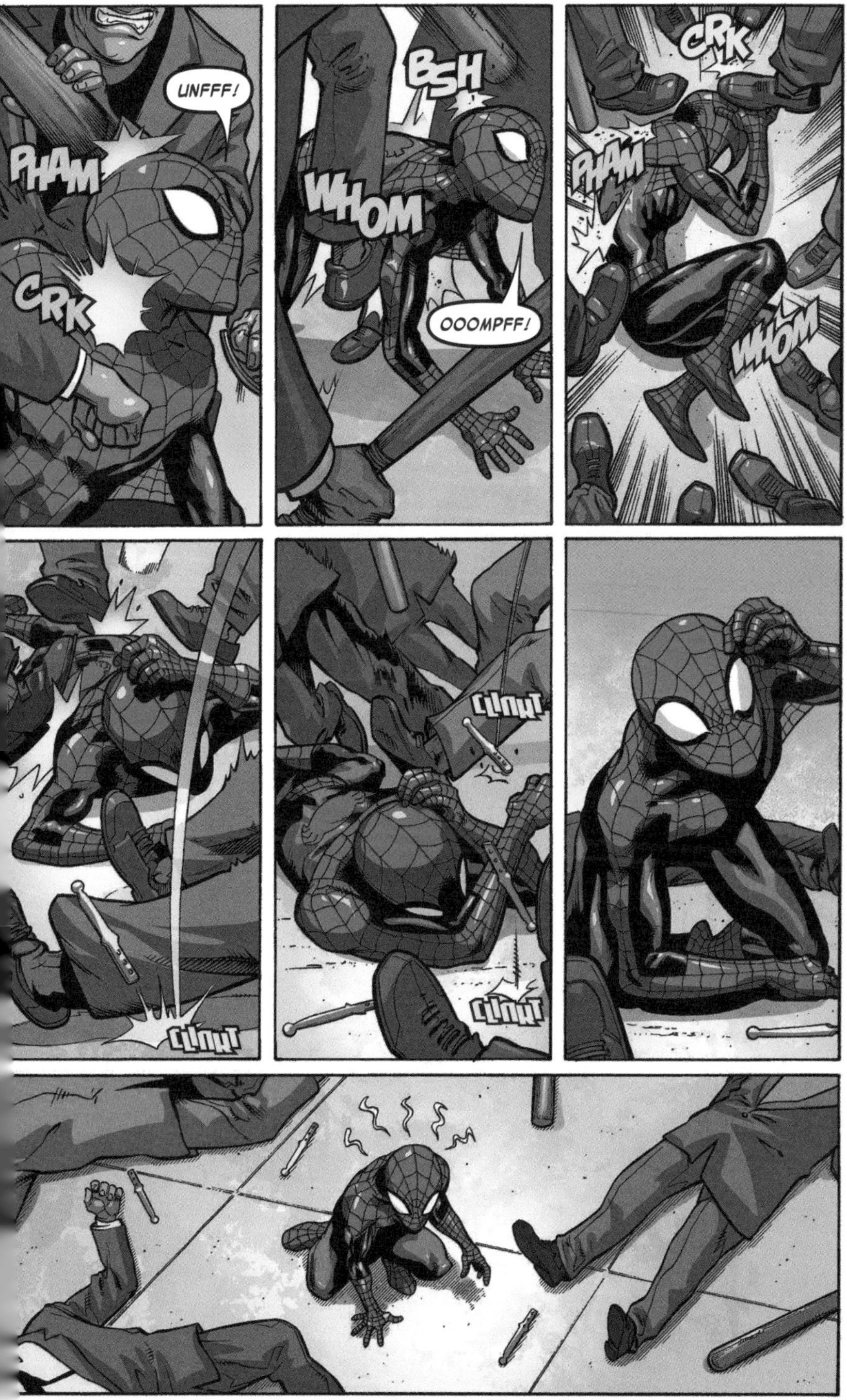
UNFFF!
PHAM
CRK
BSH
WHOM
OOOMPFF!
CRK
PHAM
WHOM
CLINK
CLINK
CLINK

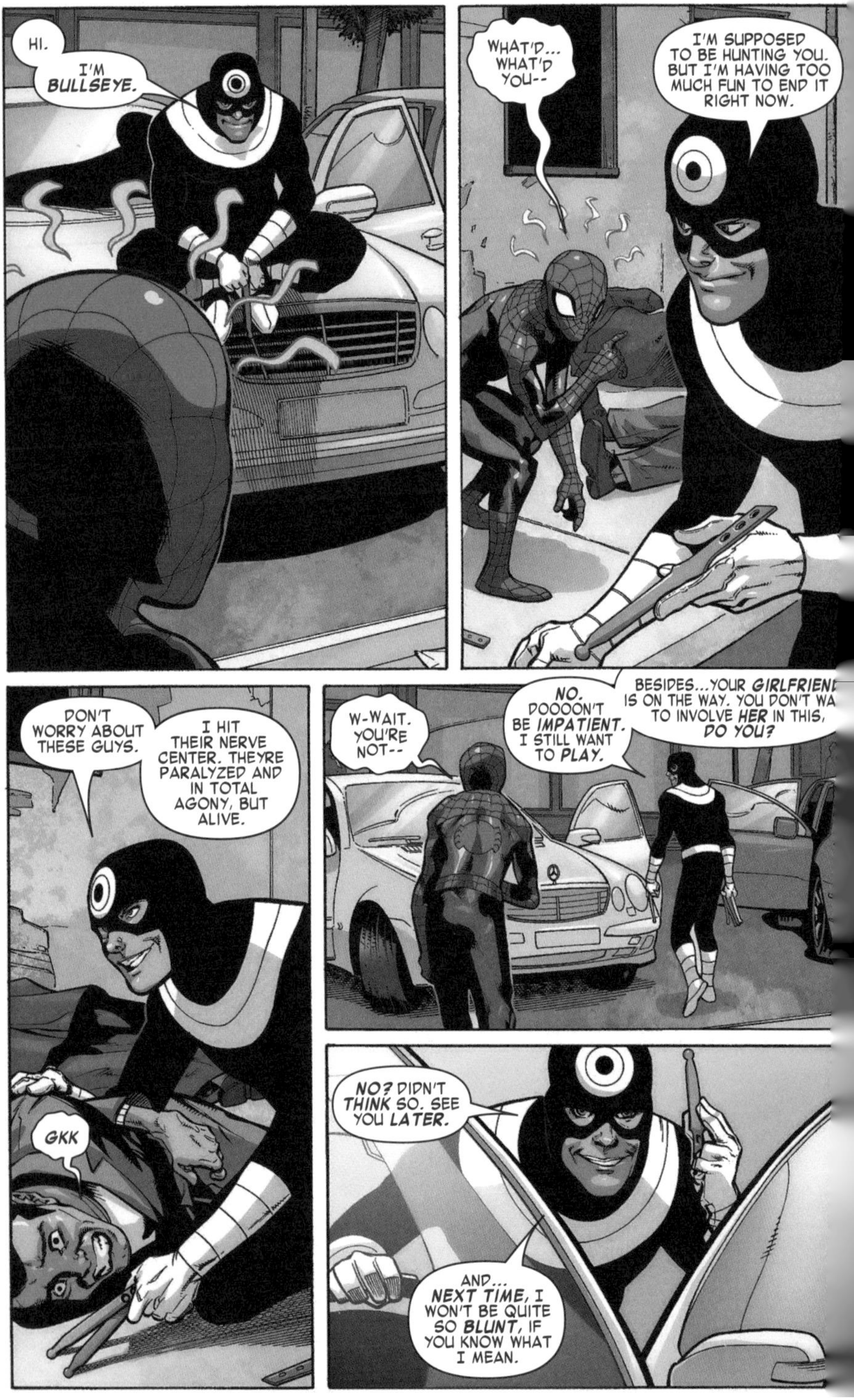
HI.
I'M BULLSEYE.
WHAT'D... WHAT'D YOU--
I'M SUPPOSED TO BE HUNTING YOU. BUT I'M HAVING TOO MUCH FUN TO END IT RIGHT NOW.
DON'T WORRY ABOUT THESE GUYS.
I HIT THEIR NERVE CENTER. THEYRE PARALYZED AND IN TOTAL AGONY, BUT ALIVE.
GKK
W-WAIT. YOU'RE NOT--
NO. DOOOON'T BE IMPATIENT. I STILL WANT TO PLAY.
BESIDES...YOUR GIRLFRIEND IS ON THE WAY. YOU DON'T WA TO INVOLVE HER IN THIS, DO YOU?
NO? DIDN'T THINK SO. SEE YOU LATER.
AND... NEXT TIME, I WON'T BE QUITE SO BLUNT, IF YOU KNOW WHAT I MEAN.

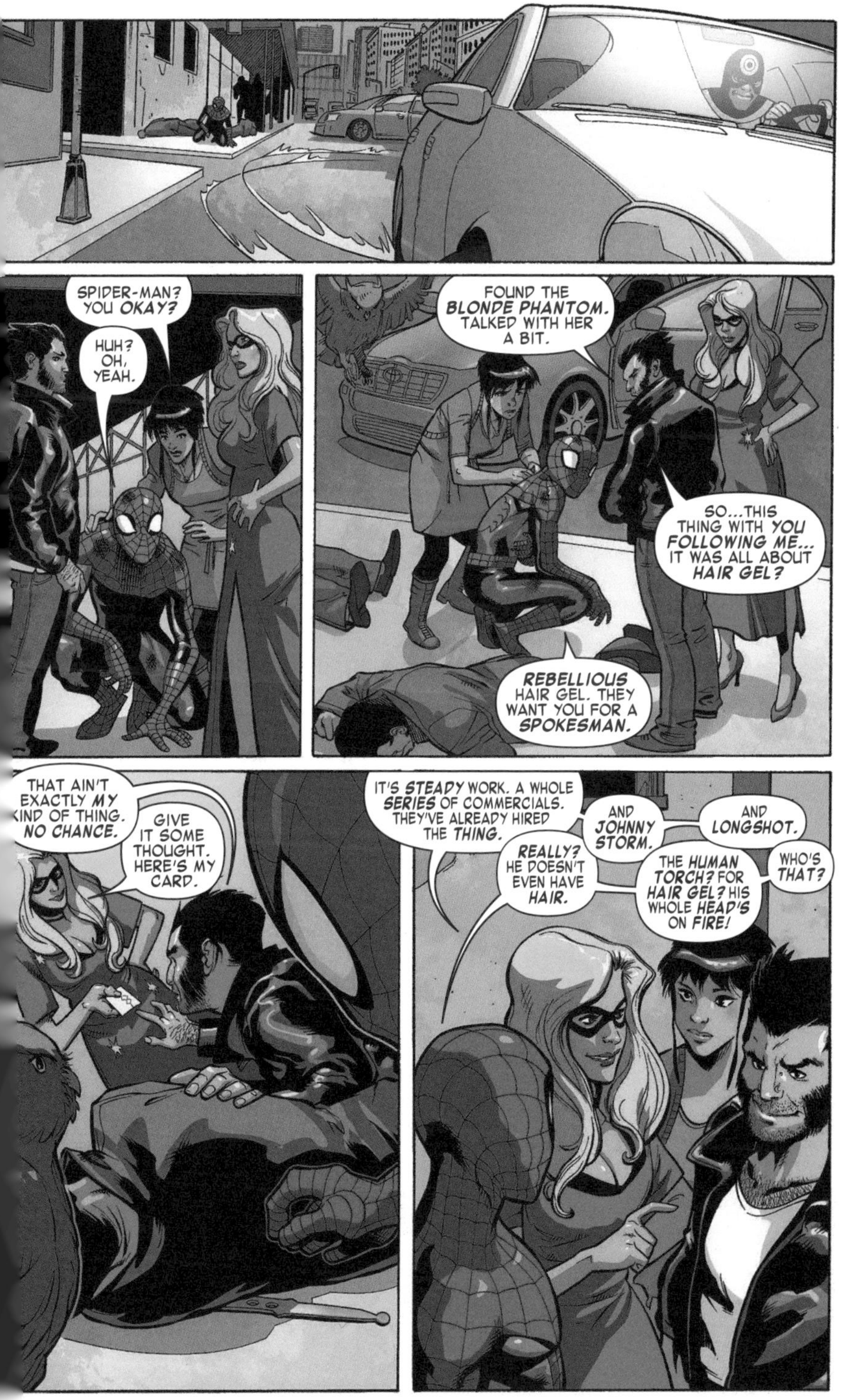

SPIDER-MAN? YOU OKAY?
HUH? OH, YEAH.
FOUND THE BLONDE PHANTOM. TALKED WITH HER A BIT.
SO...THIS THING WITH YOU FOLLOWING ME... IT WAS ALL ABOUT HAIR GEL?
REBELLIOUS HAIR GEL. THEY WANT YOU FOR A SPOKESMAN.
THAT AIN'T EXACTLY MY KIND OF THING. NO CHANCE.
GIVE IT SOME THOUGHT. HERE'S MY CARD.
IT'S STEADY WORK. A WHOLE SERIES OF COMMERCIALS. THEY'VE ALREADY HIRED THE THING.
REALLY? HE DOESN'T EVEN HAVE HAIR.
AND JOHNNY STORM.
THE HUMAN TORCH? FOR HAIR GEL? HIS WHOLE HEAD'S ON FIRE!
AND LONGSHOT.
WHO'S THAT?

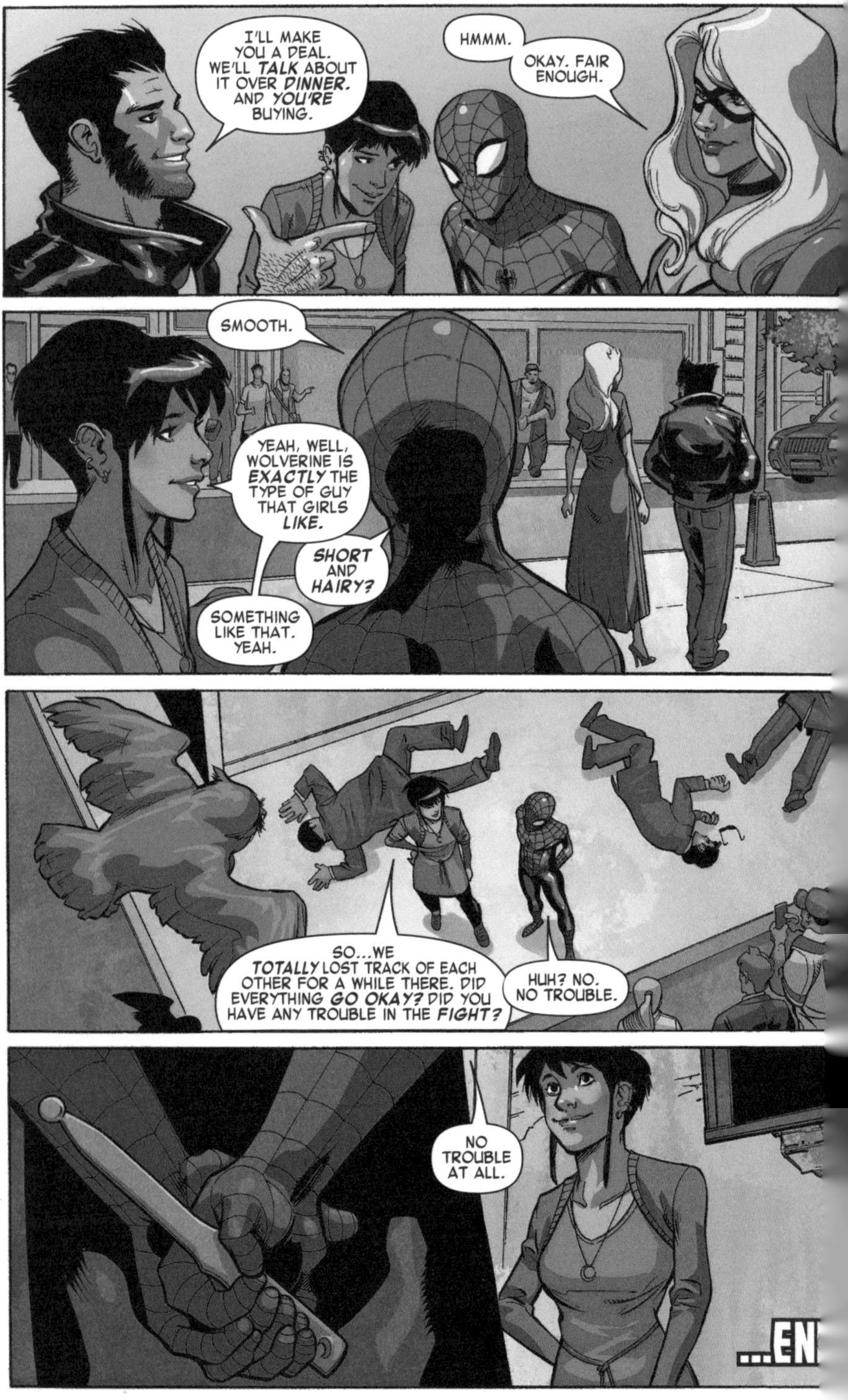

I'LL MAKE YOU A DEAL. WE'LL TALK ABOUT IT OVER DINNER. AND YOU'RE BUYING.
HMMM.
OKAY. FAIR ENOUGH.
SMOOTH.
YEAH, WELL, WOLVERINE IS EXACTLY THE TYPE OF GUY THAT GIRLS LIKE.
SHORT AND HAIRY?
SOMETHING LIKE THAT. YEAH.
SO...WE TOTALLY LOST TRACK OF EACH OTHER FOR A WHILE THERE. DID EVERYTHING GO OKAY? DID YOU HAVE ANY TROUBLE IN THE FIGHT?
HUH? NO. NO TROUBLE.
NO TROUBLE AT ALL.

BONUS PINUPS

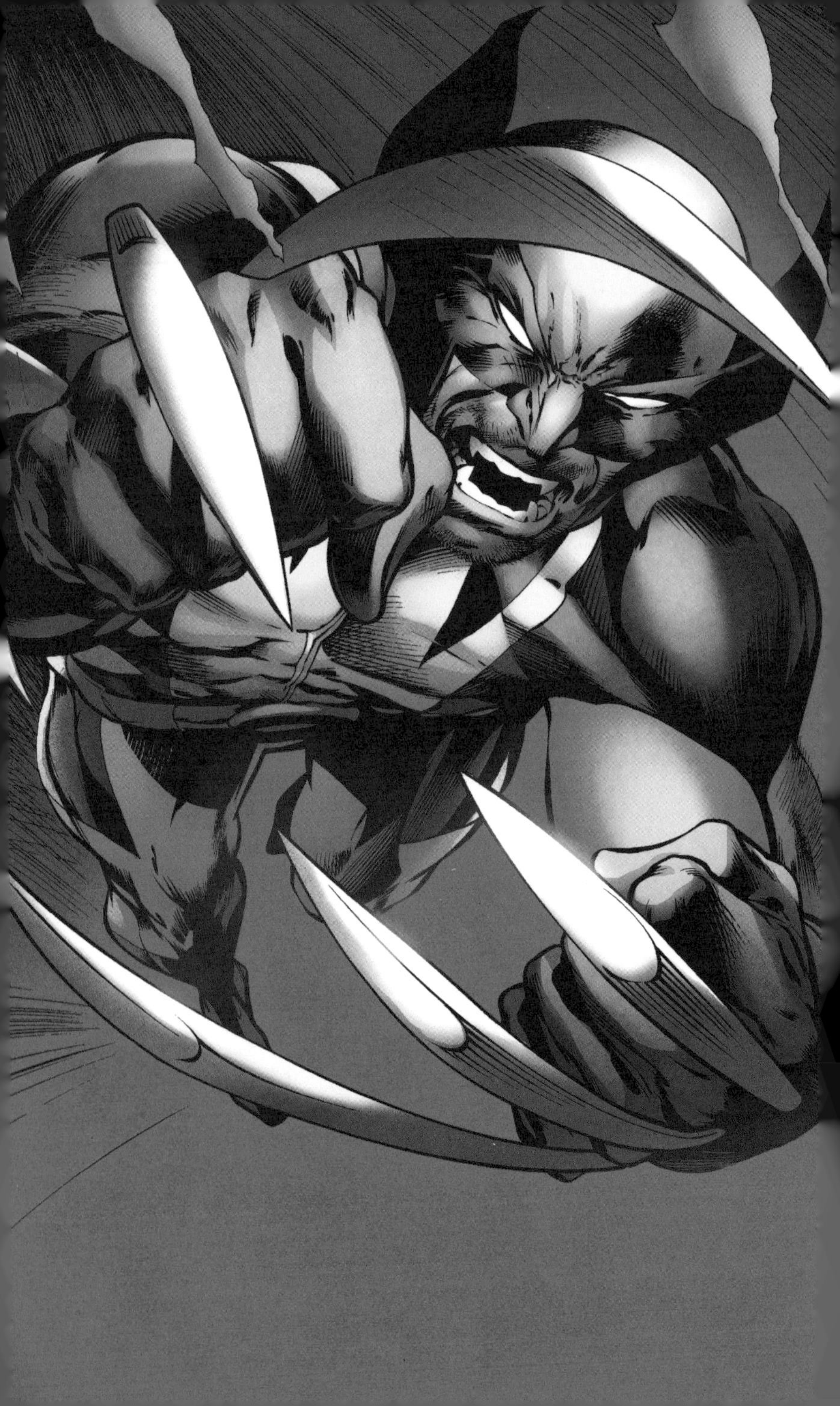

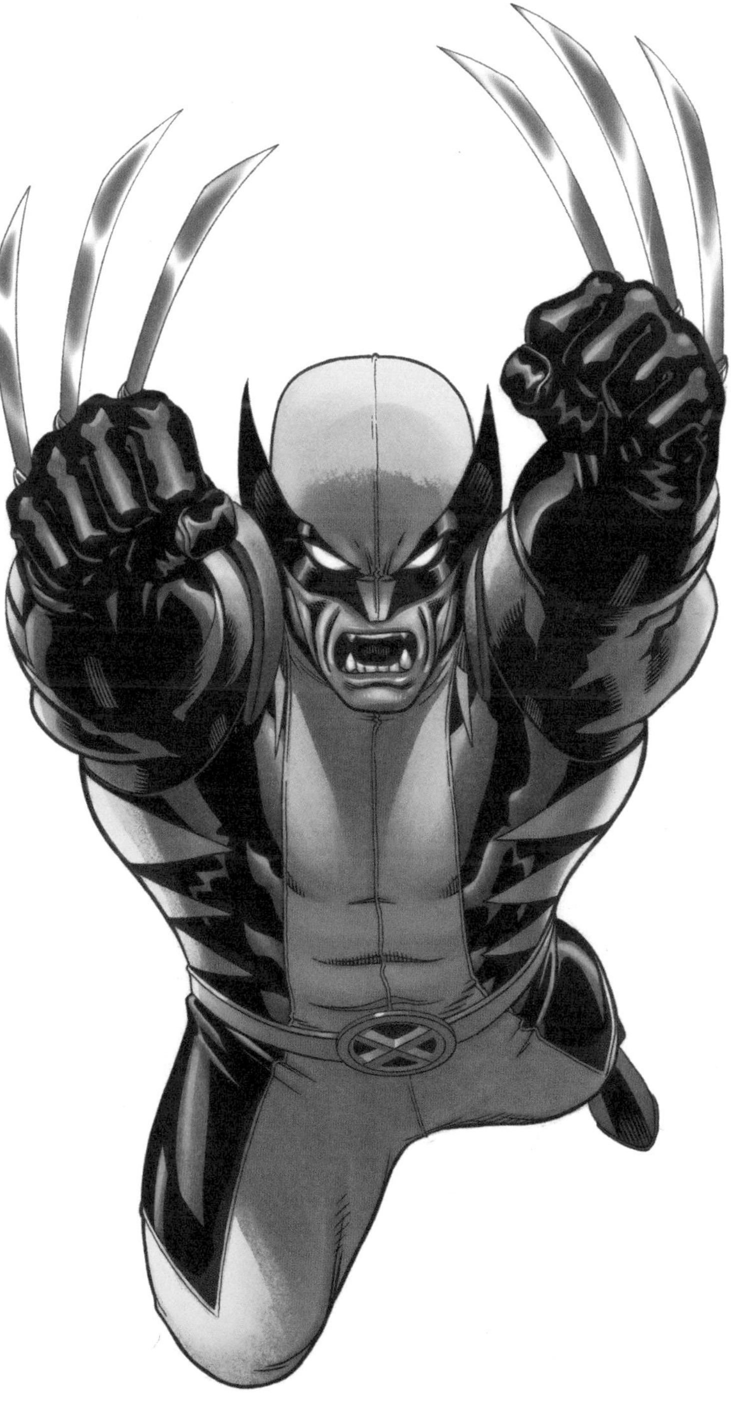

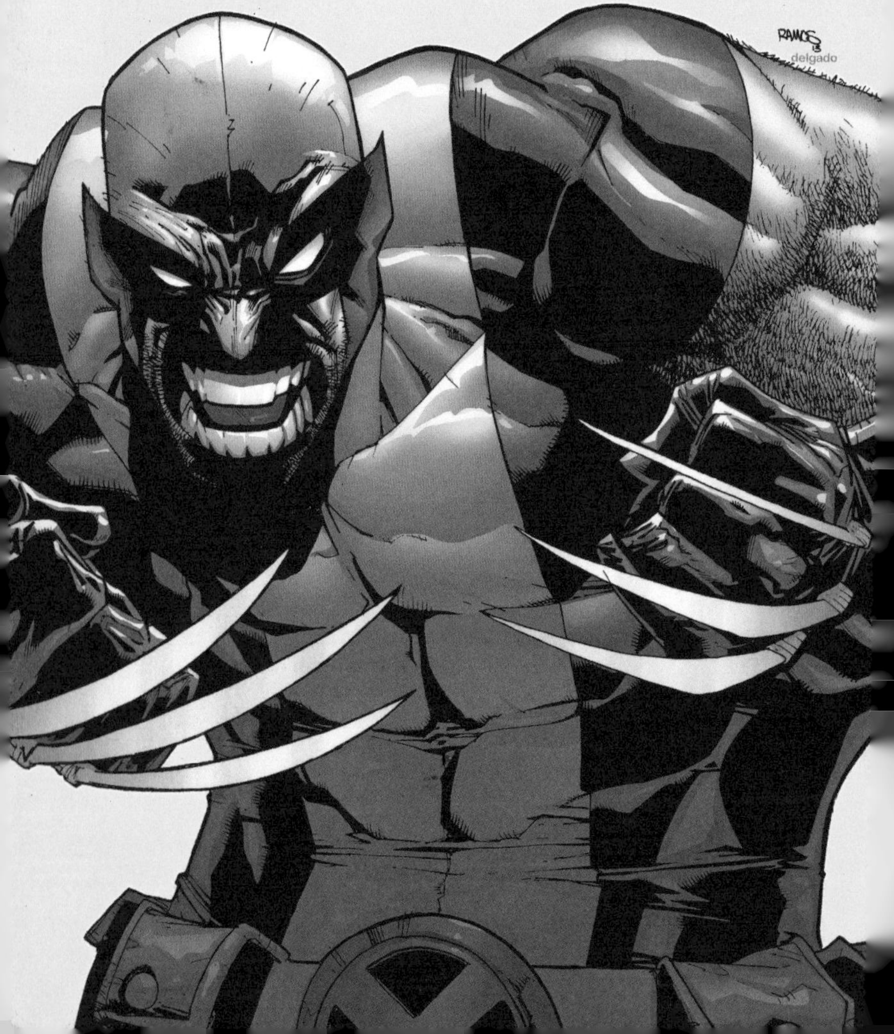
RAMOS 13
delgado